T3-BNW-601

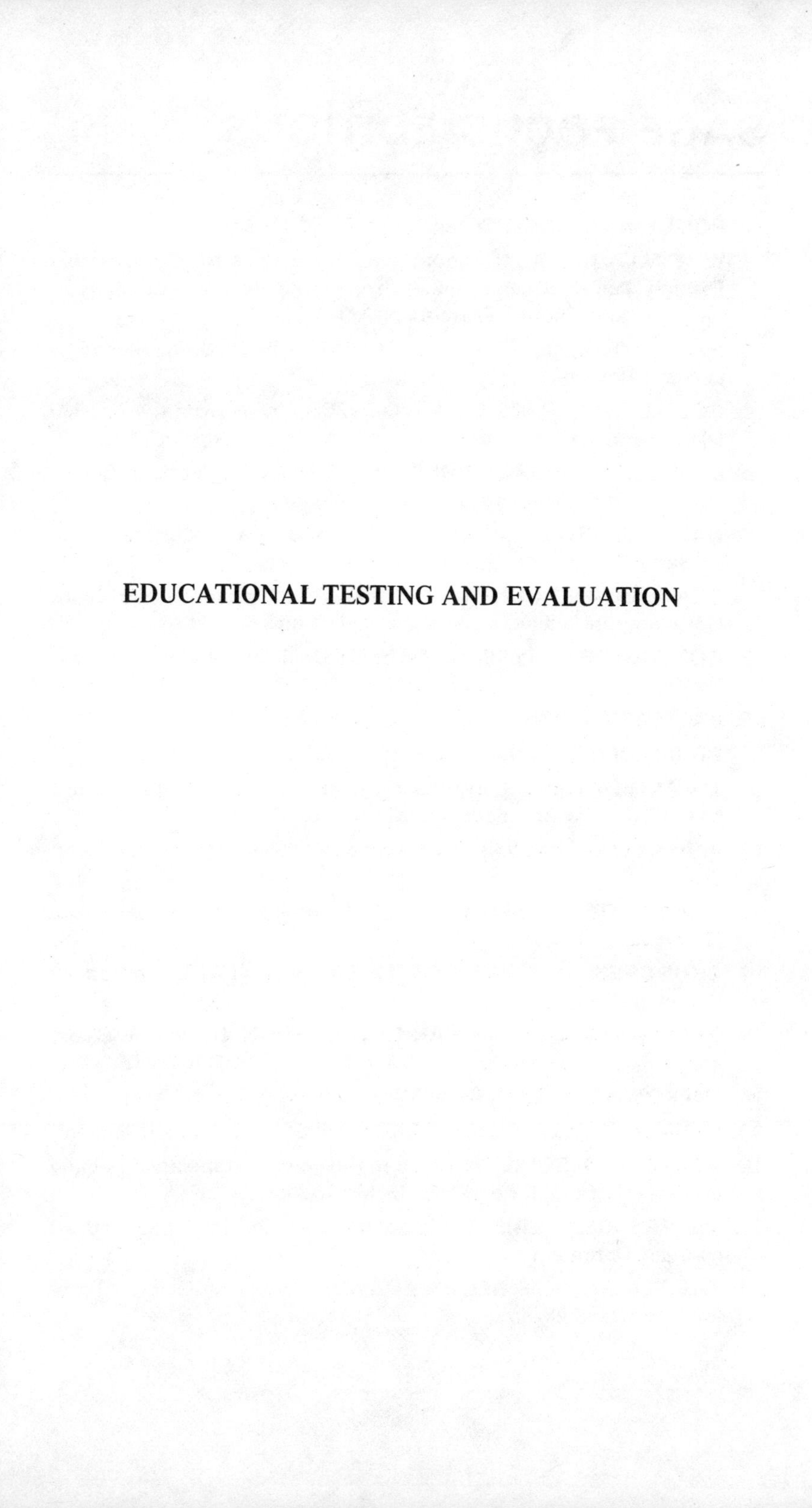

EDUCATIONAL TESTING AND EVALUATION

SAGE FOCUS EDITIONS

1. **POLICE AND SOCIETY,** edited by David H. Bayley
2. **WHY NATIONS ACT: Theoretical Perspectives for Comparative Foreign Policy Studies,** edited by Maurice A. East, Stephen A. Salmore, and Charles F. Hermann
3. **EVALUATION RESEARCH METHODS: A Basic Guide,** edited by Leonard Rutman
4. **SOCIAL SCIENTISTS AS ADVOCATES: Views from the Applied Disciplines,** edited by George H. Weber and George J. McCall
5. **DYNAMICS OF GROUP DECISIONS,** edited by Hermann Brandstatter, James H. Davis, and Heinz Schuler
6. **NATURAL ORDER: Historical Studies of Scientific Culture,** edited by Barry Barnes and Steven Shapin
7. **CONFLICT AND CONTROL: Challenge to Legitimacy of Modern Governments,** edited by Arthur J. Vidich and Ronald M. Glassman
8. **CONTROVERSY: Politics of Technical Decisions,** edited by Dorothy Nelkin
9. **BATTERED WOMEN,** edited by Donna M. Moore
10. **CRIMINOLOGY: New Concerns,** edited by Edward Sagarin
11. **TO AUGUR WELL: Early Warning Indicators in World Politics,** edited by J. David Singer and Michael D. Wallace
12. **IMPROVING EVALUATIONS,** edited by Lois-ellin Datta and Robert Perloff
13. **IMAGES OF INFORMATION: Still Photography in the Social Sciences,** edited by Jon Wagner
14. **CHURCHES AND POLITICS IN LATIN AMERICA,** edited by Daniel H. Levine
15. **EDUCATIONAL TESTING AND EVALUATION: Design, Analysis, and Policy,** edited by Eva L. Baker and Edys S. Quellmalz
16. **IMPROVING POLICY ANALYSIS,** edited by Stuart Nagel
17. **POWER STRUCTURE RESEARCH,** edited by G. William Domhoff
18. **AGING AND SOCIETY: Current Research Perspectives,** edited by Edgar F. Borgatta and Neil G. McCluskey
19. **CENTRE AND PERIPHERY: Spatial Variation in Politics,** edited by Jean Gottmann
20. **THE ELECTORATE RECONSIDERED,** edited by John C. Pierce and John L. Sullivan

EDUCATIONAL TESTING and EVALUATION

Design, Analysis, and Policy

Edited by

EVA L. BAKER and
EDYS S. QUELLMALZ

SAGE Publications Beverly Hills London

Educational Testing and Evaluation: Design, Analysis, and Policy was developed at the Center for the Study of Evaluation, University of California, Los Angeles. Copyright is claimed until December 1984. Thereafter all portions of this work covered by the copyright will be in the public domain.

Educational Testing and Evaluation: Design, Analysis, and Policy was developed under a contract with the National Institute of Education, Department of Health, Education and Welfare. However, the opinions expressed herein do not necessarily reflect the position or policy of that agency, and no official endorsement should be inferred.

Educational Testing and Evaluation: Design, Analysis, and Policy is published and distributed by Sage Publications, Inc., Beverly Hills, California under an exclusive agreement with The Regents of the University of California.

For information address:

SAGE PUBLICATIONS, INC.
275 South Beverly Drive
Beverly Hills, California 90212

SAGE PUBLICATIONS LTD
28 Banner Street
London EC1Y 8QE, England

Printed in the United States of America

Libary of Congress Cataloging in Publication Data

Main entry under title:

Educational testing and evaluation.

(Sage focus editions ; 15)
Papers presented at a conference on measurement and methodology in education, held in the winter of 1978 on the UCLA campus and sponsored by the Center for the Study of Evaluation.
1. Educational tests and measurements–Congresses.
2. Academic achievement–Evaluation–Congresses.
I. California. University. University at Los Angeles.
Center for the Study of Evaluation. II. Series.
LB3051.E34 371.2'6 79-21678
ISBN 0-8039-1361-3
ISBN 0-8039-1362-1 pbk.

FIRST PRINTING

CONTENTS

ACKNOWLEDGMENTS

We would, first of all, like to thank the authors of these pieces, many of whom contributed time and effort far in excess of our ability to compensate them. We would also like to express our gratitude to the authors and the participants at the conference for their interest and concern in assisting CSE in our programmatic efforts. The editors wish especially to acknowledge those CSE staff who assisted them in the preparations associated with this volume: first, all CSE staff who fully participated in the conference itself, and particularly Jane Beer, who supervised all arrangements; second, Marlene Henerson, who coordinated the preparation of drafts and served as liaison as well with the publisher; third, Donna Cuvelier, Irene Chow, and Dorothy Westmoreland, who prepared the manuscript; and last, Trissy Baker, who helped out in a variety of ways.

In addition, we would like to thank the NIE staff who assisted us throughout the conference preparations and supported our effort in the months following. Daniel P. Antonopolos provided much encouragement in support throughout the period of the conference, in this effort and many others. Jeffrey Schiller, Charles Stalford, Judy Shoemaker, Morton Bachrach, and Raymond F. Wormwood of NIE assisted CSE throughout the process of the book's development. Finally, we would like to thank Cheryl Tyler, of UCLA Contracts and Grants Office, for her assistance throughout this period.

–Eva L. Baker and Edys S. Quellmalz

EDITORS' NOTE: This project was supported by the National Institute of Education (NIE) under Grant No. 400-76-0029. However, the opinions and findings expressed here do not necessarily reflect the position or policy of NIE, and no official endorsement by NIE should be inferred.

INTRODUCTION

Eva L. Baker

In the Winter of 1978, on the UCLA campus the Center for the Study of Evaluation (CSE) held an invitational conference on Measurement and Methodology in Education. The work presented in this volume is the product of that experience. With support of the National Institute of Education of the Department of Health, Education, and Welfare, CSE planned the conference as a means of assessing the state of the art in educational testing and evaluation. The conference invitees were limited to a small group of highly accomplished scholars and practitioners so that informal contacts might be encouraged.

Because CSE's institutional mission is to forward research in testing and evaluation, this conference was intended to contribute to setting the agenda for long-range inquiry. Such a plan had an historical basis at CSE, for an earlier conference on the role of evaluation and instruction had been held near the outset of CSE's existence in 1967 and had led to the identification of important problems for continued scholarly attention. Thus, we felt that assembling a group at this time and structuring discussion around planned presentations would stimulate the definition of critical issues important to CSE's and the field's future productivity.

There are at least three ways to obtain "state-of-the-art" messages in the setting of a conference. One is to solicit directly such statements from the participants, and to encourage the offering of circumspect, general comments. A second is to select topics deliberately which cover a broad range of potential issues and to assign those topics to appropriate speakers. A third tactic is to ask people to write about the problems they see as critical and the lines of inquiry they see as exciting. The state of the art would be inferred from the sum and distribution of participants' attention. CSE combined the second and third approaches. We first inquired into a participant's willingness to discuss a policy, test design, or quantitative issue, next attempted to balance the program among those areas, and then allowed each participant to frame the precise nature of his/her participation personally.

We believed that this strategy was likely to yield a range of topics appropriate to a conference with goals as ambitious as ours. We saw the benefits in this approach to be the ready identification of the participants with the issues each selected to address. Elder statesman or other similarly dispassionate global assessments would be traded for a sense of immediacy and for actual experience. On the other hand, the potential deficits of such an approach were also clear, such as imbalance in topics. In fact, our plan was moderately successful. Although authors were given the opportunity to identify interests in policy, test design, or quantitative analysis, sometimes the resulting efforts seemed more appropriate for an area different from that perceived by the author. Balance and comprehensive attention to the full range of critical areas in testing and evaluation were criteria not completely satisfied by our participants' contributions.

A review of the topics which were selected in itself provides a commentary on the state of the field and the actors within it. First, a word or two is needed about the authors. All have been academicians at one time or another, although a good number are presently managing large-scale research and development efforts rather than spending all their time in research and teaching. Members of another group, which overlaps in general with the first, are not regarded principally as "measurement" or "methodology" scholars, although, again, some of their published work has been in that direction. These individuals focus their efforts on research and development in the fields of learning and instruction. Concerns relating to measurement and methodology impose on these fields but are usually treated by these educational psychologist as problems and obstacles to be overcome rather than as research goals in themselves. This group contrasts with another contingent more properly classed in the methodological category. These individuals conduct theoretical work in measurement and in the analysis and interpretation of data. Typically, these scholars focus on the abstract problem to be solved and let others pursue how solutions might apply to practical educational settings. In still another subset are those, either from learning backgrounds or from the fields of quantitative methods, who have, by virtue of interest or reputation, found themselves propelled into the field of policy.

What class of educational problems was discerned as important by these groups? In general, we can review what eluded their attention and what areas were found to be of central interest. First, relatively little, and almost no systematic, attention was given to educational policy as a legitimate focus for activity. That may be, of course, because educational policy in the United States is diffuse, conflicted, overly invoked, and meagerly studied. Perhaps, because the authors are academicians, the grand implication of "policy-relevant" research is less familiar to them; or the lack of comprehensive view may have occurred out of deliberate rejection of the world of policy. The former explanation is eminently more probable. Policy is treated in these chapters as an abstraction, but the mechanics of policy implementation are not discussed. While one participant, acting in a role of commentator, excoriates his colleagues for ignoring important issues such as school finance, desegregation, and so on, he, like all the rest, tacitly accepts that: (1) testing is an important activity; (2) testing can be improved; and (3) the lack of a comprehensive policy about testing is all right. It appears that the debate on testing and evaluation is elevated to a matter of public policy only when a serious matter occurs—"serious" defined as an item reported in *Time* or *Newsweek.* Furthermore, even where policy issues were raised, either explicitly or as a function of how the conference program was organized, the tactic for improving the policy situation was thought to inhere in a corresponding methodological improvement. Solutions proffered, such as better procedures for setting standards for students' performance, better measures for assessing classroom-level instruction, or better designs for comparing the effects of educational programs, were thought to provide a *critically* missing element, which, once in place, would permit our educational practices to go forward with more confidence. Of course, the authors are not policy analysts, perhaps a fact which prompted the discussion to be substantive. They are methodologists and educational psychologists who would naturally assume that their perspectives of the educational complex are at least as important as any other view.

Another notable omission in these efforts was the concrete expression of concern for students, those who are the data providers in most testing and evaluation efforts. While allusion to the goal of improving American education for the good of the children appears as either invocation or benediction in many of the pieces, only in a few instances was the question of the value of testing itself raised in terms of its effects on individual students. Tests and evaluation are more often described as procedures which contribute instrumentally to other aims, such as improved understanding of educational program effects, rather than as processes which significantly affect the test takers and cause both desired and unplanned consequences. The student body, therefore, is treated more like a specter, or at best a resource, rather than as a centrally affected component of technical activity.

The authors do, on a more positive note, break significant ground in their writing. In a number of chapters, they address the matter of testing in the context of a new, and thus not wholly articulated, model of testing. To contrast this model with its predecessor, a brief recapitulation of the recent intellectual history of testing is needed. The previous psychometric model referenced tests to content and regarded achievement as a general construct, exhibited in greater or lesser degrees, by students. To reference a test means to attempt to represent in the measure explicitly a range of desired subject matter, the skills interacting with the subject matter, and the achievement construct, or synthesizing idea, that unites both subject matter and skill. The general achievement construct was treated as a relatively stable feature indicated by student performance. Performance, of course, is subject to a variety of influences, including out-of-school factors, such as maturation and family background; and performance is intended to be influenced by in-school efforts. The educational influence on measures developed in this model was normally demonstrated only in the aggregate; that is, the tests were not designed to respond to every nuance of an instructional program, but rather its "total" effect. Minor quivers in the instructional index were not to affect these more general indicators, for tests of this sort were to address that which was most stable and secure in student achievement. The use of tests developed in such a model contributed to the debate about school effectiveness, including such well-known contentions as those surrounding the Coleman Report, and raised fundamental questions regarding the efficacy of American education. While it is clear from a wide range of criteria that we should not be overly sanguine about our schools and what they are purporting to do in the name of education, hanging the system on tests developed according to a psychometric model which emphasizes stability may provide only partially valid information. To illustrate, it is revealing that proponents of this model engaged in debate about the proper measurement of change, that is, differences in student performance from occasion to occasion. In such discussion, some measurement experts relegated performance differences over time, that is, change, to the same conceptual category as test unreliability, apparently an undesirable phenomenon to be controlled as much as possible.

Simple reflection suggested that an alternative model for testing was needed, and in a transition period, a substitute emerged. Largely guided by atheoretical knowledge and by clinical experience—both sources usually anathema to many methodologists—a testing model which referenced measurement to instruction was proffered. The argument for basing tests on instructional offerings instead of on the more stable achievement constructs was supported by the following premises: (1) schools are supposed to induce change via instruction; and (2) schools and programs have experienced significant changes in instructional resources and delivery, but such changes are not detected by available tests. Thus, to be a fair indicator, a test which is administered to measure the effects of schooling should be able to detect the effects of instruction. Since instruction is based on the idea of change, the orientation of achievement tests to the measurement of relatively stable and general student characteristics is inappropriate.

While the idea of a model referencing tests to instruction was intriguing (and is well represented in much of the writing in this volume), the practicality of implementing the model was a different story. Basing a test's development principally on the contents of a particular instructional program raised problems of its own. First, the charge of arbitrariness could be made. Reduced to its simplest form the question could be posed: "On what, then, is instruction based?" If instruction, as practiced in the schools, consists of an idiosyncratic amalgam of curriculum materials, pedagogical and social knowledge, personal predispositions, and resource integration—as it must in a decentralized system of education—then instruction certainly cannot provide a definable "it" to which a test, or much else, can systematically relate. One tack to deal with this concern has emerged from the work of research and development centers, educational laboratories, and other institutes through their production of coherent, discrete instructional materials and procedures and their development of corresponding tests to assess student progress. Another alternative is to develop the test first, then design instruction to represent the test. The end-product would supposedly be the same, a correspondence between test and instruction. But, of course, the overt relinquishment of responsibility for instruction to measurement experts raises philosophical issues of significance.

The existence of a definable and stable instructional treatment, however, does not solve the ineluctable issue of arbitrariness, a topic which surfaces in the following chapters predominately in the area of standard setting for competency tests. The basis for the design of instructional materials and the tests they generate should be other than convenience, habit, and analyses of subject matter.

How people best learn must be represented in the design decision. It is, of course, shocking to some that the process of learning should be of interest when the product of learning, test performance, is at issue. But without a research base relating to the processes used to incorporate and access new information and skills, the test developer is left principally with his/her own instincts about defensible ways to measure achievement.

An exciting aspect of both the conference and this book is that no fewer than five authors directly discuss the need for a model of testing which (1) accounts for change due to instruction and (2) accounts for the learning requirements of students. There is general agreement here at least that cognitive processes involved in task acquisition, memory, and integration should be linked with both instructional and measurement features, so that a general model for teaching-learning-assessment may be articulated. This model would be grounded in theory, and would properly represent both the tasks and the manner in which achievement itself is acquired. Given that at any one time alternative theories of learning and instruction may have varying credibility, the model would need to be robust enough to survive such variation.

Because an integrating model is more yearning than reality at the present time, the identification of one cogent problem for joint effort by the research community was a major outcome of the conference. What remains is to see whether effort can be directed toward the solution of this problem.

Another important set of contributions in this book derives from the quantitatively oriented scholar. While it has long been expected and accepted that methodologists talk to themselves, the array of presentations in this volume departs from tradition. In this book, without exception, the problems addressed by quantitatively oriented scholars do derive from real problems in the arenas of educational decision-making. For many critical needs, such as evaluating the effects of an innovative educational program, advancing or retaining students, and estimating the chance of being wrong in a decision with serious ramifications, it is appropriate that the most sophisticated resources be applied to elucidate solutions. The methodological chapters here provide a refreshing blend of interest in common, realistic problems, and sophistication of strategy.

Substantively, the conference combined interests across a wide range of issues in evaluation and testing and involved many well-respected scholars in the process. The scene of the conference and the character of the participation were also noteworthy. First, the conference was held in January in California, when the rest of the country was suffering a harsh winter. There was an excellent turnout from the Midwest and East Coast. Second, time was allowed throughout for discussion of the papers. While some of the discussion points have been incorporated into the epilog, the flavor of the interaction does not come through. During the conference, there was remarkable elan and good cheer. Even on matters of long-term and serious disagreement between individuals, the commentary and dialog were congenial and tolerant. Many of the individuals in attendance were longstanding colleagues, and so the atmosphere of reunion occasionally crept into the proceedings. Finally, many of the participants who did not prepare papers were of no less academic or professional standing than those who were making presentations. Thus, there was almost none of the obeisance to the god-like presenters which sometimes is evident in conferences where the participants come exclusively to learn and the presenters arrive exclusively to share their acknowledged wisdom.

Certainly, both the substantive and social functions of the conference were of benefit to CSE and to NIE. Topics were discussed which were of sufficient import to inform, and in some cases, confirm, CSE's plan for its intellectual direction. That direction includes a continuing concern for the practitioners and students who are the users of tests and a commitment to explore the testing and evaluation agenda from a stance which accounts for both the consumers' needs and for the needs and proper roles of the research community. NIE benefited because the needs and state of the art on the more technical side of testing were articulated by leading scholars in the field. Plans which include support for research and development well beyond the resources available to CSE were inferrable from the contents of these proceedings.

Of course, it is not clear what will come of our efforts to address the many problems confronting us. If we can, through reflection and scholarly dialog, influence the course of testing and evaluation and the implications these activities have for policy and for the daily lives of students, teachers, and school people, then conferences like these are worth the effort. We must prepare ourselves to be able to contend with the inevitable furor which will occur when tests and evaluation themselves are subject to the same public scrutiny as innovative educational programs attract at the present. Unless the best thinkers in our field develop ways to improve, through research and development and through education of the public, the uses of testing and evaluation, even our most well-developed methodologies will have no use in a society that sees no need for our wares.

PART I

ISSUES IN TEXT DESIGN

INTRODUCTION

The area of test design has been the long-neglected stepchild of achievement test theory, traditionally the domain of statistically oriented psychometricians, yet, insuring the content and construct validity of a test has been seen as the relatively uninteresting task of curriculum specialists. With increasing media coverage of program evaluation test results and competency testing data, however, questions have arisen and there has been scrutiny of the quality of the tests commonly used for informing important decisions about educational programs and the accomplishments of individuals. Norm-referenced tests, fortified as they are by psychometric jargon, complex statistics, and sequestered item pools, are coming under attacks because of their conceptual and psychological weaknesses. It would seem that assembling subject matter specialists to fill in a content/process matrix with items constructed according to few rules (or no rules at all) is not sufficient to produce conceptually, psychologically coherent measurement instruments. Meanwhile, criterion-referenced testing, still in its infancy, is struggling to develop defensible methodologies for specifying those dimensions of items that influence student performance in explicit skill domains.

In the controversy currently surrounding testing, several salient issues have emerged from the critiques of researchers in learning, instruction, evaluation, psychology, and linguistics. One major concern is that tests do not tap what is taught and learned. Some achievement tests omit, or disproportionately emphasize, skills taught in a school system. Often, too, item subscales are labeled so generally, e.g., "logic," "main idea," that items falling into these categories are written at widely different levels of complexity and are presented in stimulus contexts clearly different from one another and from the stimuli used to teach the skill in the classroom.

Accompanying the complexity/context problem are problems resulting from variations in the information-processing strategies students may use to respond to items presumably within the same skill domain. To the extent that test specifications do not attempt to control item information-processing requirements, students may respond to items on a basis irrelevant to the skills the test is attempting to assess.

Compounding these within-domain problems is the frequent absence of domain specifications or test blueprints used to fashion a test. Analyses of a test's design must often rely on inferences about the bases for generating test items. Surprisingly, this disturbing lack of precision in describing a test's characteristics occurs not just in state or district evaluations and assessments, but even in reported research. After meticulously describing independent variables, many studies reported in journals fail to describe in a replicable manner the dependent variable. Statements such as "a reading comprehension test" or a "computation test of a number of items was administered" further demonstrate the pervading assumption that tests are inherently valid and well designed.

A second major issue in achievement test design, then, is the need for better methodology to develop explicit, responsive, valid domain specifications. Attention is beginning to focus on the stimulus and response dimensions of items which must be carefully controlled. Not only are context, structure, and length important, but cognitive processing demands, linguistic complexity, and sociological content also influence student responses. Few testing or research programs currently include guidelines for these, subtler, aspects of item construction. Just as quality research methodology requires dependent measure descriptions sufficient to permit replication, so must testing programs and evaluations provide replicable test blueprints.

A third issue in test design is the relationship of the nature of the test specification to the breadth of test application. Relatively unexplored is the question of how the number, range, and specificity of skill domains will vary with the purpose of the test and the instructional heterogeneity of the examinee pool. For example, it is unclear how domain specifications of a curriculum-embedded diagnostic test for a three-week unit should differ from the design features of a curriculum-embedded end-of-term exam or from a cross-curricula achievement test.

In the opening paper on test design, Eva Baker describes the tenets of domain-referenced testing and proposes four criteria for judging the quality of a test: (1) that a test be meaningful; (2) that its purpose and structure be public; (3) that it gather information as economically as possible; and (4) that it address skills sensitive or amenable to instruction. Richard Schutz suggests that truly responsive assessment arises from within an empirically validated system that integrates measurement in instruction. Michelene Chi and Robert Glaser, and Lawrence Frase describe findings from cognitive learning research and discuss implications for test construction. Lee Schulman discusses teachers' views that much of testing is irrelevant to the realities of teaching and should represent only one data point in the teacher's decision-making process. All of these papers underscore the importance of convincing test designers that descriptive rigor is important and that models must be developed for communicating test design blueprints in comprehensible form to audiences as diverse as researchers, practitioners, and parents and students. Rather than floating curriculum free, globally structured, and superficially described, tests must increasingly become more systematically formulated, specifically characterized, and instructionally referenced.

–Edys S. Quellmalz

1

IS SOMETHING BETTER THAN NOTHING?

The Metaphysical Aspects of Test Design

Eva L. Baker

Like many people at my time of life, I have been asking myself questions about the meaning of experience, both personal and professional. In the course of my reflection, I have found myself thinking about my relationship with my mother. As you may know, such a tendency is not uncommon; personality theorists suggest that much of an individual's development is defined by the extent to which he or she tries either to repeat or to avoid salient characteristics of a dominant parent. Until recently, I assumed that I was an avoider. My mother is a very strong person, someone who always worked outside the home in a variety of jobs. I had always seen only differences in her work and mine; but now I detect some similarities.

My mother has been mostly a saleswoman, and has usually sold through direct sales products such as food freezer plans, aluminum siding, and water softeners. Working in these fields was lucrative, because the "pitch" used was convincing. People were encouraged not to purchase the product, but to "participate in an advertising campaign." There were testimonials provided to the effect that if a participant supplied a list of contacts to the company, he/she would be paid a bonus for each of the referrals who subsequently purchased the product. Thus, one could conceivably receive a product free, and perhaps generate funds in addition, depending upon the liveliness of the list of names provided. This sales promotion technique, to my adolescent eyes, had all the virtues of chain letters. I was disturbed by the great numbers of customers, usually in weak financial condition, who thought nothing of distributing lists of church membership, of coworkers' home addresses, and of regional girl scout personnel in hopes of securing a product for free. As you might have imagined, the actual incentive was realized for very few. Most participants ended up with an expensive product and a long-term credit arrangement.

I would like to consider whether I, as a part of the educational research and development establishment, have been guilty of making promises to the poor in the area of testing. For most of us, our efforts are made out of conviction rather than the desire for a commission. Nonetheless, our pitch goes something like this: "If you will use a certain kind of test and institute certain kinds of instructional practices, then the present state of affairs in the schools will change." As many of us know, the view of school effectiveness has been generally low, appropriately gauged or not. School people are feeling in need of solutions that are discrete and identifiable. The use of "testing" as a technique for school improvement is appealing because it combines the implicit values of high standards and productivity into an operation which requires, at the outset, very little systemic change in the overall process of schooling. In this paper, I would like to discuss the nature of the promise that testing apparently makes, and to explore how we might carry it out. I will also attempt to carry on this discussion without discernible reference to the quantitative side of testing.

Much of the research on testing has been driven by the quantitatively oriented scholars. When one listens to quantitatively skilled measurement people, they discuss the analytical procedures for inferring abilities and characteristics of students and seem sometimes to use arcane techniques. I also hear in their remarks the assumption that it's fairly easy to get a good test together. In fact, much of their work evolves from the premise that "given an appropriate test item"—a test item which relates in regular and logical ways to the curriculum, teaching, instructional exposure, or some other construct—all else follows. I believe that the task of constructing a good item and a good test consisting of items which share known, logical, and instructionally useful characteristics, is extraordinarily difficult.

Some small amount of work done at CSE and nationally has been directed to the issue of designing tests. Much of that work is based on the general impetus provided by Wells Hively and his creation of the "item form" about ten years ago. The item form was designed to function as a blueprint or specification for like items, i.e., items planned to assess similar skills on a test. The item form's components included a sample format indicating how the behavior of the student was to be demonstrated, a set of content restrictions designed to limit the substantive information or principles that the item was to reflect, and a set of conditional variables which were to be regarded as irrelevant to the performance, variables to be overcome in successful completion of the item. For instance, a variable such as "shading" might be irrelevant to a discrimination of geometric shape. The child should select a circle as the appropriate answer to the item whether it was empty, shaded, or completely colored in. The intent of manipulating item formats, content restrictions, and conditional variables was, and is, to enable the development of tests which have characteristics that are clearly described. These characteristics include:

(1) a coherent set of items measuring each identified skill;
(2) the provision of items which represent the range of performance included in the test specification; and
(3) features used in test generation which may be described and used for multiple purposes, e.g., diagnostic student placement or the design of instruction.

While various names for the elements of Hively's model have been proffered by others in this area, the use of some form of test specifications has been a defining characteristic of "domain-referenced" measurement. Although there are various interpretations of how much information one must provide in these test specifications—Hively's work representing more detailed specification than, say, Popham's—the overall intent is the same.

Because a basic tenet of the specification process is the clear description of parameters within which test items are to be developed, the charge of arbitrariness, often directed to the process of setting minimum performance standards, can similarly be directed to the limitations imposed on the content and the behavior of the item. The very act of having specifications makes it clear that the testing process assumes at least tacit control of the curriculum; certainly it is arguable that such control ought not to be arbitrary. The manner varies in which test developers attempt to diffuse this charge. Sometimes the approval of content parameters and testing formats is solicited from teachers, and often this solicitation includes a broader range of interested parties. If we can report that elementary school teachers, curriculum specialists and subject matter experts have been queried about the appropriateness of various item restrictions and concur with the test development specialists, then our worries about arbitrariness recede. Consensual arbitrariness is easier to live with.

An alternative to seeking consensus for test specifications developed by a given agency is to diffuse the development task itself, so that teachers and other practitioners are responsible for the original draft of specifications as well as for subsequent review of revised forms prepared by the test development agencies. This process is necessarily more time consuming because the participants not only must be trained in the intent of the measurement and the purposes of test specifications but also convinced that they have sufficient skill and time to undertake primary drafts. Furthermore, there are certain problems which seem to emerge when teachers are used in this process. We have observed that they experience difficulty in separating the requirements for parameters for test development, e.g., content restrictions, from their thinking about their own ideal instructional sequences. Thus, teacher-generated specifications of tests, under conditions of moderate training, more often than not appear to be specifications of platonically ideal instructional plans. The content provided is often ordered, and the sequence tends to reflect how the teacher plans to go about inculcating skills and other wisdom rather than what content the students should be able to deal with on the test. Thus, much revision and recycling may be necessary.

A third way to deal with the arbitrariness concern is to allow such arbitrariness to reside in existing material, in history, rather than to be newly created by the test developer, and thus more vulnerable to attack. For example, in an evaluation undertaken by CSE we found we could not successfully develop rules for the generation of sentences to assess oral reading skills of second- and third-grade children. We had inspected avaiable text materials as well as the research on language development and reading and found that no clear progression was either extant or recommended. As an alternative, we collected the four most popular reading text series in the state of California for that age group and sampled sentences from these texts for use on our test. We had a definitional universe of content—all sentences appearing in the four most popular reading series in California. The rules that defined how those sentences were created were unclear and certainly arbitrary, but we had a sense that the test items sampled a domain based on the reality of curriculum rather than the imagination of a test developer.

The arbitrariness issue is pervasive in the area of test specifications, and more than the stop-gap ploys described above is necessary. One can attack the problem by contrasting strategies for the development of test specifications into inductive and deductive styles. In an inductive model, one might advocate collecting samples created by individuals who, by common standards, are described as possessors of the skill in question, and samples for those who are felt to be deficient or unlikely to possess the desired skill or competency. After these samples are arrayed, they might be inspected to determine which features discriminate group membership, and from these, a set of desirable content characteristics might be inferred.

The deductive alternative, of course, is based upon the thought of those who believe in the existence of good models of curriculum. For certain areas—for instance, in the field of writing—models of process have been posited. These models, in turn, are explicated to provide hypotheses about what kinds of discriminations will be important under various conditions. Again, the basis of these discriminations would form the features of the test specifications.

The ideal treatment of arbitrariness would appear to me to be one that essentially dissolved the claim. It should be possible to demonstrate links between curricular models and models of cognitive process such that certain features of a task would meet appropriate requirements for both curricular and cognitive processing models. The use of such parameters in the ideal sense would lay to rest much of the discussion of arbitrariness, except for the particular renditions of the content selected to be measured. Much research is necessary before correspondences between cognitive and curricular models will be identified sufficiently to permit proper test specification. But it is a feasible goal.

The second major concern of the use of test specifications to generate test items relates to how one knows that the items created are any good. At present, we don't have many satisfactory solutions to this problem. Typical procedures involve asking individuals to "match" items to specifications. Most of the experimental conditions under which such studies have been conducted have been too "clean." The typical ambiquities in items and specifications have been deliberately avoided. Second, very little attention has been devoted to how to determine if a "match" exists. We know from preliminary work at CSE that items can apparently cohere or disaffiliate from one another depending upon the dimensions the rater happens to regard as paramount. Some people naturally focus on content similarities; others on item format distinctions; still others on cognitive processes required by the item. The raters' attention needs to be directed deliberately.

As a way of avoiding the problem, some researchers have tried to use empirical data to support item congruency. They look at the extent to which administered items cluster in order to determine whether the specifications used to generate items have exerted appropriate control.

Clearly, difficulty level and item clusters would be important dimensions to examine, *if* we knew for certain the instructional treatments which preceded our empirical analyses. It seems clear that defining specification-item congruency by the empirical methods described above leaves one on the rim of a tautology: what is the effect of instruction on item congruency, and how would items look under other instructional conditions? While there has been some work in the shift of factor structure of items following instructional exposure, such research has not been related to how the items were originally developed. The problem is also complicated by the concern for the nature of the instruction received. Very often, research is conducted with "instruction--no-instruction" comparisons, when what passes for "instruction" is weak. It seems to me that we must concern ourselves not only with whether or not instruction occurs, but with the quality of the instruction, the features it emphasizes, and the strength of delivery as well. These dimensions should influence the extent to which we can infer that items are "properly" clustering. Of course, everyone knows that the instructional history of learners is an important matter. But knowing and acting as if we know are two different things. I rather think that most of us behave as if tests have "properties" in and of themselves, quite apart from the instructional context in which they are embedded. Certainly, we report and use test statistics as if tests were context free.

At CSE we have been exploring some alternatives to improving the process of matching test items to the specifications which presumably spawned them. We have been extrapolating work from set theory in mathematics to help us with the issue. Simply speaking, when we try to match a test item with its set of specifications, we are attempting to assign membership to a set. The specifications create the parameters for the set; the various items serve as potential members. Of course, items are not either "in" or "out" of a set. "Belongness" depends upon stringency of requirements for membership and what dimensions are attended to in assignment. As discussed earlier, individuals provided with little guidance make rather idiosyncratic assignment of items to specifications. The field of mathematical set theory has evolved an appropriate notion called fuzzy sets. Fuzzy set theory allows one to assign membership on a zero to one continuum, with decimal values indicating the degree of "belongness." While there are other promising applications from mathematics, the fuzzy set activity suggests that we can then verify the raters' assignment values by hypothesizing empirical values under various conditions of instructional emphasis. We are beginning work in this area at CSE and hope to evolve a preliminary checklist and some procedures for helping people address this concern.

To recall my original question: "Is something better than nothing?" In testing I suppose that my answer would be "yes, if." Tests are clearly political fodder, and will be used increasingly in issues of public concern. Individuals' opportunities will hinge upon their performance on tests we develop, and thus the desire for open access to the tests will also increase. I believe that the use of test specifications provides a way for us to meet the public's desire for information about tests without placing us, as some recently suggested legislative amendments would have it, in the position of fully publishing all test items and constantly generating new items. The "if" on the "yes, if" response is *if* we can generate sets of lucid specifications which make public our intent to measure (and instruct) in certain general and important areas. The menu for satisfying the public's appetite for test information presently consists of statements of goals, objectives, skills, and standards. These strike me (mixing a metaphor) more appropriate as tone poems, for you can read them any way you like. We can be much more responsive to legitimate public pressures for testing information by providing real specifications to help all interested parties understand what they are getting into when they adopt testing as a preferred practice for instructional improvement.

A second general concern, in addition to the need for publication of test specifications, is that of economy. At minimum, this principle would suggest that we desist from requiring more tests as an automatic response to any problem. Leigh Burstein and Ward Keesling did a study which in part audited the data processing of standardized tests in the State of California. I believe their findings were that approximately half of the data collected in California for the stated purpose of providing information to the legislature on student progress never reached the computer. If you can calculate the resources involved in that annual exercise (not simply the cost per child for test purchase and scoring but the costs in time and anxiety) it seems to me that price outweighs the likely import of the findings from such tests. We need to be much more sensitive to the economics of testing. The costs are too high for purely ceremonial or symbolic benefits.

My last point is that when we give a test, we are asking people to communicate to us; they use the test to tell us, quickly, what is in their heads. Our part of the bargain should be to provide tests that are meaningful—that have merit and value *in and of themselves.* "Meaningful" is a boring, educational word, tinged with pop psychology; and with apologies to Edwin Newman and his concern for the English language, it is simply what I mean. I think test-taking situations should be meaningful. For instance, I am unshakable in the belief that if you're going to test students' writing ability, you should present an opportunity for them to write, no matter how well multiple-choice tests correlate or predict writing behavior. Because a test is very often an important event in the lives of students, we send them messages every time they are presented with an item. Thus, even when economy is the concern, it should be balanced with the need to have people understand the logical relationship between what they are asked to do on tests and the skills and competencies society expects them to exhibit. Such is the nature of meaningful testing.

The overall word which summarizes my desiderata in testing is *fair.* Fairness implies open, public, meaningful, coherent, and economic testing practices. Something is better than nothing, *if* we can be fair.

2

THE DESIGN OF MEASUREMENT IN INSTRUCTION

Richard E. Schutz

I can treat the topic of "test design" definitively and with dispatch. Solutions to all the important problems of test design in education were generated decades ago. Test design in education does not now and has not for a long time constituted a technical obstacle for those of us concerned with education or educational research and development. Some within our midst staunchly refuse to recognize the solutions so that the problem can be kept alive. But anyone concerned with the "how to" of test design and construction can acquire it by consulting any number of introductory texts in measurement and/or evaluation in education. Proficiency in test design and construction is a useful, salable skill for anyone concerned with educational research and development. But it is a skill that can be acquired by any BA-level person within a few months of on-the-job training.

Although one can say with confidence that test design is not a problem in education, this is not to say that all aspects of design and planning related to measurement and methodology have been wrapped up. The traditional view of these unresolved aspects within the measurement and methodology guild has been that they involve the use of tests by school people. That is, tests are designed and constructed. If the design and construction are sound, then the only issue remaining is their use. The wise use or appropriate use of tests is a problem that needs constant attention from measurement and methodology people, since school people and others frequently, if not typically, use tests unwisely or inappropriately. This is the position that I was born and bred on and that I promoted without qualms until very recently.

It is now clear to me that this view is outmoded conceptually and contemporarily. It really doesn't take much intelligence to conclude that aspirations to get school people to use tests wisely stand no chance, however noble or well-intentioned the aspiration might be. With the National Education Association committed to getting standardized tests out of schools and the courts questioning whether intelligence tests may be used, one doesn't have to be a genius to recognize that our best efforts to educate educators in the use of tests haven't worked, and it is too late to begin trying harder.

I don't mean to suggest that the schools are going to stop using tests. Every indicator points in the opposite direction. But the popularity of tests or the scale of their use is not the point. Under any circumstances, any aspiration to ensure that tests as such become more wisely and appropriately used is a fantasy. The fault is in the head of the measurement and methodology community, not in the hand of the school community. Fortunately, an alternative paradigm and technical means are now available that remediate the conceptual deficiency and that are in synchronization with the contemporary education context.

This brings me to the title of my paper, "measurement in instruction." The meat of the title is the preposition "in." The normal phrase is the measurement *of* instruction, and the contrast in the prepositions is one of substance rather than syntax. In both education and educational research and development, the worlds of objectives, instruction, and measurement have operated as three separate worlds. This separation is maintained in our professional organization, AERA, where we have separate divisions—B, C, and D—for objectives, instruction, and measurement. It is maintained in education operations at all levels. In school districts of any size there are typically separate staffs for the three functions. In classrooms, objectives are typically handled as one world; instructional resources are another world; and measurement is still a third world—with no functional links among the three. Such links in classroom instruction are advised by professors, and imputed by teachers, but the links simply do not show up when one actually looks for them. Statements of objectives are one matter, instructional materials are another, testing programs are another, and they do not hook up.

From a measurement and methodology position, the rationale for keeping measurement external to instruction rather than integrating the two functions has been that each instructional setting is different, and each setting includes a near-infinite number of different instructional resource options. However, when one looks at what is actually there in classrooms, a radically different understanding is also possible. To date such looks have been largely limited to the elementary school and to the subjects of reading and mathematics, but all the available evidence points to the wide generalizability of the findings, and certainly of the methodology to other subjects and age/grade levels.

There is now strong evidence that a large proportion (something like 90%) of classroom time in elementary schools in the basic subjects is referenced to a very small number (say 5 or 6) textbook series in each subject. This in no sense means that all classroom instruction is uniform. But it does mean that the matter of measurement *in* instruction is highly tractable under this condition. The situation need not be viewed as a bumbling, buzzing confusion.

Now it could be that the tractability would break down when one examines the text series, since even six series, for six grades and two subjects, provide latitude for a lot of variation. Cursory examination of the texts certainly supports the common belief that there are many differences. This is where the investigation usually stops, since in getting this far the researcher has found so many things which appear faulty in the text that further examination is seen with aversion. However, if you chain researchers to their benches for a few years doing various kinds of analyses, what begins to come through is that the big differences are *within* age/grade levels of the texts rather than *between* age/grade levels, when these within-year differences are collapsed. A second source of differences derives from the pet notions and the rhetoric of different author teams. These are highly promoted by the series but can be subordinated for measurement purposes.

This same situation holds for instructional intentions. When you ask people about instructional intentions ordered by age/grade levels, you get remarkable agreement. Where people differ is in their emotional attachment to elements of the structure and in the pedagogy they bring to it.

What it boils down to is that instrumentation can be designed and developed that each text publisher and each school person will regard as consistent with "their" program and that can be used *in* instruction to provide credible information on instructional accomplishments at the class, school, and district level. The instrumentation yields customized reports and appropriately aggregated data for teachers, principals, and district administrators at the beginning, midpoint, and end of each school year. The full cost of the goods and services for a year for a subject ranges from about twenty-five cents a child, if schools use their own computer, to about a dollar if they use the mails and the developer's computer (the biggest cost item is mailing).

This instrumentation directly integrates measurement and instruction. SWRL refers to this product system category as Instructional Accomplishment Information (IAI) systems. From the perspective of the schools, the measurement incorporated into IAI directly references what is being accomplished in a given class, school, or district, and is a sound mechanism for acknowledging those accomplishments. From the perspective of the research community, IAI is powerful and versatile instrumentation for investigating all kinds of interesting aspects of instruction under natural conditions.

Thus, the educational research and development community now has the instrumentation and processing technology minimally required to provide measurement *in* instruction, compatible with instruction as it is now operating rather than with a conjectured view of how it should or could operate.

The characteristics of an Instructional Accomplishment Information system constitute a minimal form of integration of measurement in instruction. This is certainly not the only way to effect such integration. As a matter of fact, our R&D at SWRL effected the means of a more sophisticated and efficient form of integration before we did the type of IAI system I've been talking about. We refer to this better product system category as Comprehensive Products for Instruction (CPI). From a design view, all aspects of CPI instrumentation are better than those of IAI instrumentation, since a CPI product system embodies all the features of IAI and goes on to include resources for obtaining instructional accomplishments, rather than simply acknowledging them.

A CPI product system thus incorporates the resources necessary and sufficient to make "high quality instruction" an operational rather than a rhetorical matter. SWRL has performed the research and development to generate such resources in several subjects for the full K-6 level, and our data to date indicate that a CPI product system has powerful potential for both the school community and the research and development community.

For example, with the CPI in reading, the research and development community can now provide the school community with the resources required to teach all children to read, excluding only children with an identifiable physiological deficiency. That is a bold statement which both the research and development community and the school community will find hard to accept. Educational research and development particularly and education generally have expanded during the past ten-twenty years on the basis of failure rather than success. Failure conditions have become a standard way of life, and we have adapted to the conditions as if they were permanent. Just as the method of invention had to be invented to make industrial research and development feasible, so now accomplishment of research and development successes now has to be learned in education. But the instructional requisites for this professional learning are currently in place.

IAI and CPI instrumentation both have nice features for researchers as well as for teachers. For one, the instrumentation pins down the benefits of criterion-referenced tests. These benefits have heretofore been elusive, since such tests have a way of sliding or being pushed into the norm-referenced test context. For another, the instrumentation extends and advances the formative evaluation/summative evaluation distinction. Summative evaluation need no longer be treated as a one-shot matter following the completion of development. The measures that are incorporated into a CPI system provide technically sound feedback mechanisms that carry through with the "treatment" in its natural use. This in turn permits longitudinal studies of instruction using as units of analysis classes, schools, and districts as well as individual students.

IAI systems and CPI systems only begin to scratch the surface of the design potential when one begins to view and operate with measurement in instruction rather than of instruction. The test design considerations take one beyond the realm of psychometrics, but no one said we had to stay within those boundaries. True scores will never die; but they were really never more than theoretical fictions from the beginning.

3

THE MEASUREMENT OF EXPERTISE: Analysis of the Development of Knowledge and Skill as a Basis for Assessing Achievement

Michelene T. H. Chi and Robert Glaser

We would like to propose that the effective measurement of achievement requires that test developers have information about the psychological characteristics of advanced competence and expertise in the knowledge and skills taught in school. In school instruction, effort is often concentrated on the early stages of acquisition because failures in learning are generally attributed to deficiencies in grasping the fundamentals on which further learning must build. While it seems reasonable to concentrate on these early stages, there are reasons why such a strategy is not necessarily an optimal one for attaining advanced levels of proficiency. It is apparent that the performance of the beginner and the novice is very different from the performance of the skilled and knowledgeable individual. The mistakes and cumbersome routines of the novice are a necessary stage of learning. But, if we knew more about the stages and processes involved in the

AUTHORS' NOTE: This research program, conducted at the Learning Research and Development Center, is supported in part by Contract No. N00014-78-C-0375, NR157-421 of the Office of Naval Research, and by the National Institute of Education.

changes from novice to expert performance, it would then be possible to devise achievement measures more directly focused at efficient educational strategies—strategies that perhaps would take the novice through a different succession of stages, yield fewer failures of learning, and bring about the attainment of higher levels of achievement.

Past studies of knowledge and skill acquisition may have devoted too much effort to describing the way in which learning occurs, without sufficient information about what is involved in high-level competence and expert performance. Based on these past studies, the instructional sequences laid out in textbooks and teaching procedures seem logical enough; but too frequently, the results of instruction lead to failures of retention and transfer, and the instructional process itself is often unnecessarily inefficient. The question that needs to be asked is whether the assessment procedures and related teaching sequences currently in use have any relation to sequences that would be optimal for producing not only beginning but advanced levels of achievement.

In order to deal with this question, we need, for research purposes, to go beyond our usual practices of specifying educational objectives. We need to analyze the cognitive processes involved in transforming a novice into an expert, in terms of an adequate cognitive theory of the nature of this transformation. When the structure and process characteristics of learning that facilitate high levels of competence are understood, then new advances in techniques of instructing and assessing this competence should occur.

Toward this objective, we suggest that studies be undertaken of the changes that take place as individuals attain increasing competence in various subject matters, and that particular emphasis be placed on defining the differences between novice and expert performance. These investigations should be designed to understand overt changes that appear as the competence level of individuals increases—changes, for example, that are of the following kind: (a) variable and crude performance that becomes consistent, relatively automatic, and precise; (b) small unitary algorithmic acts that change into larger response integrations and overall strategies; (c) change in the ability to perform in simple stimulus contexts to the ability to handle complex patterns in a noisy context of events; (d) changes whereby performance becomes increasingly symbolic and covert, where the learner responds increasingly to internal representations of an event and to internalized standards and strategies for problem solving; (e) the increasingly skillful acceptance and rejection of rules when they are applicable and inapplicable in certain situations; and (f) the increasing ability to learn from the events of one's own experience.

THE NATURE OF EXPERT-NOVICE DIFFERENCES

As a starting basis for examining the differences between the achievement of the expert and novice, we propose possible dimensions of the expert-novice distinction that can guide this work. Our framework for understanding the nature of this difference is to characterize human information processing in terms of two components: one, a knowledge structure or content component that can be represented as a network of concepts and relations; and two, an assembled set of cognitive processes for performing a sequence of actions with the content (Anderson, 1976; Greeno, 1977; Norman and Rumelhart, 1975). Although it may ultimately be misleading to differentiate between content and processes (since well-developed processes can become retrievable items of knowledge), it is heuristically useful, at least initially, to consider content and processes as separable components. Hence, in what follows, we outline some of the important dimensions of content structure and processes that may provide a basis for differentiating novice from expert performance.

KNOWLEDGE DIFFERENCES (CONTENT)

To be an expert in a subject domain means that one knows more; expert performance in a domain makes imposing demands upon knowledge in that domain. One of the tasks we face is to find out what it means to know more. One way to conceptualize this notion is in terms of current psychological models of memory in which, for the most part, knowledge is represented in the form of semantic networks. Knowing more means several things in the framework of such models. For a particular domain of knowledge it means: (a) having more central concepts or conceptual nodes in memory, (b) more relations (or features) defining each node, (c) more relations interrelating the nodes, and (d) more robust relations in terms of their strength for retrieving related nodes. In other words, a simple way to characterize the semantic network of an expert's knowledge base is to say that his network is dense, containing clusters of related information, whereas the network for the novice is sparse, with relatively few highly interrelated clusters.

The notion of a dense network for the expert is intuitive and, in some ways, it is also trivial to compare the density of an expert's network with that of a novice's. For example, we can determine whether the first postulate is true, that is, whether the expert has more nodes in memory about the subject-relevant knowledge, by a simple assessment through tests of the relevant concepts. For a given subject domain such as physics, having more nodes simply means that there are more physics concepts that the expert can define and recognize as compared to a novice. Suppose we let each physics concept, such as mass, density, acceleration, etc., be represented by a node. An expert would have additional related concept nodes of force, momentum, etc., whereas a novice would not.

The second postulate, that there are more relations defining each concept node for the expert, means that the expert's node has more features and properties related to a given concept node. To take the same example again, for the novice, the properties of mass may involve only the concepts of weight and density, whereas for the expert, the concept of mass may include the additional features of acceleration and force, etc.

The third postulate, more relations interrelating nodes, means that each concept is connected with a greater number of other concepts (for the experts) than for the novice. This essentially implies that there are multiple routes relating one concept to another. One way to quantify these multiple relations is to look at the amount of cross-referencing. For example, Shavelson (1972) has demonstrated this by comparing a physics student's free association to physics concepts before and after instruction. After instruction, it was clear that not only were more terms associated to each physics concept (by means of a free-word association test), but more indexing occurred.

The fourth postulate, more robust relations between concepts, means that the probability is higher of a concept evoking other concepts, as well as evoking its defining features. The retrieval of chess chunks and the retrieval of equations in bursts in solving physics problems are evidence of the robust relations that can exist between concepts. For example, in a memory task testing for the recall of chess positions, Chase and Simon (1973) found that chess masters can retrieve several chess pieces before pausing, whereas novices pause after retrieving one or two pieces. Similarly, Larkin (1977a) also found that expert physicists can retrieve several typical equations consecutively before pausing. Novices, on the other hand, retrieve physics equations sporadically, such that they are randomly distributed over time. Such a retrieval pattern suggests that the robust relations may selectively exist only among concepts that are relevant to each other. In chess, for example, a robust relation may exist only between the king and rook of the same color (because of repeated experience with the castle position), whereas a weaker relation may exist between the queen and the rook. It is precisely this differentiation of strength of relation that may not exist in the novice's network.

In addition to conceptualizing the knowledge base as a semantic network of concepts, we can also postulate, as does Anderson (1976) that the knowledge base contains procedures. That is, knowledge is represented as a procedure for "how to" do or execute something (Norman and Rumelhart, 1975). One technique for representing procedural knowledge is in terms of a production system (Newell, 1973). A production system is a set of rules, each rule containing some conditions which, if satisfied, result in execution of the action side of the rule. For example, one's knowledge about how to solve a physics problem can be captured by a set of rules, where each rule specifies the conditions under which a given physics equation will be applied to the problem. If this is the conceptualization of an expert's knowledge base, then we would want to know in what ways an expert's knowledge base is superior to that of a novice's. We would hypothesize that an expert's knowledge base (a) contains many more productions than a novice, (b) discriminates more finely among productions, and (c) orders the productions within any given production system in a different way from the novice's.

According to this view, we could speculate that the superior problem-solving abilities of experts arise from the existence of a production system that has been prestored. Hence, solving a standard physics problem requires no direct problem-solving skill, but merely matching and retrieving the "right" production system. An important aspect of studies that we plan to carry out will be to substantiate whether such standard production systems are already prestored in the memory base of an expert. Alternatively, one could think of problem solving as a constructive process whereby a set of productions have to be organized to handle each problem. In this case, we would want to know how the complex data structure of an expert permits the assembly of a more elaborate and efficient set of productions to handle the problem-solving task.

At the moment, we speculate that both of the above processes occur. That is, for the expert, a standard problem requires only the retrieval of prestored production systems, whereas a novel or a difficult problem may require the organization of a new set of productions. For the novice, however, every problem may require the latter type of constructive assembly process to reach solution. The question is, how does a large repertoire of knowledge facilitate the organization of an efficient set of processes that is used to arrive at a solution?

STRATEGY OR PROCESS DIFFERENCES

Another component differentiating expert and novice performance may be characterized as processing differences. By processing differences we mean differences in cognitive strategies that are not immediately attributable to content knowledge, although they may be a function of differences in the knowledge base–for example, we refer to differences in the use of planning, the amount of self-inquiry, and the type of solution paths. For certain tasks, the cognitive strategies that experts use are quite different from those of the novice. They may be similar only at a superficial macrolevel, but they are very different when analyzed in detail. Observable strategy differences that can provide the focus for the initial studies we suggest can be described in terms of solution strategies, planning strategies, and strategies for self-inquiry.

Solution Strategies. Investigators in the field of problem solving have described such solution strategies as forward versus backward search, means-end analyses, hill climbing, etc. When these strategies are studied in the context of solving physics problems, it appears that there is a difference in the solution strategies of the expert versus the novice. For simple problems, the expert physicist in the Simon and Simon (1978) study uses a forward strategy. That is, he simply evokes equations in succession for which the values of the variables are known and then solves for the unknown variable. In this systematic manner, the solution is quickly obtained. The novice, however, appears to be using the more "sophisticated" solution of working backward. That is, a goal is first defined, and then equations are set up to solve for a subgoal. However, the expert's less sophisticated forward strategy is used because he is more certain that his path will lead to a solution. For more complicated problems, however, an expert's problem-solving behavior is characterized best by the more sophisticated means-ends analysis. In general, the solution strategy of the expert compared with that of the novice appears to differ in terms of the following aspects: The expert physicist uses fewer equations, his solution procedure is shorter, and it is ordered differently from that of the novice (Simon and Simon, 1978). The important research question is how this advanced solution strategy develops–why are experts able to assemble their existing relevant knowledge and skill into higher-order strategies, whereas the novices cannot?

In answer to this question, three aspects of processing mechanics appear to be involved in an expert's ability to come up with efficient problem solving strategies: (a) a competent performer can detect and encode the details of a problem in ways that indicate a particular order of substrategies; (b) he or she is able to scan for features of the problem situation that can be linked to available concepts or solution routines in memory; and (c) the expert is able to successively reanalyze and redefine the subgoals of the problem, as applicable and inapplicable solution routines are retrieved from memory. Hence, these aspects of performance become candidates for components of ability to be assessed in achievement of this kind.

A fourth candidate, as evidenced from past work, is that the expert's effective solution strategies arise from his/her ability to encode a problem by parsing key words in a given problem statement. An effective strategy may arise as a result of a powerful parsing ability, where certain key words readily evoke the appropriate solution routines. Consonant with this notion, it has been shown that students can categorize algebra word problems into types simply after having read a fifth of the problem (Hinsley, et al., 1978). This ability to categorize a problem appears to be facilitated by a strategy of reading key words.

Planning. Planning strategies provide another dimension of differences between expert and novice. Planning refers to activities that occur prior to the actual solving of the problem. The "actual" problem-solving activities refer to the application of operators that transform the initial situation to the final goal state. Planning, on the other hand, refers to various activities, such as (a) setting goals, (b) deciding which approach to use for parsing the problem statement, (c) deciding whether or not to seek an isomorphic problem where familiar routines already exist, and (d) assembling a set of processes for applying the operators to the problem.

The problem-solving behavior of experts can indeed be characterized by planfulness. For example, compared with beginning students in physics, experts do not directly proceed to quantitative equations. They pause and formulate their plans; they carry out what has been called an intervening *qualitative analysis* (Larkin, 1977a) before proceeding with their problem-solving behavior. Such qualitative analysis is usually accompanied by an understanding of the problem in terms of its real-world physical representation.

There are several ways to assess whether or not problem solvers are planning. One way is to infer the existence of planning behavior by the way they read a problem. For example, in the solution of algebra word problems, some individuals read the entire problem before formulating their plan of attack, whereas others translate each sentence of the word problem line by line (Hinsley et al., 1978; Paige and Simon, 1966). One could speculate that those individuals who read the entire problem first before attempting to solve the problem are more likely to plan than those individuals who translate each line of the problem directly into an equation. Another more direct approach is simply to examine the thinking-aloud protocols of subjects who are asked to solve problems. In such verbal protocols, one can detect explicit planning strategies, such as finding problem isomorphs, setting goals, and laying out a sequence of operators to be applied.

However, there may be another aspect of an expert's planning processes that may not be as observable through subjective introspection as through the medium of verbal protocols. This planning phase may be conceived of as a rapid initial analysis. In the domain of chess, this initial analysis lasting about fifteen-thirty seconds has been called *assessment* (Simon and Barenfeld, 1969). In the domain of musical sight reading, it is named *preconception* (Wolf, 1976). It seems that such initial categorization or planning of the problem is necessary for efficient problem solution as carried out by experts.

Another way to look at this planning process is not whether individuals can categorize problems correctly or bring to bear the appropriate schemata of problem types, but rather, whether they can detect similarities in the features of a to-be-solved problem so that they can transform it into a problem for which they already have a solution routine (Resnick and Glaser, 1976). Simon (1969) cites an example of such problem transformation. He discusses a problem called number scrabble that is analogous to a tic-tac-toe problem. In order to rapidly develop a strategy to play number scrabble efficiently, all one needs to do is to perceive that it is a modified version of tic-tac-toe. In another context, Larkin (1977b) found that for difficult physics problems, most of the expert's activity is involved in finding the appropriate way to think about the problem. In other words, planning can be conceived of as a process to represent the problem in such a way "so as to make the solution transparent" (Simon, 1969: 77). A "transparent" representation of a problem may be interpreted as one that permits the direct retrieval from memory of a prestored solution algorithm. In our investigations of this kind of behavior, we shall attempt not only to understand whether experts tend to participate more in planning than novices, but what the nature of these planning strategies are. An important point to note is that planning has only been grossly analyzed experimentally.

Self-Inquiry and Metacognition. Closely related to the idea of planning are the apparent differences among individuals in their use of executive control functions such as checking their solutions to problems, interrogating themselves about possible errors, and hypothesizing the possible goals of the problem. Experts appear to make fewer metacomments about their solution processes and strategies than do novices; novices are much more uncertain about their solution strategies, and hence are constantly asking themselves questions about the procedure they are using and about the accuracy of their computation (Simon & Simon, 1978).

Another interesting piece of evidence is that if problem solvers are required to hypothesize the goals of the problem, as well as to verbalize their plans, they are more likely to succeed in solving the problems (Pellegrino and Schadler, 1974). In many problem-solving situations, it may be that low-achieving problem solvers do not lack the necessary knowledge but rather they need to be reminded of goals and possible actions so that they can obtain the appropriate information. If this is the case, then diagnostic assessment of this inability might be helpful for instruction.

SUMMARY

We recommend and are carrying out research that can provide a theoretical and empirical basis for the assessment of performance through investigation of the development of competence in knowledge and skill. In particular, we suggest experimental studies designed to identify expert-novice differences and their implications for the measurement of achievement and the conduct of instruction. These studies can be carried out in terms of the two major interacting components of the human information-processing system: content, that can be investigated in terms of the quantitative and qualitative aspects of knowledge structures, and cognitive processes, that can be investigated in terms of problem solution strategies, planning, self-inquiry, and other such processes that become apparent from this work.

The success of such a research program should be judged eventually by whether or not it enables more individuals to attain high levels of competence as a result of formal instruction and on-the-job training and work experience. In order to really focus on this matter, it is necessary to consider the kinds of knowledge and skill that facilitate learning from long-term experience. The essential educational task is to provide individuals with knowledge structures and cognitive process capabilities that are more susceptible to long-term development than are learning outcomes that are based upon education for short-run levels of competence.

The significance of the research that has been recommended lies in this distinction between instruction based upon knowledge of the long-term changes that occur with experience and practice versus instruction based upon knowledge of the more immediate products of short-range learning. Our task is to obtain knowledge about the nature of these long-term changes so that the design of instructional and assessment procedures need not rely primarily on knowledge of short-term learning and achievement. One important implication of the qualitative changes in the long-term development of competence is that different modes of learning are active at different stages of the acquisition of skilled performance. As a result, the level of performance attained needs to be assessed and then matched with appropriate instructional conditions in order for further expertise to be developed.

Lack of knowledge of the phases of development of complex performance can result in educational conditions that place artificial limits on performance that serve as detriments to the learning of advanced competence. In an instructional situation, individuals can cease to show improvement not because they are incapable of further learning, but because some conditions of performance imposed by instruction restrict the opportunity for the development of expertise. Furthermore, the lack of knowledge of exactly what to measure as an indication of expertise results in the use of criteria of performance on tests which may not adequately measure advanced capabilities, or capabilities that provide a basis upon which competence can be achieved as a result of further experience.

At the present time, we can only generally indicate the implications for revised training and assessment practices of research on the novice-expert distinction, because our knowledge of the nature of advanced competence is limited. The long-range goal of the recommended research program is to obtain knowledge about skills that are complicated enough to require years before expertise is achieved, and then to theoretically and experimentally determine how performance of these skills can be best achieved and maintained for a greater number of individuals.

REFERENCES

ANDERSON, J. R. (1976) Language, Memory, and Thought. Hillsdale, NJ: Lawrence Erlbaum.

CHASE, W. G. and H. A. SIMON (1973) "Perception in chess." Cognitive Psychology 4: 55-81.

GREENO, J. G. (1977) "Process of understanding in problem solving," in N. J. Castellan, D. B. Pisoni, and G. R. Potts (eds.) Cognitive Theory (Vol. 2). Hillsdale, NJ: Lawrence Erlbaum Associates.

HINSLEY, D.A., J. R. HAYES, and H. A. SIMON (1978) "From words to equations: meaning and representation in algebra word problems," in M. A. Just and P. A. Carpenter (eds.) Cognitive Processes in Comprehension. Hillsdale, NJ: Lawrence Erlbaum.

LARKIN, J. H. (1977a) "Processing information for effective problem solving." Unpublished manuscript, University of California at Berkeley.

--- (1977b) "Skilled problem solving in physics: a hierarchical planning model." Unpublished manuscript, University of California at Berkeley.

NEWELL, A. (1973) "Production systems: models of control structures," in W. G. Chase (ed.) Visual Information Processing. New York: Academic Press.

NORMAN, D. A. and D. E. RUMELHART (1975) Explorations in Cognition. San Francisco: Freeman.

PAIGE, J. M. and H. A. SIMON (1966) "Cognitive processes in solving algebra word problems," in B. Kleinmuntz (ed.) Problem Solving. New York: John Wiley.

PELLEGRINO, J. W. and M. SCHADLER (1974) "Maximizing performance in a problem solving task." Unpublished manuscript, University of Pittsburgh.

RESNICK, L. B. and R. GLASER (1976) "Problem solving and intelligence," in L. B. Resnick (ed.) The Nature of Intelligence. Hillsdale, NJ: Lawrence Erlbaum.

SHAVELSON, R. J. (1972) "Some aspects of the correspondence between content structure and cognnitive structure in physics instruction." Journal of Educational Psychology 63: 225-234.

SIMON, D. P. and H. A. SIMON (1978) "Individual differences in solving physics problems," in R. Siegler (ed.) Children's Thinking: What Develops? Hillsdale, NJ: Lawrence Erlbaum.

SIMON, H. A. (1969) The Sciences of the Artificial. Cambridge, MA: MIT Press.

--- and M. BARENFELD (1969) "Information processing analysis of perceptual processes in problem solving." Psychological Review 76: 473-483.

WOLF, T. (1976) "A cognitive model of musical sight-reading." Journal of Psycholinguistic Research 5: 143-171.

4

THE DEMISE OF GENERALITY IN MEASUREMENT AND RESEARCH METHODOLOGY

Lawrence T. Frase

CONCERN ABOUT TEST SCORES

Today, we hear a great deal about test score declines. Federal and state agencies hum with concern about the decline in students' performance on standardized tests. Broad-reaching proposals to develop and institute tests of competence in various areas are underway, with the prospect that our children will be confronted with an endless variety of tests as they move through school and from school to work.

I'm concerned about this, first, because of my assumptions about the proper use of tests, but also because there is a certain irrationality in the response to test score declines. We do not yet understand the nature and extent of test score declines, much less their causes. We need to be

AUTHOR'S NOTE: This paper was presented at the Center for the Study of Evaluation Winter Invitational Conference on Measurement and Methodology, Los Angeles, January 1978. The opinions expressed here are the author's, and they do not necessarily reflect the official opinions or policies of the National Institute of Education. The author is now at Bell Laboratories, 6 Corporate Place, Piscataway, New Jersey 08854.

thoughtful and cautious about the consequences of our testing proposals. If they are taken seriously, they will alter our educational goals and resources in complex ways.

Confusions about the nature and extent of declining test scores arise in part because the psychometric tradition has given administrators the tools for assessing potential for academic success without tying those assessments of intellectual performance to an analytic conception of how people learn and how they adapt to the demands of school and work tasks.

As a consequence, one can predict success or failure, in a general sense, but there are too few clues in our assessment to tell us what to do to remedy potential failures. Paradoxically, in an era of concern for the welfare of individuals, we are in danger of stressing the evaluation of people without a means to encourage relevant changes in their behavior. The danger is that management tools will proliferate without a careful sharpening of their rationales. We may become very good at condemning children but not very good at helping them.

I assume that the most defensible use of tests is not to manage or predict, but rather to assess specific areas of intellectual functioning—assessments that point to actions that can be taken to modify skills. We need different kinds of test items; items that issue from what we know about the skills that allow students to function in classroom study activities and in related contexts. To do this, test development needs the support of cognitive and developmental theory.

The step from test items that reflect particular skills or processes to instructional methods that encourage those skills or processes requires a nontrivial leap—and probably a good deal of practical teaching experience. I'm more sanguine about our capacity to build items that test certain skills than I am about our ability to translate such items into instructional methods. Nevertheless, if we don't develop tests that relate to some broad conceptions of human learning, and link such conceptions to instructional methods, twenty years from today we will find ourselves managed by tests that float free of the realities of our everyday lives.

In this paper I will do three things. First, in contrast to the note of alarm on which I began, I'll express some optimism about the decline of superficial analyses in testing and research methodology. But even here there is a need for caution lest our tendency toward precision makes us lose sight of the broadly adaptive characteristics of human behavior that cut across learning tasks.

Second, I will review a model of learning skills that might be used to link specific performances to test items, and to link test items to instructional methods. This is only one model that could provide a domain focus for item writing, but it has a strong research base and it communicates with the kinds of activities that are encouraged in reading comprehension programs.

Third, I will review some complexities of inferring processing activities from performance on test items. This analysis suggests that we can learn a great deal about tests and about people by concentrating on the strategies that test takers use to arrive at the information (or data base) presumed to support test-taking performance. The problem is that test-taking performance is often governed by factors (like motivation and world knowledge) which have little to do with the nominal task presented by a test item.

NORM-REFERENCED TESTS, CRITERION-REFERENCED TESTS, AND COGNITIVE PSYCHOLOGY

Fortunately, in the educational measurement community there has been a decline of interest in general methods of assessing individual and group achievements; instead, there is a movement toward a criterion-referenced test technology. For instructional purposes, we should encourage criterion-referenced tests because of the need to relate the content to be tested to the elements of specific educational programs. As Hambleton and Gifford (1977) point out, the discrepancy between norm-referenced tests and the content covered in educational programs is a major drawback to norm-referenced tests that might otherwise be used to evaluate educational programs. Given that criterion-referenced tests could be used in a normative fashion, it seems the wiser alternative to supplement current tests with those which tap specific skills and performances. To do this, we have to give up, to an extent, our psychometric leanings to select items on the basis of their ability to discriminate among individuals when the basis for that discrimination is not clearly related to specific educational performance.

This general movement toward greater specificity in educational measurement and evaluation is paralleled by a greater emphasis on specificity in research methodology. In 1972 Anderson wrote an article called "How to Construct Achievement Tests to Assess Comprehension." Anderson reviewed 130 research articles in which comprehension tests were employed. His findings were embarrasing, and they suggest some reasons why progress in educational psychology has been slow. Although 82% of the articles reported the number of test items used, only 33% gave any rationale for their selection. And 51% of the articles gave no information about the relations of the test items to the experimental conditions. Anderson's summary, that "conclusions about methods, variables, or procedures can hardly be taken seriously," is a strong indictment of the status of educational research. So there appears to be a need to sharpen research methodologies that support educational research; i.e., a need for test methodologies that specify the component operations of general concepts like comprehension.

Recent research developments, even if they do not completely fill the breach in research methodology, at least may retard the advance of unfriendly troops until the cavalry arrives. If we put our ears to the ground, we can hear the approaching hoof-beats of cognitive psychologists. A number of provocative articles appear in Klahr's book, *Cognition and Instruction* (1976). The book deals primarily with the analysis of competence in specific domains, such as algorithmic descriptions of the representation of semantic concepts and the process of answering questions (Greeno, 1976). But, as Resnick (1976) points out, most research deals with only two of three important elements. These two elements are the structure of subject matter and the routines that describe performance on a given task. A third element, which is only weakly represented in cognitive psychology, provides methods for describing performances in the context of specific subject matters. But it is still a problem to relate these methods to teaching and acquisition routines. It is a great step forward to be able to describe specific performances in different subject matter areas, and certainly our notions of comprehension have become more precise. But the decline of generality in the negative sense of looseness of thinking about cognitive performance, has brought with it an apparent decline of generality in the positive sense of telling us about the learning skills that cut across subject matters. From time to time we might step back and look at these more general skills. They represent a level of discourse that can help us better to communicate the relations between teaching and cognition, and to assess the significance of different processes for activities like test taking.

LEARNING AND STUDY SKILLS

I'd like to discuss some candidates for those learning activities that have a fairly broad research base and which have some implications for testing.

I'll stick closely to performance in verbal tasks since many of our tests have strong verbal components.

PRELIMINARY MODEL

In Chapter 1 of the 1975 volume of the *Psychology of Learning and Motivation,* I outlined a model of the skills entailed in reading study activities. The model was divided into three general areas. The first area involved the task environment, representing immediate stimulus conditions for performance. This area included things like task directions, the sequence of information, and so forth.

The second area concerned the different kinds of performances that might be brought to bear on information. These performances were linked to information in either working memory or long-term memory. (The different memory components comprised a third area of the model.) The performances were arranged in levels such that long-term memory was more implicated in performance at the higher levels. Part of the contribution of cognitive psychology has been to show how subjects' long-term memories (or world knowledge) influence learning, and I tried to clarify processing activities that are more or less relevant to these long-term memories.

The first level of performances I called content and performance sets. These include factors that limit or expand the engagement of other kinds of performances. They were conceived to issue most strongly from the immediate task demands. Another kind of performance, at the second level, involved the encoding of task information which might vary according to the reader's set or disposition to respond. For instance, whether a reader scans a text for letters, words, phrases, or implications determines the kinds and amount of information that is represented internally. A third level of performance included rehearsal and text integration activities which are conceived to operate primarily on items available in working memory. Rehearsal activities increase residence time of items in working memory and hence transfer to long-term memory. Integration involved the bringing together of propositions or other elements of text to provide coherence to discourse and to make possible deductive reasoning activities. Finally, a fourth level involved the retrieval of information from long-term memory and the relation of that information to items in working memory or to other items in long-term memory. In short, the model included task elements, a memory system, and some specific processing activities that operate on items in memory or in the task.

The chapter also reviewed the literature and described a number of original studies to support the claim that the performances of encoding, rehearsal, integration, retrieval, and relation are implicated in a variety of learning tasks and test-taking activities. In regard to test-taking skills, we know that certain stimulus characteristics are coordinate with different performances, i.e., we can identify stimulus factors that support, supplement, and control certain processing activities. For instance, encoding activities are strongly influenced by the directions given to subjects. These constrain the items that a person selects as relevant in a task and what other performances are brought to bear on those selected items. Subjects make either shallow or deep semantic contact with materials, whether lists of words or extended texts, depending on the task instruction. For instance, requirements to make fine categorical discriminations make contact with long-term memory and result in high recall for task materials.

Another example concerns phrase segmentation. Part of a reader's encoding activities has to do with the segmentation of text into meaningful phrases. These phrases represent elements that can be stored and manipulated more efficiently than meaningless fragments of text. The activity of segmentation can be altered by changes in text format. We were able to increase reading speed by about 20% by redesigning texts so that each line of the text ended at a pausal boundary (Frase and Schwartz, 1979). The texts looked odd–something like poetry–but they nonetheless facilitated reading.

In the same way, rehearsal can be supported by repetition of items in a text and integration can be supported by grouping related information together in various ways. Retrieval and relation can be supported by prompts for recall, varying the familiarity of items, and so forth.

My point is that if we can identify stimulus characteristics that support specific intellectual performances, then we can use them to write test items that impose clearly defined processing requirements on subjects. These might also be linked to instruction. For instance, Weaver (1976) has shown that anagram task training generalizes to other reading tests. Schallert (1977) reported data showing that phrase segmentation training improves comprehension performance. We should look carefully into the current research literature for school-related intellectual operations like these and draw out the implications of testing procedures for instructional methods.

CONCLUSIONS FROM AND MODIFICATIONS OF PRELIMINARY MODEL

As for the preliminary model of processing activities that I have reviewed, there are some changes that need to be made. For instance, most of the performances that I've suggested seem to be subskills that are assembled according to higher-level executive processes. A separate group of executive processes should be added; and I would move the category of performance sets into that executive grouping. For instance, how a person sequences the different subskills could influence reading speed and memory. Research by Flavell et al. (1970) and by Brown (1975) suggests that meta-comprehension skills, like memory monitoring, change in interesting ways as reading skills develop. These activities could become grist for an expansion of our current test repertoire, a repertoire that might better reflect the state of the art in cognitive and instructional psychology.

One of the most impressive factors that emerged from our studies was the strong role of encoding activities on subjects' learning. That is, even before we worry about tracing out complex semantic linkages among items represented in the mind, we ought to consider whether and how subjects pay attention to the material before them. I'd like to pursue this problem in greater detail and boil my model down into just two factors.

TWO ELEMENTS OF INTELLECTUAL PERFORMANCE: BUILDING A DATA BASE AND PERFORMING OPERATIONS ON IT

The model that I have described can be thought of as two broad properties of intellectual performance. The first has to do with building an internal data base of information upon which to operate (the representational problem); the second has to do with the operations performed on that base. When a person selects a multiple-choice answer on a test, for instance, a reading comprehension test or a reasoning test, we often assume that the answer is related to the information on the page given in support of the alternatives. This may not be true; and if not necessarily true, it places a great limit on our ability to draw detailed inferences about human performance from test items. To the extent that a test-taker imports simplifying strategies into the test-taking situation, we do not know what data base provides the context for performance. In the remainder of this paper, I'll disregard the problem of how people manipulate information that is completely extracted from a test item and accurately represented internally. I'll concentrate on the complexities of determining whether information presented in a test item ever arrives internally at all. We can achieve a deeper understanding of test-taking performance by concentrating on what may appear to be lower-level skills, skills that at another time might have been called "paying attention" or some such. They reflect the encoding portion of the model that I described.

To explore this problem, I'd like to concentrate on the solving of syllogistic reasoning arguments of the form, "All S are M. All M are P. Therefore, all S are P." The subject's task is to determine whether the conclusion follows logically from the premises. The test response format might vary, and the content of the premises and conclusion might vary from the schematic form in my example to something like ordinary text. In the literature there is a preponderance of multiple-choice formats as response items. But these details of experimental procedures seem less important than the major points that I want to make.

THE REPRESENTATIONAL PROBLEM

Achieving an adequate representation of the propositions presented in premises of a syllogism or of sentences in a text relates closely to problems of reading comprehension. There are two subproblems concerning representation. I call these the problems of *partial representation* and *optional representation.* Partial representation is concerned with whether all relevant features of a sentence are or need to be encoded. Optional representation is concerned with the form of representation, given that a proposition is completely represented.

Partial Representation. Consider first whether a reader responds to entire sentences or just to parts of them. Revlis (1975) has described a feature election model of syllogistic reasoning. The model deals with the representation of syllogistic premises as an outgrowth of the selection of partial features of quantity and polarity, where quantity refers to the universal or particular characteristics of a proposition, and polarity refers to whether it is affirmative or negative. The logical problem solver is conceived to store this rudimentary information from sentences and to combine this information from different sentences to arrive at conclusion according to certain rules. The model does not talk about complex internal representations of class inclusion statements. This alogical selective mechanism neglects a significant portion of the "meaning" of propositions, but it makes fairly accurate predictions about syllogistic errors. Revlis's data suggest that errors on syllogisms occur as a consequence of this simplifying strategy of processing the test items.

I doubt that we should call a feature selection model unreasonable, even though it is alogical. One can reject many syllogisms as invalid, without dealing with a complete representation of the set inclusions implied, by matching the quantifier in the conclusion with the quantifiers in the premises. This could be done on the basis of knowing the logical rule: "If one premise is particular, the conclusion is particular; if both premises are particular, there is no conclusion." It might also be done on the basis of an intuitive feeling that if there is some uncertainty in the premises (one or both are particular), then the conclusion should not be too certain (universal). With the latter intuitive feeling, a person can correctly evaluate the validity of 96 different syllogisms. When we talk with subjects, they sometimes tell us they proceed on such intuitions.

I am suggesting that the strategies of test takers that bring the assumptions of our test items into question represent useful information about the adaptive abilities of students. One of the problems is to determine the reduced cues that subjects use to perform a particular task. Studies that we conducted (Frase, 1972) suggest that the reasoning performance of fourth-grade children can be improved by cueing them to the few critical features of relationships that are embedded in a text. For instance, the children read texts in which were embedded sentences of the form, "The small thing was red. The red thing was a bag. The bag was full of money." The children read texts and verified sentences like, "The small thing was a bag," which entails using two sentences mediated by the word "red." Performance on these problems averaged 64% for uncued subjects. Cueing the subjects before they read to pay special attention to critical terms, like the "red thing," raised performance to 94%. In short, specific reasoning failures and successes may have something to do with the ability to select relevant information with the array of information given.

But not all simplifying strategies result in improved performance. In 1962 Henle found two particularly common strategies of reasoning. These reflect partial representation strategies. One strategy was the omission of a premise from the argument to be evaluated. Another strategy was to ignore both premises entirely and to evaluate the content of the conclusion alone based upon what the subject knows about events in the world. Errors like this, if we choose to call them errors, reflect ways in which a subject tries to simplify the task presented, or ways in which the subject brings our experimental task into alignment with reality. Scribner's (1975) syllogistic studies, with African subjects, indicate strong cultural biases to perform according to the task or according to extratask knowledge.

Optional Representation. A variety of reasoning studies suggests that the premises of a syllogism may be completely represented, but they are represented in a form which departs from the correct or intended meaning. Ceraso and Provitera (1971) have described the possibilities of interpreting assertions such as, "All A's are B's." This might be interpreted to mean that A is a subset of B, or that A is coextensive with B. Chapman and Chapman (1959) found that subjects frequently interpret "All A are B" to mean that "All B are A." We conducted several studies (Frase, 1969) in which sorites (extended syllogistic arguments) were embedded in texts, and we found conversion errors to be quite frequent. Dawes (1966) also conducted studies in which set relations were embedded in prose. He found that distortions tended strongly toward overgeneralizations, that is, recalling a disjunctive relation as nested. Dawes considered these distortions to be simplifications of the material read, because a disjunctive relation (as he used the term) is complex in the sense that two sets in a disjunctive relation have elements in common, but neither set is included in the other. To Dawes, distortions of a text apparently move in the direction of less qualified propositions, i.e., simplified structures.

As far as the syllogism goes, we might assume, along with Ceraso and Provitera (1971), that reasoners fully represent the premises of syllogism, and that errors in reasoning arise from the fact that some propositions have multiple interpretations. As the number of potential interpretations of the two premises increases, then errors in reasoning should increase. If the product of the two premises generally determines the difficulty of evaluating a conclusion, then the form of the two premises should interact to produce more or fewer errors in reasoning, depending upon how many alternative possibilities for interpretation there are. We collected error data on all 256 standard syllogisms. Analysis of these data shows that the forms of the premises do not interact, although the form of each premise interacts strongly with the form of the conclusion. These findings suggest to me that, considering the full domain of syllogistic arguments, many are solved with a strategy that entails matching of potential conclusions with part of the premise information given. In short, reasoning frequently proceeds on the basis of partial representation of the information given rather than optional representation of that information.

If we could clarify the contributions of partial and optional representation in testing, I believe that we would have learned some useful facts about subjects' adaptive strategies. If we found that partial representation was a major cause of errors in performance, then we would concentrate our efforts on subjects' attentional processes. If we found that optional representation was a more potent factor, we might shift our attention to the semantic and interpretive dimensions of subjects' activities.

We will probably find interesting differences between novices and experts (see Chi and Glaser, this volume) on these two dimensions of performance. Experts appear to concentrate on the critical elements of a task whereas the novice founders in a sea of irrelevant information. The expert is skilled at simplifying the task into those relevant elements, whereas the simplifying strategies of the novice may be based on features irrelevant to problem solution. The optional representations selected by the expert expand and elaborate the dimensions of the task in useful ways; the optional representations of the novice overgeneralize and are inaccurate in other ways. Optional interpretations operate at the level of entire discourse structures, not only sentences (Anderson et al., 1977), hence they have important implications for reading comprehension.

Ceraso and Provitera (1971) found that simplified versions of premises, which constrained the representation of premises, improved reasoning performance considerably. Griggs (1976) also found that careful instructions about how to interpret sentences improved reasoning. These studies suggest that optional representation is a useful factor to consider in test performance.

Other Complications. I'd like to consider a few other things, aside from partial representation and optional representation, that are implicated in performance on test items. Once a proposition is correctly represented in working memory, it begins to decay unless special steps are taken to insure its stability. And in reasoning and other performances, there are momentary disruptions of processing even when we know that the conditions for correct performance are available. It could be that some of these failures are due to the inability to manipulate stored information; on the other hand, the support or interference that performance gets from indirectly related information in the task is also important. A variety of studies show that the recall of propositions is determined by the context in which the propositions are embedded. Rothkopf (1972) cites data showing that recall for text is inversely related to the number of irrelevant facts in the text. But suppose that the additional information in the text consists of the inferences which can be drawn from the premises stated in the text. We can think of this as structurally related information. Stetson (1974) had children learn texts which varied in the number of inferences that were explicitly stated in the text along with the premises. In an extreme condition, 50% of the text consisted of inferences. Stetson's data showed that under conditions of high structural redundancy, subjects not only learned the inferences, but their retention of the premises was high.

The data base problem is a tricky one. Even when subjects have sufficient information to solve a problem and the skills to manipulate the information, they may fail. On the other hand, when they have insufficient information, they may succeed. In a series of studies (Frase, 1973), we had subjects read sentences which described the attributes of various sailboats. For instance, two sentences might be: "The Winston Churchill had a green hull. The Winston Churchill's speed was 12 knots." After reading, the subjects were asked questions that required the recall of the text sentences. They were also asked questions that required the integration of information from different text sentences. An integration question might be: "What was the speed of the ship with the green hull?" We found that if responses to one or neither of the required text sentences were correct, the proportion of correct integrations was about .55. If both text sentences were recalled, the proportion of correct integration scores went to .89. A related study by Stetson (1974) with children, showed that the proportion of correct inferences, or integrations, given that the premises were in memory, was .91. It was .65 if the text items were not in memory. Chance scores in Stetson's task were .50.

These data are troublesome. Although it is clear that knowing the text helps integration performance, knowledge of the basic text, from which higher level outcomes should be drawn, is neither a completely necessary nor a sufficient condition for correct performance. Stetson's subjects performed above chance without correctly responding to questions about the premises. In none of the studies was performance perfect given that the necessary text was in memory. So the notion of the text data base as a necessary or sufficient condition for performance must be approached cautiously.

SUMMARY OF THE DATA BASE PROBLEM

Important encoding activities, that we know influence performance, are conceptually prior to the full algorithmic representations that our leanings toward cognitive psychology might encourage us to develop. At least for a certain class of problems that I've reviewed, simplifying strategies that ignore semantic knowledge are available. Where world knowledge is pertinent, one still has the problem of which representation from among several might be relevant to a particular performance. In short, although the cavalry may be coming, the engagement of cognitive theorists with the analysis of test-taking performances needs the perspective that human adaptive behaviors are sometimes based upon relatively simple factors. Things like the amount of irrelevant information in a problem, the sequence in which a subject reads response alternatives, the precision of problem statement and so forth, all control test performances. How to distinguish which of these is most important, and when it is necessary to proceed with a deeper analysis, will determine the kind of theory that we think most adequately characterizes test-taking and study performance. We need to encourage multiple levels of analysis.

CONCLUSION

It seems most important to me that we sharpen our conception of learning theory, that we analyze the skills entailed in specific subject matters, and that we explore ways to relate these skills to instructional methods and outcomes. Data that I reviewed suggest that we explore not only our idealized conceptions of what cognitive processing is, but the adaptive behaviors of test takers that simplify and convert nominal stimulus materials into something other than they are intended to be.

Perhaps it is true that part of the reason for test score declines is that the background knowledge of students who now take standardized tests has changed, and that some cultural backgrounds do not support concern for how one scores on a test. If so, then it is all the more important for us to characterize and explore partial and optional representational processes, since these have to do with motivational and cultural factors which are logically prior to many of the performances that our test items attempt to measure.

REFERENCES

ANDERSON, R. C. (1972) "How to construct achievement tests to assess comprehension." Review of Educational Research 42: 145-170.

---, R. E. REYNOLDS, D. L. SHALLERT, and E. T. GOETZ (1977) "Frameworks for comprehending discourse." American Educational Research Journal 14: 367-381.

BROWN, A. L. (1975) "The development of memory: knowing, knowing about knowing, and knowing how to know," in H. W. Reese (ed.) Advances in Child Development and Behavior (Vol. 10). New York: Academic Press.

CERASO, J. and A. PROVITERA (1971) "Sources of error in syllogistic reasoning." Cognitive Psychology 2: 400-410.

CHAPMAN, L. J. and J. P. CHAPMAN (1959) "Atmosphere effect re-examined." Journal of Experimental Psychology 58: 220-226.

DAWES, R. M. (1966) "Memory and the distortion of meaningful written material." British Journal of Psychology 57: 77-86.

FLAVELL, J. H., A. G. FRIEDRICHS, and J. D. HOYT (1970) "Developmental changes in memorization processes." Cognitive Psychology 1: 324-340.

FRASE, L. T. (1969) "A structural analysis of the knowledge that results from thinking about text." Journal of Educational Psychology Monographs 60: No. 6, Pt. 2.

--- (1972) "Maintenance and control in the acquisition of knowledge from written materials," in J. B. Carroll and R. O. Freedle (eds.) Language Comprehension and the Acquisition of Knowledge. Washington, DC: V. H. Winston.

--- (1973) "Integration of written text." Journal of Educational Psychology 65: 252-261.

FRASE, L. T. (1975) "Prose processing," in G. H. Bower (ed.) The Psychology of Learning and Motivation (Vol. 9). New York: Academic Press.

--- and B. J. SCHWARTZ (1979) "Typographical cues that facilitate comprehension." Journal of Educational Psychology 71: 197-206.

GREENO, J. (1976) "Cognitive objectives of instruction: theory of knowledge for solving problems and answering questions," in D. Klahr (ed.) Cognition and Instruction. Hillside, NJ: Lawrence Erlbaum Associates.

GRIGGS, R. A. (1976) "Logical processing of set inclusion relations in meaningful text." Memory and Cognition 4: 730-740.

HAMBLETON, R. K. and J. A. GIFFORD (1977) "Development and use of criterion referenced tests to evaluate program effectiveness." Laboratory of Psychometric and Evaluative Research Report No. 52. Amherst, MA: University of Massachusetts.

HENLE, M. (1962) "On the relation between logic and thinking." Psychological Review 69: 366-378.

KLAHR, D. [ed.] (1976) Cognition and Instruction. Hillside, NJ: Lawrence Erhlbaum Associates.

RESNICK, L. B. (1976) "Task analysis and instructional design: some cases from mathematics," in D. Klahr (ed.) Cognition and Instruction. Hillside, NJ: Lawrence Erlbaum Associates.

REVLIS, R. (1975) "Two models of syllogistic reasoning: feature selection and conversion." Journal of Verbal Learning and Verbal Behavior 14: 180-195.

ROTHKOPF, E. Z. (1972) "Structural text features and the control of processes in learning from written materials," in J. B. Carroll and R. O. Freedle (eds.) Language Comprehension and the Acquisition of Knowledge. Washington, DC: V. H. Winston.

SCHALLERT, D. (1977) "Empirical investigations of the effects of differences between oral and written language on comprehension." Presented at the 27th Annual Meeting of the National Reading Conference, New Orleans, December.

SCRIBNER, S. (1975) "Recall of classical syllogisms: a cross-cultural investigation of error on logical problems," in R. J. Falmagne (ed.) Reasoning: Representation and Process. Hillside, NJ: Lawrence Erlbaum Associates.

STETSON, P. C. (1974) "Verbal transitivity in children" (Doctoral dissertation, University of Delaware, 1974). Dissertation Abstracts International 35: 2064-A.

WEAVER, P. A. (1976) "Sentence anagram organizational training and its effect on reading comprehension." Dissertation Abstracts International 37: 1312-A. (University Microfilms No. 76-20, 188.)

5

TEST DESIGN:
A View from Practice

Lee S. Shulman

I have spent the last ten years studying two types of expertise–in medicine and in teaching–and attempting to understand the relationship between them. One of the things practitioners in these two fields share is a constant involvement with tests. Yet, in studying how, why, and with what degree of trust, confidence, and commitment practitioners in medicine and teaching employ tests, some striking and, at first glimpse, paradoxical contrasts are found.

STUDIES IN MEDICINE AND TEACHING

We began in the late 1960s to study in depth the cognitive processes of experienced peer-nominated internists in order to understand how they

AUTHOR'S NOTE: The work reported herein is sponsored by the Institute for Research on Teaching, College of Education, Michigan State University. The Institute for Research on Teaching is funded primarily by the Teaching Division of the National Institute of Education, United States Department of Health, Education, and Welfare. The opinions expressed in this publication do not necessarily reflect the position, policy, or endorsement of the National Institute of Education (Contract No. 400-76-0073).

perform their medical work. The many studies conducted and the array of findings are reported in *Medical Problem Solving: The Analysis of Clinical Reasoning* (Elstein et al., 1978). We tried to identify the characteristics of expert performance—what an expert does. We wished to discover how to build both curriculum and evaluation in a way that corresponds to how experts actually perform rather than to the content of traditional medical lore regarding how physicians ought to perform.

As we studied physicians, dealing with cases across different domains of internal medicine, we found that they exhibited nongeneralizability of performance from one domain to another. We had assumed, without thinking in terms of formal domain specification and domain referencing, that internal medicine was a unitary domain. Just as items are generated to sample any other field, we felt we could generate cases to sample expertise in internal medicine. It did not much matter which cases we selected as long as each one, to use the terms we used in our research, was a high fidelity representation of problem solving in that domain. We expected significant positive correlations among performance measures across cases. Instead, what we found was that for all practical purposes, performance in one case domain provided no basis for predicting performance by the same physician in another case domain. That finding had several consequences. It led us to collaborate and communicate with other research teams which had been studying similar processes, and we discovered that they were reporting similar findings. But, like small children in their early years of sexual development, each team thought it was something that only happened to them.

For example, Christine McGuire (McGuire and Babbott, 1967) and her group at the University of Illinois Medical School have for many years been developing patient-management problems in medical reasoning, medical diagnosis, and treatment. During this time they have been struggling with the problem that performances of physicians and medical students do not correlate highly across cases. For years, they treated this as a measurement problem, a problem of unreliability. Something had to be fundamentally wrong with their measurement procedures; had they written good simulations, they believed, the cases would have had the same intercase characteristics as items on a test have with one another.

Another example was the American Board of Internal Medicine, which, after many years, terminated use of its oral examination. This was an examination conducted by taking candidate physicians to the bedsides of patients and actually conducting oral examinations across the bed. The candidates were observed as they examined the patient, and were themselves examined on their understanding of the case—a process only slightly less mortifying for the patient than for the candidate.

The major reason the board abandoned oral examinations was the incidence of unreliability of ratings among the judges. The board found that the identify of the oral examiner accounted for a higher proportion of the variance in outcome than did any other single aspect of the examination or candidate. It was only through later research conducted on the computer-based examination for internal medicine by the American Board of Internal Medicine that a group from the Oregon Research Institute led by Paul Hoffman and Robyn Dawes (Hoffman, 1974) tried to disentangle problems of tester unreliability from problems of case or domain specificity. In all those years of oral examination, the examiner had been confounded with the case. A different examiner conducted the examination for each case, since everyone assumed that the domain was singular and all cases were sampled from it. Clearly then, differences among judges could be attributed only to differences in judgment.

When Hoffman and Dawes (Hoffman, 1974) disentangled these two factors, they found that judges given the opportunity to observe a candidate on the *same* case had an acceptably high interrater reliability of judgment. The performers themselves—the experienced board-eligible internists—varied dramatically and significantly form case to case and were the reason for the apparently inconsistent judgments.

These three examples, from McGuire, from Dawes and Hoffman, and from our own research, illustrate how we can totally misconstrue the nature of the domain of expertise we are attempting to assess merely by making unwarranted assumptions about the domain or universe, rather than doing systematic studies of how that expertise is, in fact, put to use. I believe that more must be known about the topography of expertise in different areas—how that expertise is arranged and organized. Expertise in different domains is likely to be cognitively organized in different ways, therefore requiring very different strategies of domain specification, universe designation, and hence, test design.[1]

An example of curricular consequence of misconstruing a domain through misunderstanding the development of the expertise can be found in the classical medical school curricula inspired by Abraham Flexner, one of the most influential persons in the history of twentieth-century medical education.[2]

In the "Flexner curriculum" medical students refrained from clinical work until they had spent two full years studying basic biological sciences. It was asserted that students needed a broad, solid foundational base in all of the relevant biological sciences before they could profit from clinical work.

As we began to see the results of our own research on medical expertise, and the domain specificity of that expertise, we began not only to reexamine our assumptions regarding evaluation of performance in medicine, but also our assumptions about how curriculum should be organized to produce that expertise. If the expertise was domain specific, then perhaps students would not have to know all of biochemistry, physiology, anatomy, microbiology, or pharmacology before doing clinical work. Rather, instruction could be vertically organized and coordinated to permit the beginning of clinical work much earlier. For any particular domain of clinical work there is only a limited area of prerequisite understanding. We designed curricula at Michigan State that reflected this idea, where medical students began doing clinical work in the first *week* of their first term in medical school. To the amazement of our own faculty, the students did very well.

IMPLICATIONS FOR TEST DESIGN

Certain parallels can be drawn between our medical studies and research by Berliner (Berliner and Rosenshine, 1976), Wiley (this volume), and others on the relationships among time expended on instructional tasks, content covered, and achievement. In describing this research, Rosenshine (1976) observed that when pupils have fallen (in terms of standardized achievement tests) three years below grade level, instructional time somehow must be found to make up for that difference. In one sense, it requires three years of time to make up for three years of cumulative deficit. Through better quality instruction, of course, it may be possible to compress the calendar time, but the pupils must somehow traverse the content that has to be covered in order to reach grade level. Where will that instructional time come from, if not via special summer programs? It can only be taken away from the teaching of science, mathematics, social studies, art, or music.

How does our earlier work in medicine correspond to the problem of teaching children who have fallen behind? The question to ask might be: What if the expertise represented in the contents of third- and fourth-grade performance tests, which we simply assume is prerequisite to fifth-grade performance, is not, to use one of Chi and Glaser's (this volume) concepts, really the way the second-grade novice becomes a fifth-grade expert?

Indeed, perhaps that sequence of content is merely a curricular convention—the sequence which instruction has always followed—so is assumed to be the best way. I am suggesting that this is one of the kinds of implicit assumptions about the relationships between types or levels of achievement that very often condition test design and ought to be subjected to scrutiny. One way to accomplish this is through the developmental studies of expertise that Chi and Glaser have described.

A potentially dangerous vertical monopoly, one that I am increasingly uncomfortable with, has developed in the education industry: the same companies are producing both the standard curriculum materials and the standardized tests. Therefore, what constitutes average expected performance at a given grade level in a subject area by some remarkable coincidence corresponds to what the curriculum makers have chosen to define as the content of that grade level. I wonder if we are confronting a problem that is a consequence of how the process of education has become organized both politically and entrepreneurially. I trust that the work of Porter, Schmidt, Floden, Freeman and their colleagues (Porter et al., 1978) at the Institute for Research on Teaching may help us understand more fully the links between curriculum content and testing.

DIAGNOSTIC EXPERTISE AND TEST DESIGN

At the Institute for Research on Teaching (IRT), we study the *expert* as a basis for sensibly defining domains for our work. We are doing studies similar to those we conducted on medical diagnosis. Diagnostic work in the areas of reading and learning disabilities is being done in an attempt to understand how the diagnostic process works in these areas (Vinsonhaler et al., 1978). Our computer simulations of diagnostic work closely correspond to the characteristics of expertise that Chi and Glaser described. We find expertise composed of two components—clinical strategy and clinical memory. Subdividing clinical memory into its components as we do in the simulations, our formulations are also very similar to Chi and Glaser's.

How do the experts feel about tests and test design? Referring again to our studies of medical expertise, it is easy to recognize how starkly contrasting test use and attitudes about tests are between the fields of medicine and teaching. The Center for the Study of Evaluation (CSE) has conducted surveys to study teacher use of tests, observing that when teachers are asked about tests, they tend to dislike, mistrust, and disbelieve them.

The IRT sponsored a set of studies in San Jose by Greta Morine-Dershimer (1979) and Bruce Joyce (1979a,b) which involved intensive study of ten teachers as part of a Teacher Corps experience. Morine-Dershimer and Joyce observed the reactions of the teachers when a set of domain-referenced diagnostic tests that the state had mandated was returned for each of the classroom teachers' use. Performance of each pupil was keyed to each objective and, if pupils were low, the printout specified what kind of curriculum materials could be used to remediate the deficiency. The investigators waited until two weeks after the tests had come back to interview the teachers because they wanted to study how teachers' conceptions of their pupils had changed since the beginning of the year, especially after this marvelous new set of information had arrived. It turned out, however, that not a single one of the ten teachers had looked at those test results. They simply did not find them useful. They were convinced that they already knew more about their students than any one of those tests could possibly detect. Most of the teachers did not believe the tests were of any value at all.

Such observations are striking when compared to the situation in medicine, where a major problem is overcommitment to tests. Probably the single factor that is contributing most to increasing the cost of medical care is that clinicians typically order more tests than they need for a diagnosis. A study by Oskamp (1965) showed that if clinicians are provided with a few tests results, asked for their diagnostic assessment and treatment plan, and then given further increments of test information, the clinicians' diagnostic accuracy and the quality of their treatment plan, after a fairly small number of tests, reaches asymptote. They are doing as well as they ever will long before they stop ordering tests. Although diagnostic accuracy levels off, it can be seen that a clinician's *confidence* increases as he or she orders more tests. This procedure has been replicated by Slovic (1975) with horserace handicappers, who, given five or six pieces of information, are about as accurate as they can be in predicting the outcome of horseraces, but continue asking for more information because they seem to feel better that way. More recently, and most disturbingly, Sisson et al. (1976) have found that additional increments of information can *reduce* the quality of medical decisions. More information is not without its own dangers.

TESTS ARE NOT ENOUGH

Given such abiding faith in tests among other professionals, why is it that teachers do not use, trust, or like tests very much? It matters not whether the test is domain- or norm-referenced,[3] though for a long time we argued that teachers make little use of tests because norm-referenced tests cannot tell teachers what they want to know. That does not seem the answer. I would like to suggest several hypotheses to account for the contrast between the professions. I reject what may be an obvious explanation, which is that tests in medicine are far more reliable. They are not. There have been studies on the reliability of laboratory tests in medicine whose results are frightening. Medicine has serious reliability problems. Educators, in contrast, have the most reliable tests in the world. Thus, reliability is not the problem.

My hypotheses are the following: In general, the kinds of tests we use are inconsistent with, and in many cases irrelevant to, *the realities of teaching.* And the realities of teaching are quite different from *the logic of instruction.*

First, it is clear that no physician ever treats a laboratory test as self-standing, as being sufficient by itself. No physician would ever conduct an inquiry about a patient using only tests, expecting the test to provide all the information necessary to make the diagnostic classification or general assessment judgment. Medical practitioners know that the test is only part of the assessment procedure. *Clinical tests cannot be made clinician-proof!* Yet our strategy in educational test design and development has been to attempt to design tests that are *sufficient* portrayers of student performance, not subject to frequent modification or rescaling by the teachers who spend months at a time with the examined pupils, instructing, observing, and interacting with them. Nevertheless, we must remember that the test is but a very small behavior sample, extremely well calibrated but contextually restricted.

The physician uses observation, interview, touching and feeling, as well as testing, and develops an assessment and a plan by aggregating across those sources of information rather than by giving almost total weight to any one source and subordinating the others to it. A similar strategy might work better in the field of educational test design. Rather than attempting to develop tests that assess everything that is relevant to student performance in the classroom (bemoaning the fact that moving higher up in Bloom's [1956] cognitive taxonomy, or from cognition to affect, or from more to less advantaged youngsters, the tests don't do quite as well), why not treat the test as only one part of the assessment procedure and begin working on ways of helping teachers document in a better calibrated manner the other observations which they make so frequently and richly in the classroom? In that way, assessment need not depend solely on tests, but will be better informed by tests.

Another hypothesis for why teachers do not use or trust tests is related to work conducted on teacher planning (Zahorik, 1975; Yinger, 1977; Clark and Yinger, 1978; Peterson et al., 1978). This work, replicated and extended in other areas, has shown that teachers *do not* focus on outcomes. They *do not* focus on objectives. They *do not* focus on goals, though the goals are probably there implicitly as discussed by Wiley in his suggestion that curriculum affects goals. Teachers focus on *activities* and *content*. Their attention is directed to the questions *what will we do* and *what will we cover.*

For years those of us in educational research, especially in evaluation and measurement, have been insisting that teachers learn to think straight educationally. By that we meant they have to learn to think of outcomes stated in terms of behavioral objectives. However, if generations of practitioners do *not* think in such a way, an alternative consideration might be that there is something adaptive in focusing instead on activities and content covered. Teachers appear not to evaluate their day-to-day activity in terms of general assessments of achieved outcomes, but rather attend to variations in student *involvement.* When we ask teachers, "What did you achieve today?" they are inclined to say, "Well, we covered three more pages of math, and the kids were really involved." We then become critical and berate teachers for not thinking in terms of objectives–which ones they achieved and which not. I believe we have to treat the teachers' observations as data rather than as sources for blame. That is how teachers evaluate what they do. When they plan their instruction, they plan for such things as grouping, pacing, and involvement.

Barr and Dreeben (1978) have pointed out that in areas like mastery learning, where we prescribe instruction, diagnostic tests are used to help pace that instruction. Teachers in classrooms without mastery learning technology, as reported by Dahloff (1971) and Lundgren (1972) in Sweden, appear to use "steering groups." They attend to particular subgroups of pupils in the classroom to detect cues to help them decide whether to speed up, slow down, reiterate, or change topics. If that is one of the decisions teachers are most concerned about, but our tests are not measuring anything relevant to it, then should we be at all surprised that the practitioner finds our tests of little use?

One possibility may be that what the standardized tests measure and what teachers are evaluating are really two parallel and somewhat independent systems. Being in a classroom is similar to being on a cross-country train. The high correlation between pretest and posttest achievement scores over an entire year suggests that pupils are on a trajectory, and there is little chance that instruction can produce great changes in that trajectory. If such is the case, the day-to-day events that teachers can and must monitor need not be a very good indicant of the shape of that trajectory. The job of the teacher is to deal with life *on* the train and make it the most involving and most meaningful in a day-to-day sense. The teacher's first priority would not be to accelerate dramatically the progress of the train into the station. In the field of test design, we seem to have focused our efforts on providing data most useful from the perspective of those who are scheduling the trains, rather than from the perspective of the people who are conducting them.

Yet, are teachers likely to be totally oblivious to student progress in academic achievement? In the recent California BTES studies of teaching, researchers have sought the best possible process variable to predict achievement. They have concluded that the best proxy for achievement is *academic learning time,* a combination of *content covered* and degree of *engagement* or *involvement.* I find it ironic that the best available predictor of ultimate student performance is a combination of precisely those two indicators that teachers already intuitively use to monitor student progress. Our researchers and test developers have plenty to learn from the wisdom of practitioners.

CONCLUSION

The principles of test design have typically led to our selecting items for tests in a manner that throws out or rewrites items if they appear unstable. If they seem to fluctuate in important ways from day to day or week to week, we try to develop tests that lessen those fluctuations. But the job of the teacher is to deal with the fluctuations, to make sense of them, and to make the environment in which those fluctuations constantly occur sensible and educative. It is conceivable that in designing tests that are relatively immune to the variations in experience and response that characterize pupils during the course of an instructional experience, we throw out precisely those sorts of test items that the teacher might dearly love to use. We may have here another example of Cronbach's (1957) "two-disciplines" paradox. Cronbach observed that what was error variance for the correlationists was true-score variance for the experimentalists and vice versa. It may be that the test designers' error is the teachers' true-score in the day-to-day workings of the classroom. Unless designers begin to focus on the realities of teaching, the ways in which teachers do their work in classrooms, they are fated to learn twenty years from now, in yet another CSE study, that teachers continue to dislike, distrust, and feel uncomfortable with tests.

Those who would design educational tests must see themselves as inhabiting the interstices between two domains of expertise. Expertise of the first kind is the achievement of pupils who are being educated in the system, which is the subject of Chi and Glaser's research. Expertise of the second kind is the expertise of pedagogues—the teachers who must monitor, make sense of, and guide the development of that first expertise. All of us in our first psychology course were taught as a proposition that learning is an internal process in the learner, unobservable, which we infer from indices of learner behavior. If learning is an inferred process, then teaching is a profession rooted in the ability to use cues of various kinds to make inferences about that process in order to guide learning. The well-designed test can be an extraordinary tool to inform the expertise of that judge—the teacher—in making necessary inferences about the developing expertise of the learner. So far, tests have not fulfilled that promise. I suggest that this might be part of a new agenda for the field of test design.

NOTES

1. As a footnote to Chi and Glaser's (this volume) observations on studying the development of expertise, a group that has been closely associated with ours (Barrows et al., 1978) at the McMaster School of Medicine in Hamilton, Ontario, has been studying novices, more experienced medical students, and experts on the same cases. The group has been studying the students longitudinally as they go through medical school to obtain data on the development of medical expertise.

2. Ironically, Flexner was neither a physician nor a Ph.D. He was a former school principal whose *Flexner Report* (1910) revolutionized the teaching of American medicine.

3. The terms *domain-* or *criterion-referenced* tests and *norm-referenced* tests have taken on a variety of meanings. In this context, I define criterion-referenced tests as those in which an individual is assessed relative to a certain standard, whereas norm-referenced tests assess the individual's performance relative to other individuals or to a group average.

REFERENCES

BARR, R. and R. DREEBEN (1978) "Instruction in classrooms," in L. S. Shulman (ed.) Review of Research in Education (Vol. 5). Itasca, IL: F. E. Peacock.

BARROWS, H. S., J. W. FEIGHTNER, V. R. NEUFELD, and G. R. NORMAN (1978) "Analysis of the clinical methods of medical students and physicians" (A report submitted to the Province of Ontario Department of Health and Physician's Services Inc. Foundation). Hamilton, Ontario, Canada: McMaster University, March.

BERLINER, D. C. and B. ROSENSHINE (1976) "The acquisition of knowledge in the classroom," in Beginning Teacher Evaluation Study (Technical Report Series). San Francisco: Far West Laboratory for Educational Research, February.

BLOOM, B. S. [ed.] (1956) Taxonomy of Educational Objectives; The Classification of Educational Goals. Handbook 1–Cognitive domain. New York: David McKay.

CLARK, C. and R. J. YINGER (1978) "Research on teacher thinking" (Research Series No. 12). East Lansing: Michigan State University, Institute for Research on Teaching, April.

CRONBACH, L. J. (1957) "The two disciplines of scientific psychology." American Psychologist 21: 11.

DAHLOFF, U. S. (1971) Ability Grouping, Content Validity, and Curriculum Process Analysis. New York: Teachers College Press.

ELSTEIN, A. S., L. S. SHULMAN, and S. A. SPRAFKA (1978) Medical Problem Solving: The Analysis of Clinical Reasoning. Cambridge, MA: Harvard Univ. Press.

FLEXNER, A. (1910) "Medical education in the United States and Canada" (Bulletin No. 4). New York: Carnegie Foundation for the Advancement of Teaching.

HOFFMAN, P. (1974) "Physicians appraise other physicians: improving the decisions of a medical specialty board. "Oregon Research Institute, Research Bulletin 14, 4.

JOYCE, B. (1979a) "Teachers' thoughts while teaching." Research Series No. 58. East Lansing: Michigan State University, Institute for Research on Teaching.

--- (1979b) "The teaching styles at South Bay School." Research Series No. 57. East Lansing: Michigan State University, Institute for Research on Teaching.

LUNDGREN, U. P. (1972) Frame Factors and the Teaching Process: A contribution to Curriculum Theory and Theory on Teaching. Stockholm: Almquist & Wiksell.

McGUIRE, C. and D. BABBOTT (1967) "Simulation technique in the measurement of problem solving skills." Journal of Educational Measurement 1967 4: 1-10.

MORINE-DERSHIMER, G. (1979) "Teacher conceptions of pupils." Research Series No. 59. East Lansing: Michigan State University, Institute for Research on Teaching.

OSKAMP, S. (1965) "Overconfidence in case study judgments." Journal of Consulting Psychology 29: 261-265.

PETERSON, P. L., R. W. MARX, and C. M. CLARK (1978) "Teaching planning, teacher behavior, and student achievement." American Educational Research Journal 15, 3: 417-432.

PORTER, A. C., W. H. SCHMIDT, R. E. FLODEN, and D. J. FREEMAN (1978) "Impact on what? the importance of content covered" (Research Series No. 2). East Lansing: Michigan State University, Institute for Research on Teaching.

ROSENSHINE, B. (1976) "Classroom instruction," in N. L. Gage (ed.) The Psychology of Teaching Methods: Seventy-Fifth Yearbook of the National Society for the Study of Education. Chicago: Univ. of Chicago Press.

SISSON, J., R. SCHOOMAKER, and J. ROSS (1976) "Clinical decision analyses–the hazard of using additional data." Journal of the American Medical Association 236: 1259-1263.

SLOVIC, P. (1975) Personal communication.

VINSONHALER, J. F., C. C. WAGNER, and A. S. ELSTEIN (1978) "The inquiry theory: an information-processing approach to clinical problem-solving research and application" (Research Series No. 1). East Lansing: Michigan State University, Institute for Research on Teaching.

YINGER, R. J. (1977) "A study of teacher planning: description and theory development using ethnographic and information processing methods." Unpublished doctoral dissertation, Michigan State University. (Also available as Research Series No. 18 from the Institute for Research on Teaching, Michigan State University, East Lansing, Michigan.)

ZAHORIK, J. A. (1975) "Teachers' planning models. "Educational Leadership 33, 2: 134-139.

PART II

QUANTITATIVE THEORY AND APPLICATIONS

INTRODUCTION

Chapters 6 through 11 address issues related both to large-scale assessment methodology and to the methodology for examining the statistical properties of mastery tests. The most critical of these issues is the degree to which the failure of evaluations to detect program effects may be attributable to the nature of the tests and the analytical techniques employed.

As a set, the papers reflect the diverse character of current technical efforts in measurement and methodology in evaluation contexts. Topics range from a reconsideration of units of analysis in determining the analytical model for a program evaluation through a new formulation for judging program effectiveness based on pupil performance on individual test items. The common thread throughout is a conviction that conventional treatments of quantitative data in evaluation may be failing to provide evidence of program effects because of methodological inadequacies. There is also a shared willingness to expand the measurement and methodological repertoire to encompass quantitative techniques more logically consistent with substantive questions under investigation.

In "Analyzing Multilevel Educational Data: The Choice of an Analytical Model Rather than a Unit of Analysis" Leigh Burstein challenges the conventional atheoretical approach to the choice among competing units of analysis in educational research and evaluation. He argues that phenomena of importance occur at multiple levels of the educational system, e.g., pupil, classroom, school, etc., and that these phenomena should be identified and examined. Burstein recounts the highlights of a debate on units of analysis problems that took place at the 1967 CSE Conference on Evaluation of Instruction and maintains that viewpoints expressed at that conference are a foundation for much discussion of the topics in education today. He makes a case for the use of multilevel methods in identifying the effects of educational programs and points to recent work that shows promise for achieving a better fit between analytical procedures and the effects they are intended to identify.

Peter M. Bentler and J. Arthur Woodward in their chapter point out the complexity of assessing program effects in large-scale quasi-experiments and, in doing so, acquaint the reader with some recent advances in methodology. They describe a reanalysis of Head Start data which Jay Magidson interpreted as evidence for the program's positive effects. Through the use of covariance structure analysis methods based on Karl Jöreskog's LISREL model, Bentler and Woodward in their research were unable to detect positive effects for Head Start. They maintain that unequivocal statistical evidence of the program's benefits remains to be found.

While the Burstein and Bentler and Woodward chapters emphasize analysis and interpretation issues, the chapters by Robert Floden et al., and Robert Linn focus on issues in the choice and use of standardized achievement tests as measures of program effects. Floden et al., discuss the consequences of standardized test selection. They argue that the effects of test selection, both on the interpretation of results and on the content of instruction, have been oversimplified, denied or ignored. This point is emphasized by evidence that four major standardized achievement tests (the Stanford Tests of Basic Skills, the Iowa Test of Basic Skills, the Metropolitan Achievement Tests, and the CTB/McGraw-Hill Comprehensive Tests of Basic Skills) differ in the content they cover. The authors explore the consequences of these differences in items and how they affect both the assessment of a school district's progress and the content of instruction in the district's classrooms.

Robert L. Linn provides empirical evidence of the technical problems in combining data from many standardized achievement tests in evaluations of program effectiveness. Recent excursions into this aspect of the test equating controversy result from the efforts of the U.S. Office of Education to use the Norm Curve Equivalent system (NCE) and the common set of evaluation models developed by RMC Corporation (Talmadge and Horst) in the aggregation of test results from local Title I evaluations. Linn discusses the basic methodological concerns raised by the use of the NCE system for evaluating Title I programs and illustrates how misleading the results from such an attempt can be.

Rand Wilcox and Chester Harris examine statistical problems inherent in assessing the properties of criterion-referenced tests, particularly those used for mastery decisions. Wilcox reviews recent statistical developments in judging the consistency of decisions from mastery testing. He points to theoretical and statistical resolutions of several thorny problems in this area. His results should prove useful to measurement personnel who are confronted with the difficult task of documenting the psychometric properties of mastery tests used for proficiency and minimal competency testing.

Harris summarizes his recent work on a new theory of achievement testing. The theory uses a probability model framework to integrate evidence on individual and group performance on test items generated from an algorithm for a well-specified content domain. According to Harris, the application of this methodology will lead to better information about instructional sensitivity of achievement. The topics addressed by these authors, then, reflect the issues of serious concern to quantitative analysts. Further exploration of these concerns should permit future methodological decisions to be made—such as choice of measure, design, and statistical technique—so that the purpose of the investigation is more adequately served.

—Leigh Burstein and Frank J. Capell

6

ANALYZING MULTILEVEL EDUCATIONAL DATA:

The Choice of an Analytical Model Rather than a Unit of Analysis

Leigh Burstein

It is fitting that issues concerning units of analysis be addressed at a CSE conference on methodology. Some of the most enlightened thinking by educational researchers on this topic occurred ten years ago at a CSE conference on the evaluation of instruction (Wittrock and Wiley, 1970). Several of the presenters for the 1978 Measurement and Methodology Conference participated in the earlier discussions. That earlier exchange serves as a catalyst for current CSE efforts and for this paper.

1967 CONFERENCE REVISITED

Some general comments about the 1967 conference help provide the context for current concerns about units of analysis. The presentations and discussions at the 1967 conference were remarkable in their highly creative and reflective thought about evaluation theory and methodology.

On the one hand, there is little known today that was not envisioned by the participants at the earlier conference. At the same time, there has been great progress in recognizing and struggling with the complexity of evaluation as a social and political as well as a methodological and psychological activity. The character of the design and measurement issues considered in the 1978 conference reflects a sense of history and of rational evolution in the focus of evaluation methodology.

THE UNITS OF ANALYSIS DEBATE

The considerations surrounding questions of units of analysis reflect that history and evolution. At the 1967 conference, Wiley introduced the issue in the context of his paper on the design and analysis of evaluation studies. Harris and Husek were the designated discussants, but at one time or another, Bloom, Glaser, Glass, Messick, Lortie, Lumsdaine, and Wittrock contributed to what might politely be called a huge difference of opinion. Direct quotes from the Wiley presentation and some of the comments it generated help illustrate the debate over units of analysis.

The remarks by Wiley (Wittrock and Wiley, 1970) that sparked the greatest debate were as follows:

> If the object (educational program, procedure, or components thereof) of evaluation is a typical classroom instructional program where instruction is received simultaneously by all students in the class, then the appropriate vehicle (or sampling unit) is the *class* and not the *individual pupil.* This is equivalent to the standard definition of the experimental unit: *if two pupils in the same class may not receive different instructional treatments,* the classroom is the appropriate unit . . . traditional instruction is by nature classroom based since if it were not it would be tutorial (p. 264, emphasis added).

Wiley's statement about the collectivity as the unit caused Bloom (Wittrock and Wiley, 1970) to remark:

> There must be heresy in this someplace. . . . I am a little concerned that . . . [the methodologists] . . . are telling the instructor, the psychologist, the evaluator, what it is that he may or may not do . . . kids . . . react differently to a particular teacher, a particular set of material; they react differently at different times. I think you people are telling us that this isn't really a problem that we can attack, and I am trying to say that maybe we ought to push you to ask, "How can we go about attacking some of these questions . . . ?"
>
> First of all I want to know, what have I done to this particular child. . . . Then I want to go beyond that and know what I can do

with this kind of child, teacher, material, purpose. But I want to start with one teacher and one kid and keep working up to thousands of teachers, thousands of kids, and thousands of sets of materials (pp. 276-277).

Lumsdaine added that, according to Fisher:

The unit of analysis is always the unit of assignment. . . . The unit of assignment should be the smallest unit . . . that will let us get away from serious reactive effects. . . . For the usual introduction of an instructional package in a school, depending on the sociology of the school, it should be either the classroom or the whole school; in a few instances, where a major procedure is involved, I think the unit of assignment has to be the school district (pp. 281-282).

Glass pushed Lumsdaine's point further by elaborating Fisher and Cox's treatment of the unit of analysis and modifying their definition to suit conditions in behavioral research. For Glass (Wittrock and Wiley, 1970):

the units of analysis should be the smallest unit where the experimental materials are randomly assigned to conditions and allowed to react or respond independently for the duration of the experiment (p. 282).

In response to Stake's concern about whether Wiley considered pupil behavior to be an adequate criterion to use for evaluation, Wiley (Wittrock and Wiley, 1970) stated that it was not enough and added:

When we talk about the effects of a treatment on the classroom, we are talking about something fundamentally different from the effects of the treatment on the individuals in the classroom . . . pupils react differently in the classes than they do by themselves. That is fundamental enough to require discussions of the effect on the collectivity rather than the effect on the individual and to be asking questions at a different level (pp. 283-284) .

Harris disagreed with Wiley and commented:

How do you distinguish the collectivity from the individuals in the collectivity? . . . you would still get the data from the individuals (p. 284).

Lortie, in support of Wiley, responded:

we confuse the fact that we get the data from individuals with the notion that all behavior is individualistic (p. 284).

At this point the discussion changed focus slightly as Wittrock pointed out a crucial methodological problem in designating a unit. Glaser and Lortie then engaged in an exchange which seemed to delineate the fundamental distinction between how an instructional psychologist and a sociologist view the social psychological system embodied in the classroom. First, Wittrock (Wittrock and Wiley, 1970) remarked:

> I see advantages to using the class as a unit. But with research in instruction, this unit raises new problems of generalization, especially in longitudinal research.
>
> A given class in a school is a tenuous unit. . . . What does this do to my attempts to generalize my results, to my attempts to do longitudinal research extending over one or more years of time?
>
> If I can talk about individuals in a class and still have some basis for assuming that the errors are independent within that class, I am on a better basis to make generalizations than if I have to work with the class as a unit (pp. 284-285).

We will return to Wittrock's point later.

The Glaser-Lortie (Wittrock and Wiley, 1970) exchange, beginning with Glaser, was as follows:

> *It is still true that no one has ever taught a class.* You teach *an individual in the context of a class,* but no one has ever taught a class. It is impossible to teach a class. You teach individuals whose behavior changes.
>
> The class is a convenient artifact so that the teacher can reach one student (p. 285, emphasis added).

To which Lortie replied:

> Only two million people are constrained by that, two million Americans we call schoolteachers (p. 285).

Glaser's response was:

> All right. But they teach to the class only as a manageable way of changing the behavior of a single individual (p. 286).

And Lortie countered with:

> That's what you want them to do, but that is not what many of them conceive as their responsibility (p. 286).

THE HIDDEN RESOLUTION

The extensive quotes from the 1967 discussion clearly demonstrate the division of opinion among a group of enlightened researchers/evaluators concerning the choice of a unit of analysis. Had the participants at the 1967 conference enjoyed the ten years of hindsight that we share today, and had they paid more attention to a second set of key points in Wiley's remarks on analysis, the discussion on units of analysis need not have been so divisive. Elaborating his declaration that the appropriate vehicle for evaluation is a collectivity such as a classroom or a school, Wiley pointed out some options in instrumentation, measurement, and data analysis afforded by this judgment. Of particular interest to the present paper is that Wiley (Wittrock and Wiley, 1970) foresaw the multifaceted manner in which the effects of educational programs might be manifested:

> the objects of instruction might well affect other characteristics of a unit than the mean level of achievement. They might, in fact, affect the *distribution of achievement in the collectivity.* . . . Another relevant kind of measure that may be produced is a contrast among subpopulations. . . . When the contrast is a result of a continuous variable it may be considered a rough estimate of the regression coefficients of the original criterion variable with respect to the continuous variable.
>
> This logic might lead one to the use of regression coefficients as new criterion measures for evaluating the differential effect of the treatment on individual pupils (pp. 267-268, emphasis added).

Wiley's notion that class outcome characteristics other than the mean level of achievement might be affected by instruction suggests a means for capturing the dynamic properties of group composition. Additionally, his identification of within-group regression coefficients as a potential criterion measure for assessing the effects of within-group processes foreshadows our current interest (Burstein, 1976, 1977; Burstein and Linn, 1976, 1977; Burstein, Linn, and Capell, 1978; Linn and Burstein, 1977). We elaborate on the concept of slopes as indicators of within-group processes in a later section.

THE CHOICE OF ANALYTICAL MODEL: AN EVOLUTION OF THOUGHT

The question of choice of units of analysis or appropriate unit of analysis has evolved over the years into a more general methodological concern: how to analyze data that are derived from the multiple levels of the educational system—pupil, teacher/classroom, school, school district.

This focus on the substantive analytical model rather than on making a choice among competing units of analysis is the more reasonable perspective to take if one is to learn something about the question one sets out to answer. But having said the easy, and perhaps the obvious, it is necessary to add that the choice of analytical model is, to a large degree, constrained by the type of study one is conducting and the types of outcomes and processes under investigation. This seemingly obvious declaration, however, also warrants clarification, which the following observations attempt to provide.

Observation 1. By nature, most of the quantitative empirical research on the educational process and most reasonable-scale educational program evaluations (such as Project Follow Through) are quasi-experimental or nonexperimental. As with other methodological and measurement issues, experimental paradigms for the selection of the unit of analysis and, thereby, the analytical model, run afoul of the complications inherent in large-scale quasi-experiments and nonexperiments. Experimental design paradigms lead one to focus on the wrong set of potential choices—on power and significance—rather than on description, estimation, and hopefully, explanation. Description, estimation, and explanation should provide the methodological core for the study of the educative process within the context of the sociopolitical organizations that are our classrooms and schools. Again quoting Wiley (Wiley and Wittrock, 1970: 276): "The social context and its influence on response in a classroom . . . should be a substantive focus of study for evaluation because it is fundamental to our evaluative inferences."

If we accept Wiley's focus, then it is natural to look to quasi- and nonexperimental methodology and to what is currently called qualitative methodology in order to derive tenable analytical models for educational research and evaluation.

Observation 2. Wittrock (Wittrock and Wiley, 1970: 284-285) was essentially correct when he implied that what may be a reasonable analytical model for the effects of instruction or of a program on a shortrange outcome (e.g., an achievement test at the end of an instructional unit) loses its salience when one wishes to make generalizations, especially time-dependent ones. While the instructional psychologist interested in the impact of a well-circumscribed instructional unit may easily choose a reasonable analytical model and unit of analysis, the sociologist studying school effects, the evaluator investigating program effectiveness, or the stratification theorist focusing on the educational determinants of occupational and income inequality deal with a much more complex educational history that cannot be simply described by observing a single classroom or, for that matter, a single school at a given point in time. When the phenomenon under study is dynamic rather than static, the prerequisite frame of reference and analytical model specification (and hence units of analysis decisions) are much more complex.

Observation 3. If we learn how to create educationists sufficiently hybrid to be at once psychologists, sociologists, anthropologists, and methodological theorists, we may be able to understand the educative process and its effects and develop an analytical methodology suitable for their empirical clarification and communication. Once that is accomplished, we will cease to hear about the nonissues of choice of unit of analysis.

With these observations in mind, the present focus on choice of analytical models as opposed to selection of the units of analysis can be clarified and illustrated.

JUSTIFICATION FOR FOCUS

The effects of education can exist both between and within the units at each level of the educational system. Yet the majority of studies of educational effects have restricted their attention to between-student, between-class, or between-school analyses.

Cronbach (1976) argued that the majority of studies of educational effects conceal more than they reveal, and that "the established methods have generated false conclusions in many studies" (p. 1). His concern is foreshadowed in the educational literature by the exchange cited earlier (Wittrock and Wiley, 1970), and by Haney's (1974) review of the units-of-analysis problems encountered in the evaluation of Project Follow Through.

When faced with the analysis of multilevel data, most researchers, on the basis of theory or statistical considerations, have tried to make a choice among alternative units of analysis. Unfortunately, those who resort to theory either reject plausible alternative models (Brophy, 1975; Bloom in Wittrock and Wiley, 1970; Stebbins et al., 1977; Wiley in Wittrock and Wiley, 1970) or find themselves unable to choose (Cline et al., 1974; Haney, 1974; McBee and Fortune, 1977; Walberg and Singh, 1974). Selecting the appropriate unit on the basis of statistical considerations can also leave the choice unresolved due to competing alternatives (Burstein, 1975; Burstein and Smith, 1977; Glendening, 1976; Haney, 1974).

Haney (1974) has elaborated the range of alternative units of analysis considerations in the context of the evaluation of Project Follow Through. He cites four general types of considerations: the purpose of the evaluation (questions to be addressed), the evaluation design (nature of treatments, independence of units and treatment effects, appropriate size), statistical considerations (reliability of measures, degrees of freedom, analysis techniques), and practical considerations (missing data, policy research, multiple year comparisons, economy). Haney was unable to choose among units because the purpose of the evaluation dictated the child as the unit, but the unit of treatment was the classroom; moreover, the multiyear character of Follow Through made classrooms impractical as units of analysis. Furthermore, considerations of random assignment offered no relief since there was no random assignment at any level and the comparison children were not equivalent to treatment children.

Apparently, thinking of multilevel analyses as problems in the choice of unit of analysis is not a very penetrating perception. Phenomena of importance occur at all levels and need to be described and subjected to inference making (Burstein, 1978; Burstein and Linn, 1976, 1977; Burstein, Linn, and Capell, 1978; Cronbach, 1976). Once again, Haney's (1974) arguments are succinct and to the point:

> Investigators ought to have a strong bias for studying various properties of the educational system at the level at which they occur; . . . variation in attributes of interest ought to be studied at those levels (or between those units) at which it does (or is expected to) occur. . . . If the hypotheses are explicitly stated in terms of mathematical models, the impact of shifting levels of analysis from one unit of analysis to another will be much more easily assessed than if they are not (pp. 96-97).

ALTERNATIVE MEASURES OF GROUP OUTCOMES

Haney's methodological point is clear: different types of analyses of multilevel data address different questions, and research on schooling typically asks questions at multiple levels. Moreover, as Wiley (Wittrock and Wiley, 1970) suggested, once it is determined that the questions of interest and/or statistical considerations warrant analyses of aggregated data, the types of between-group effects one expects to find remain to be specified. In particular, when one's purpose is to determine factors affecting pupil performance, it is possible that the analyses of between-group (class, school, etc.) means can hide important differences in the within-group distribution of pupil outcomes and educational inputs.

Several aspects of current schooling practices lead us to expect that within-school and within-class distributions of pupil performance vary. First, schools (classes) do differ in the distribution of educational performance as well as in mean performance. Moreover, schools with the same mean outcome often exhibit different distributions of performance within school, and an analysis of means alone could not be expected to account for such distributional differences.

Second, a variety of educational theories about the effects of specific schooling practices on within-group behavior argue for an examination of distributional properties other than group means. Obviously, the variability of performance is of interest in studies comparing individualized, competency-based, or open educational instructional programs with more traditional instructional practices. Also, research on the interaction between teaching style and learning style would lead one to expect variability of outcomes for pupils with similar entering characteristics and preferences who are taught by teachers with differing instructional styles.

Finally, using distributional characteristics in addition to the mean as criterion measures has been shown empirically to merit consideration (Lohnes, 1972; Klitgaard, 1975; Brown and Saks, 1975a, 1975b). In his analyses of data from the Cooperative Reading Project, Lohnes (1972) found that standard deviations and skewness indices added to the explanatory power of means. Klitgaard (1975) and Brown and Saks (1975a, 1975b) found that school district standard deviations exhibited more significant relations with school characteristics than did school and school district means.

Though they sought answers to different questions and used different methodologies, Lohnes, Brown and Saks, and Klitgaard apparently share Wiley's and our belief that educational outcomes are multifaceted and are incompletely measured by simple group averages. There also seems to be consensus that educational theory can be developed which will link pupil entering characteristics and characteristics of the educative process to distributional properties of educational outcomes.

We (Burstein, 1976, 1977; Burstein and Linn, 1976, 1977; Burstein, Linn, and Capell, 1978; Burstein and Miller, 1978a, 1978b; Linn, 1977; Linn and Burstein, 1977) have elaborated a theory for the use of within-group slopes of outcomes on inputs as criteria in educational effects studies. (Karweit and Fennessey [1977] have independently suggested that differences in slopes across schools deserve further consideration.)

Our justification for considering within-group regressions as outcomes derives much of its impetus from research on aptitude-treatment interactions (Snow, 1976) and from prior experience with distinctions among colleges (Rock, Baird, and Linn, 1972). In its simplest form, it is expected that, given similar distributions of entering pupil performance or characteristics, different teachers and different instructional practices will result in differing distributions of educational outcomes. For example, it might be hypothesized that teachers (or classrooms) who are equally effective in terms of means might yield varying slopes because of different instructional practices. Some teachers use compensatory instructional practices which emphasize the improved performance of lower-ability students and thereby produce a flatter slope, while other teachers allow each child to learn at his/her own rate and thereby produce a steeper slope. We (Burstein and Linn, 1976, 1977; Burstein, Linn, and Capell, 1978) compared alternative analytical models for identifying educational effects in the presence of hypothetical heterogeneous, within-class regressions. For the conditions studied, the key findings were that heterogeneous within-class slopes were shown to make important differences in identified effects, differences which were not swamped by sampling variability in the estimation of slopes, and that certain analytical strategies exhibited good properties even in the presence of heterogeneity.

Although within-group slopes are conceptually appealing indices of educational effects, three points warrant further examination. First, it must be determined that slopes are sufficiently stable. Second, it must be determined that slopes are potentially distinct from other group indices (e.g., pre- and post-test means and standard deviations) in realistic situations. Third, realistic cases must be found in which slopes are related to school and class characteristics after controlling for other background measures and other group indices. We have already begun to investigate all three points, but for the present we focus on the last and, to me, most provocative.

Interpretations from some of our recent empirical investigations are helpful here. Preliminary results of an analysis of science achievement data on U.S. 14-year-olds in the IEA study (Burstein, 1977, 1978; Burstein and Miller, 1978a, 1978b) provided tantalizing evidence of the possible payoff from investigating the relation of within-group slopes to measures of school and classroom process. We found that within-school slopes of science achievement on a verbal ability measure (assessed concurrently) were significantly and positively related to school mean responses of pupils on indices of exposure to science instruction and the degree to which pupils reported instructional practices which emphasized exploration (discovery methods of instruction). See Table 6.1.

The results fit in well with other recent research on informal/open/individually guided/unstructured instruction (see particularly Rosenshine, 1978; Stebbins et al., 1977). Instruction which emphasizes student self-direction (selection) of learning goals and methods tends to exacerbate preexisting differences in pupil skills. Higher-ability students tend to make more appropriate choices and achieve at a faster rate than lower-ability

Table 6.1 School-Level Regressions of Means, Standard Deviations, and Slopes on School Means on Background and Schooling Characteristics for Science Achievement of U.S. 14-year-olds (N=107 schools)

	Dependent Variables[b]					
	Unstandardized			Standardized		
Independent Variables[a]	Mean	S.D.	Slope	Mean	S.D.	Slope
RWK	.957* (7.02)[c]	.134 (1.45)	.912* (4.05)	.452	.154	.440
SEX	-6.955* (4.42)	-2.297* (2.16)	-.566* (2.18)	-.219	-.176	-.182
POPOCC	.752* (2.70)	.197 (1.04)	.002 (.04)	.188	.120	.005
BOKHOM	3.729* (3.78)	1.673* (2.51)	-.024 (.15)	.273	.298	-.018
GRADE	1.062 (1.28)	-.559 (1.00)	-.119 (.87)	.071	-.091	-.082
SCISTUDY	.317* (2.33)	.165 (1.80)	.068* (3.03)	.123	.157	.272
EXPLORE	.351* (2.19)	.265* (2.44)	.073* (2.75)	.112	.206	.238
R^2	.77	.34	.37			

* Coefficient exceeds twice its standard error.

a. The variables included are: raw word knowledge score (RWK), sex of student (SEX), student's report of father's occupation (POPOCC), student's report of number of books in the home (BOKHOM), grade in school (GRADE), student's report of exposure to science (SCISTUDY), student's report of degree of use of exploration in science in instruction (EXPLORE).

b. The overall mean, the between-student standard deviation, and between-school standard deviation of RSCI are 34.11, 9.47, and 4.57, respectively, in a weighted analyses (mean=33.47 and s.d.=5.00 for between-schools unweighted analysis). The mean and standard deviation of the within-school slopes are .92 and .49, respectively.

c. t-statistics in parentheses.

Source: Burstein and Miller, 1979.

students. The steeper within group slopes with greater opportunities for exposure to instruction and with greater emphasis on discovery approaches are consistent with expectations from other research and suggest the need for similar investigations with other data sets.

CONCLUSION

The work described above is a subset of a broader range of issues and problems which require more attention of the CSE Multilevel Analysis Project. It is unclear what form the final products of the investigation of the analysis of multilevel data will take, but it is possible to imagine the following scenario. As a preamble, we point to a trend developing in educational evaluation for the conduct of what Glass (1976) has termed "meta-analyses" (see also Light and Smith, 1972). People conducting meta-analyses seek to accumulate knowledge about the impact and characteristics of a particular educational innovation by aggregating findings across numerous investigations of the phenomena.

There would seem to be a natural parallel to meta-analyses which is relevant to the examination of alternative methodological approaches for the analyzing of multilevel data. In this context, there are two key dilemmas in the development of appropriate methodologies. First, the available methodological approaches vary greatly in the degree to which they are theory based as opposed to ad hoc. And second, all currently available empirical data sets suffer from a variety of inadequacies which would limit their utility for comparing alternative methodological approaches.

It is important to identify analytical approaches which are practically viable as well as theoretically sound and which are usable with actual data. We propose, therefore, that in addition to the studies of the variation in analytical properties across approaches with hypothetical data, alternative approaches be applied to a wide variety and sizable number of actual data sets, each with a potentially differing set of inadequacies. In this way, more can be learned about the methods (e.g., which are more generally usable; which behave similarly for specific kinds of data sets) and the influence of data limitations on methods (e.g., the exclusion of types of information makes different approaches impractical or unattractive).

The final product of the exercise described above could take the form of a meta-analysis of methodologies for analyzing multilevel data which has parallels to Glass's (1976) meta-analysis of psychotherapies. Hopefully, it would point to better strategies for the conduct of research and evaluations involving multilevel educational data.

REFERENCES

BROPHY, J. E. (1975) "The student as the unit of analysis." Research Report No. 75-12. Austin: University of Texas.

BROWN, W. and D. H. SAKS (1975a) "The production and distribution of cognitive skills within schools." Journal of Political Economy 83: 571-593.

——— (1975b) "Proper data aggregation for economic analysis of school effectiveness." Public Use Data 3: 13-18.

BURSTEIN, L. (1975) "Data aggregation in educational research: applications." Technical Report No. 1. Consortium on Methodology for Aggregating Data in Educational Research. Milwaukee, WI: Vasquez Associates. (Also, paper presented at the Annual Meeting of the American Educational Research Association, Washington, D.C., April, 1975.)

——— (1976) "Assessing the differences of between-groups and individual regression coefficients." Presented at the Annual Meeting of the American Educational Research Association, San Francisco, April.

——— (1977) "Three key topics in regression-based analyses of multilevel data from quasi-experiments and field studies." Presented at the Institute for Research on Teaching, Michigan State University, East Lansing, Michigan, December 16.

——— (1978) "The role of levels of analysis in the specification of educational effects." Commissioned by the Educational Finance and Productivity Center, Department of Education, University of Chicago, under contract from the National Institute of Education.

——— and R. L. LINN (1976) "Detecting the effects of education in the analysis of multilevel data: the problem of heterogeneous within-class regressions." Presented at the Conference on Methodology for Aggregating Data in Educational Research, Stanford, California, October.

——— (1977) "Alternative analytical models for identifying educational effects in the presence of heterogeneous within-group relations of input to outcome." CSE Report Series. Los Angeles: Center for the Study of Evaluation, University of California.

———, and F. CAPELL (1978) "Analyzing multilevel data in the presence of heterogeneous within-class regressions." Journal of Educational Statistics 4: 347-383.

BURSTEIN, L. and M. D. MILLER (1978a) "Alternative analytical models for identifying educational effects: where are we? Presented at the Annual Meeting of the American Educational Research Association, Toronto, Canada, March.

——— (1978b) "Selected topics in regression-based analyses of multilevel educational data." CSE Report Series. Los Angeles: Center for the Study of Evaluation, University of California.

——— (1979) "The use of within-group slopes as indices of outcomes." Presented at the Annual Meeting of the American Educational Research Association, San Francisco, April.

BURSTEIN, L., and I. D. SMITH (1977) "Choosing the appropriate unit for investigating school effects." Australian Journal of Education 21: 65-79.

CLINE, M. D. et al. (1974) Education as Experimentation: Evaluation of the Follow Through Planned Variation Model, Vols. 1A, 1B. Cambridge, MA: Abt Associates.

CRONBACH, L. J. with assistance of J. E. DEKEN and N. WEBB (1976) "Research on classrooms and schools: formulation of questions, design, and analysis." Occasional Paper, Stanford Evaluation Consortium, July.

GLASS, G. V. (1976) "Primary, secondary, and meta-analysis of research." Presidential address of the Annual Meeting of the American Educational Research Association, San Francisco, April.

GLENDENING, L. (1976) "The effects of correlated units of analysis: Choosing the appropriate unit." Presented at the Annual Meeting of the American Educational Research Association, April.

HANEY, W. (1974) "Units of analysis issues in the evaluation of Project Follow Through." Unpublished report. Cambridge, MA: Huron Institute.

KARWEIT, N. and J. FENNESSEY (1977) "A pragmatic framework for studying school effects: Estimation experiments using actual and simulated data: a progress report." Baltimore: Center for Social Organization of Schools, John Hopkins University, April.

KLITGAARD, R. E. (1975) "Going beyond the mean in educational evaluation." Public Policy 23: 59-79.

LIGHT, R. J. and P. V. SMITH (1971) "Accumulating evidence: procedures for resolving contradictions among different research studies." Harvard Educational Review 41: 429-471.

LINN, R. L. (1977) "Descriptors of agregates." Presented at the Annual Meeting of the American Educational Research Association, New York, April.

and L. BURSTEIN (1977) "Descriptors of agregates." Based on a paper presented at the Annual Meeting of the American Educational Research Association, New York.

LOHNES, P. (1972) "Statistical descriptors of school calsses." American Educational Research Journal 9: 547-556.

McBEE, J. K. and J. C. FORTUNE (1977) "Use of distribution parameters of achievement scores for teacher placement." Presented at the Annual Meeting of the American Psychologist Association, San Francisco.

ROCK, D. A., L. L. BAIRD, and R. L. LINN (1972) "Interaction between college effects and students' aptitudes." American Educational Research Journal 7: 109-121.

ROSENSHINE, B. V. (1978) "Formal and informal teaching styles: a review of S. N. Bennet's, teaching styles and pupil progress." American Educational Research Journal 15, 1: 163-169.

SNOW, R. E. (1976) "Learning and individual differences," in L. S. Shulman (ed.) Review of Research in Education, Vol. IV. Itasca, IL: F. E. Peacock.

STEBBINS, L. B., R. G. ST. PIERRE, E. C. PROPER, R. B. ANDERSON, and T. R. CERVA (1977) Education as Experimentation: A Planned Variation Model, Vol. IV-A. An Evaluation of Follow Through.

WALBERG, H. J. and R. SINGH (1974) "Teacher quality perceptions and achievement in Rajasthan." Alberta Journal of Educational Research 20: 226-232.

WITTROCK, M. D. and D. E. WILEY (1970) The Evaluation of Instruction: Issues and Problems. New York: Holt, Rinehart & Winston.

7

A HEAD START REEVALUATION:
Positive Effects Are Not Yet Demonstrable

Peter M. Bentler and J. Arthur Woodward

In an exciting recent report a causal modeling approach was taken toward evaluating the effect of a summer Head Start program on white first-graders' cognitive ability (Magidson, 1977). It was proposed that the use of a new, general causal model for the analysis of the data would, finally, permit an appropriate adjustment to be made for preexisting differences among the participant groups. Of particular interest was the question of whether the new analysis would reverse the conclusions of previous analyses, which found the Head Start program to be ineffective. Magidson reported the impressive result that positive estimates of effect could be shown for this sample, which yielded among the most negative of all of Westinghouse's reported effects (Cicirelli et al., 1969). The implication is that other samples would show even stronger positive effects of the Head Start program. Unfortunately, as we shall demonstrate, a careful reevaluation of these same Head Start data must lead to the conclusion that there

AUTHORS' NOTE: This investigation was supported in part by a Research Scientist Development Award (K02-DA00017) and a research grant (DA01070) from the U.S. Public Health Service. The assistance of B. Barnow, M. Hee, and D. Weeks is gratefully acknowledged.

is no demonstrable Head Start effect. The Magidson report is, at the very least, misleading; in some respects, it is simply wrong. In view of the controversial nature of this material, as documented by Magidson (1977: 403-404), our conclusions require public scrutiny. This is particularly true since there is the implication in Magidson's report (despite his formal disclaimer), via footnotes, that numerous famous methodologists have reviewed and agreed with his conclusions.

The basic data for the Magidson study, taken from Barnow (1973), are reported in Table 7.1. The main dependent variables of the Head Start program are represented by Y_1 and Y_2, where Y_1 is a posttest score on the Illinois Test of Psycholinguistic Abilities and Y_2 is a posttest score on the Metropolitan Readiness Test. It can be seen that these two dependent variables are substantially correlated with each other–they measure something in common. Participation in the Head Start program, given by Z, was coded 1, 0 for treatment vs. control condition, so that participation in Head Start yielded lower cognitive test scores. The problem is to determine whether this observed negative effect of Head Start can be explained by a model assuming some biasing effects of sample selection and, if so, whether a more unbiased, positive effect can be detected.

Table 7.1 Correlation Matrix for Head Start Data (N=303)

	Y_1	Y_2	X_1	X_2	X_3	X_4	Z
Y_1	1.000						
Y_2	.652	1.000					
X_1	.259	.275	1.000				
X_2	.246	.215	.468	1.000			
X_3	.217	.255	.241	.285	1.000		
X_4	.116	.190	.297	.209	.407	1.000	
Z	-.097	-.094	-.118	-.084	-.220	-.179	1.000

NOTE: Y_1 = Illinois Test of Psycholinguistic Abilities
Y_2 = Metropolitan Readiness Test
X_1 = Mother's Education
X_2 = Father's Education
X_3 = Father's Occupation
X_4 = Income

Four indicators of socioeconomic status (SES) were found to correlate positively with the postprogram dependent variables, as seen in Table 7.1. These indicators are measures of mother's education (X_1), father's education (X_2), father's occupation (X_3), and income (X_4). These indicators, furthermore, correlate negatively with program participation. The possibility arises that, if the irrelevant variables $X_1 \ldots X_4$ could be controlled statistically, there might be a positive effect of Program Z on the dependent variables Y_1 and Y_2. Ordinary analysis of covariance was not able to demonstrate this effect since the variables contain measurement error; Magidson's "general alternative to ANCOVA" (analysis of covariance) presumably did uncover it. Let us analyze Magidson's "general" model first, place it into perspective, then look at the specific Head Start model, and finally evaluate the Head Start program by more careful methods. This sequence is appropriate since Magidson specifically considered the Head Start results as only illustrative of his general approach.

MAGIDSON VS. JÖRESKOG

Magidson indicates that he presents a "general alternative" to the analysis of covariance that corrects any estimates of treatment effects for measurement errors, in the context of a model that hypothesizes latent factors which influence overt variables and each other. The overt variables are treatment, dependent, and covariate control variables. Other than such a general and vague statement of the basic idea, however, it must be emphasized that Magidson does not present a mathematical statement of any new, general model. His general alternative to ANCOVA turns out to be–upon careful reading–no more or less than a recommendation that Jöreskog's (1973) LISREL model be used in ANCOVA situations. While Magidson (1977: 405, 413) indeed credits Jöreskog, there is a strong implication, perhaps unintended, that he is doing more than simply applying Jöreskog's model to a set of data. Such an implication is totally inappropriate, in spite of the wide-ranging title of his paper.

Since Magidson basically applied Jöreskog's (1973) model to the data of Table 7.1, we can review this work in the context of Jöreskog's notation. However, since Jöreskog's (1973) model has been incorporated into a newer model, we shall use the more recent model (Jöreskog, 1976; Jöreskog and Sorbom, 1977). Our own reanalyses are carried out with the relevant, publicly available computer program LISREL III (Jöreskog and Sorbom, 1976), and our results are labeled to be consistent with LISREL

III so that they can be replicated or evaluated easily. The program used by Magidson is no longer available. For an introduction to Jöreskog's model, see Wheaton et al. (1977). For a technical summary of this model in matrix notation, and its relationship to an alternative, more general model (Bentler, 1976), see the appendix.

MAGIDSON'S HEAD START MODEL

It must be stated that Magidson *did* develop a creative model to explain Y_1, and another to explain Y_2, in the context of a procedure that allows the identification of Head Start effects and irrelevant effects. Tables 7.2 and 7.3 present the parameter estimates and standard errors of these models, as obtained from our analyses using LISREL III. These results produce virtually the same parameter estimates as obtained by Magidson, and the same χ^2. Absolute equivalence to Magidson's results, however, cannot be guaranteed since his equations do not correspond to his path diagram, and neither is consistent with his text. Furthermore, he did not indicate that he obtained a Heywood case, requiring fixing an unknown, surely positive error variance, to zero. Finally, our computer program is not identical to his.

The independent variables in the model of Table 7.2 are the control variables $X_1 \ldots X_4$ and the treatment variable Z. These variables are related to four underlying factors $\xi_1 \ldots \xi_4$. The estimated factor loadings are given by the Lambda X matrix. In this and all later matrices, if no

Table 7.2 Parameter Estimates and Standard Errors (in parentheses) for Model Y_1

	Lambda X				Theta		Phi			
	ξ_1	ξ_2	ξ_3	ξ_4	Delta		ξ_1	ξ_2	ξ_3	ξ_4
X_1	.48(.10)	.59(.14)	0	0	.42(.24)	ξ_1	1.0			
X_2	.47(.09)	.42(.11)	0	0	.61(.09)	ξ_2	0	1.0		
X_3	.46(.08)	0	.31(.07)	0	.70(.07)	ξ_3	0	.30(.11)	1.0	
X_4	.24(.11)	0	.97(.04)	0	0	ξ_4	-.39(.13)	.14(.15)	-.09(.07)	1.0
Z	0	0	0	1.0	0					
Gamma	.55(.12)	0	0	.11(.10)						
Lambda Y = 1.0	Theta Epsilon = .74(.11)									

$\chi^2_{(3)} = 4.00$

standard error appears in parentheses next to the parameter estimate, that value was taken as known and fixed at the given value. The first factor, ξ_1, is a general SES factor, while factors ξ_2 and ξ_3 are more specific SES factors. As can be seen in the Phi matrix, which gives the factor intercorrelations, these factors were constrained such that factor ξ_1 was not allowed to correlate with factors ξ_2 and ξ_3, while ξ_2 and ξ_3 were allowed to correlate with each other. Factor ξ_4, it can be seen, is synonymous with the treatment variable Z. The predictors $X_1 \ldots X_3$ were assumed to have uncorrelated error factors, whose proportion of standardized variance is given in the Theta Delta column; it can be seen that X_4 and Z are taken as error-free. For the reader unfamiliar with LISREL, Lambda X, Phi, and Theta Delta represent an ordinary factor analytic model with correlated factors. The dependent variable Y_1 is seen as Lambda Y to be related to a latent factor of its own, while Y_1 has an estimated unique variance, Theta Epsilon, of .74.

The important Head Start relevant information in Table 7.2 lies in the vector Gamma. It shows that factor ξ_1 influences an estimated true Y_1 with a weight of $\hat{\gamma}_1$=.55, while factor ξ_4, which is identical to Z, has a weight of $\hat{\gamma}_4$=.11. The latter weight is positive, thus leading Magidson to the conclusion that treatment has a small positive effect on the cognitive variable Y_1. The three degrees of freedom model fits, with $\chi^2_{(3)}=4.00$, and probability p=.26. The two LISREL parameter matrices Beta and Psi, not relevant to the current model nor given in Table 7.2, are fixed at 1.0 and 0.0, respectively.

The parameter estimates of Table 7.2 can easily be translated into the general LISREL model. The measurement model [1] is given by such equations as $X_1 = 48\,\xi_1 + .59\,\xi_2 + \delta_1$, where the estimates of the variance of δ_1 is .42. The correlation of (ξ_1, ξ_4) is -.39. Also, $Y_1 = 1.0\,\eta + \epsilon$, where the estimate of the variance of ϵ is .74. The structural equation model [2] provides the regression $\eta = .55\,\xi_1 + .11\,\xi_4$. Similar equations complete the model.

An immediate question about Magidson's conclusion can be raised by noting the standard error of .10 for the estimated treatment effect. Thus, the treatment effect is obviously not two standard errors greater than zero, which we might demand before accepting the value of .11 as statistically nonzero. A more exact result will be presented later.

A similar model for the dependent variable Y_2 is given in Table 7.3. The parameter specification is the same as in the previous model, and the results are virtually the same. The model again fits, with $\chi^2_{(3)} = 4.80$, p = .19. Since the estimated treatment effect is again small but positive (.14),

Table 7.3 Parameter Estimates for Standard Errors (in parentheses) for Model Y_2

	Lambda X				Theta		Phi			
	ξ_1	ξ_2	ξ_3	ξ_4	Delta		ξ_1	ξ_2	ξ_3	ξ_4
X_1	.48(.09)	.62(.07)	0	0	.38(.19)	ξ_1	1.0			
X_2	.42(.09)	.42(.13)	0	0	.64(.11)	ξ_2	0	1.0		
X_3	.51(.08)	0	.24(.08)	0	.68(.07)	ξ_3	0	.19(.12)	1.0	
X_4	.37(.11)	0	.93(.05)	0	0	ξ_4	-.40(.13)	.14(.13)	-.03(.08)	1.0
Z	0	0	0	1.0	0					
Gamma	.57(.12)	0	0	.14(.11)						
Lambda Y = 1.0	Theta Epsilon = .72(.11)									

$\chi^2_{(3)} = 4.80$

Magidson concluded that Head Start did have a positive influence on the cognitive variable Y_2. Nonetheless, the standard error of .11 makes this conclusion questionable as well.

THE HEAD START EFFECT

The procedure of fitting a model with many parameters and, when it fits by a significance test, drawing conclusions about a specific parameter—here, the Head Start effect—is not an appropriate way of evaluation whether that parameter is truly nonzero. A more correct way of evaluating the treatment effect must consist of (1) specifying a model that differs from the previous models only in that the treatment effect (γ_4) is fixed at zero, (2) estimating the parameters of the model under this restriction, and (3) evaluating the hypothesis of a zero treatment effect via statistical methods.

Tables 7.4 and 7.5 present the results of estimating models Y_1 and Y_2 when γ_4 is set at zero. The Y_1 model of Table 4 fits statistically, with $\chi^2_{(4)}$=5.17, p=.27. Similarly, the Y_2 model of Table 5 fits acceptably, with $\chi^2_{(4)}$=6.44, p=.17. Since both of these models cannot be rejected statistically, using Magidson's approach one would have to conclude that there is no treatment effect; after all, the model specifying that there is no treatment effect is able to account for the data adequately. However, as pointed out above, a more exact procedure is available. This is based on the χ^2 test.

Since the models of Table 7.2 and Table 7.4 are identical except for the treatment parameter, the difference in χ^2 fit of the two models provides a significance test for treatment on cognitive variable Y_1. Specifically, we have $\chi^2_{(4)} = 5.17$ for the four degrees of freedom model of Table 7.4 and $\chi^2_{(3)} = 4.00$ for the three degrees of freedom model of Table 7.2; thus $\chi^2_{(4)} - \chi^2_{(3)} = \chi^2_{(1)} = 1.17$ is a one degree of freedom χ^2 test for Head Start treatment. It can be seen that this value does not exceed tabled cutoff values for typical a-level statistical hypotheses, so that one cannot reject the hypothesis that the treatment effect, γ_4, is zero. A similar procedure concerned with evaluating the effect of Head Start on cognitive variable Y_2 yields the result $\chi^2_{(1)} = 1.64$. Again, the null hypothesis of no Head Start effect cannot be rejected. There is no statistical evidence to support Magidson's conclusions regarding the effectiveness of Head Start.

The LISREL III program provides an indicator as to whether the final solutions provided by the program are appropriate solutions under the model and the statistical estimation method. In all cases reported in this paper, the indicator concluded that an appropriate optimizing solution had been reached. A careful study of the solution of Table 7.5 reveals, however, that the error variance associated with variable X_1 was negative (-.04), so that it might have been appropriate to modify Magidson's model by setting this value to zero in both models in Tables 7.3 and 7.5. When this procedure was carried out, the results again demonstrated that no statistically significant Head Start effect could be detected [$\chi^2_{(1)} = 1.13$].

Table 7.4 Estimates of Model Y_1 of Table 7.2 with Gamma 4 Set to Zero

	Lambda X				Theta		Phi			
	ξ_1	ξ_2	ξ_3	ξ_4	Delta		ξ_1	ξ_2	ξ_3	ξ_4
X_1	.47(.10)	.65(.18)	0	0	.36(.22)	ξ_1	1.0			
X_2	.50(.10)	.36(.13)	0	0	.62(.09)	ξ_2	0	1.0		
X_3	.47(.09)	0	.31(.07)	0	.68(.07)	ξ_3	0	.30(.14)	1.0	
X_4	.23(.12)	0	.97(.05)	0	0	ξ_4	-.26(.09)	.03(.11)	-.12(.06)	1.0
Z	0	0	0	1.0	0					
Gamma	.48(.09)	0	0	0						

Lambda Y = 1.0 Theta Epsilon = .77(.09)

$\chi^2_{(4)} = 5.17$

Table 7.5 Estimates of Model Y_2 of Table 7.3 with Gamma 4 Set to Zero

	Lambda X				Theta		Phi			
	ξ_1	ξ_2	ξ_3	ξ_4	Delta		ξ_1	ξ_2	ξ_3	ξ_4
X_1	.47(.09)	.91(.73)	0	0	-.04(1.34)	ξ_1	1.0			
X_2	.46(.09)	.28(.25)	0	0	.71(.13)	ξ_2	0	1.0		
X_3	.55(.09)	0	.21(.09)	0	.65(.08)	ξ_3	0	.14(.17)	1.0	
X_4	.39(.12)	0	.92(.06)	0	0	ξ_4	-.27(.08)	.01(.07)	-.08(.07)	1.0
Z	0	0	0	1.0	0					
Gamma	.48(.09)	0	0	0						

Lambda Y = 1.0 Theta Epsilon = .77(.09)

$\chi^2_{(4)} = 6.44$

ALTERNATIVE HEAD START MODELS

Magidson's models for the Head Start data are specific to each of the two dependent variables Y_1 and Y_2. It is entirely possible that a more comprehensive model that includes both Y_1 and Y_2 in a single analysis would yield a statistically significant effect of Head Start participation. This would be particularly true if a model could be developed that decomposed the variance of the dependent variables into reliable (or, common) and error (or, unique) variance, and regressed the reliable cognitive variance on treatment in the context of a model that encompassed the irrelevant covariates. One such model is presented in Table 7.6 and a variation of it is given in Table 7.7.

In Table 7.6 it will be obvious immediately that the structure of the variables $X_1 \ldots X_4$ and Z is identical to the previous models. However, there are now two dependent variables Y_1 and Y_2 that have their own common factor. Their error of unique variances (Theta Epsilon) were set to be estimated as equal. (In this model, as before, the parameter Psi was set at zero, and Beta at one.) It will be seen that $\hat{\gamma}_4$=.38, implying a quite substantial, positive Head Start effect. The standard error of .44, however, makes the conclusion questionable, and a strict test of the null hypothesis of no treatment effect cannot be rejected. The model of Table 7.6 has $\chi^2_{(9)}$ = 8.38, while the model of Table 7.7, identical to the previous one with the exception of the forced zero treatment effect, has $\chi^2_{(10)}$ = 9.06. The

Table 7.6 Parameter Estimates for a Y_1 and Y_2 Model

	Lambda X				Theta		Phi			
	ξ_1	ξ_2	ξ_3	ξ_4	Delta		ξ_1	ξ_2	ξ_3	ξ_4
X_1	.33(.07)	.64(.10)	0	0	.48(.11)	ξ_1	1.0			
X_2	.28(.07)	.59(.09)	0	0	.57(.10)	ξ_2	0	1.0		
X_3	.34(.06)	0	.52(.10)	0	.61(.09)	ξ_3	0	.48(.10)	1.0	
X_4	.24(.07)	0	.63(.10)	0	.55(.12)	ξ_4	-.51(.36)	.09(.17)	-.09(.20)	1.0
Z	0	0	0	1.0	0					
Gamma	.93(.23)	0	0	.38(.44)						

Lambda X		Theta Epsilon
Y_1	1.0	.35(.03)
Y_2	1.0	.35(.03)

$\chi^2_{(9)} = 8.38$

Table 7.7 Estimates of Model Y_1 and Y_2 of Table 7.6 with Gamma 4 Set to Zero

	Lambda X				Theta		Phi			
	ξ_1	ξ_2	ξ_3	ξ_4	Delta		ξ_1	ξ_2	ξ_3	ξ_4
X_1	.33(.06)	.64(.10)	0	0	.48(.11)	ξ_1	1.0			
X_2	.29(.06)	.59(.09)	0	0	.57(.10)	ξ_2	0	1.0		
X_3	.29(.06)	0	.58(.08)	0	.61(.09)	ξ_3	0	.51(.09)	1.0	
X_4	.19(.06)	0	.61(.09)	0	.55(.12)	ξ_4	-.12(.06)	-.11(.08)	-.29(.07)	1.0
Z	0	0	0	1.0	0					
Gamma	.81(.04)	0	0	0						

Lambda Y		Theta Epsilon
Y_1	1.0	.35(.03)
Y_2	1.0	.35(.03)

$\chi^2_{(10)} = 9.06$

difference in χ^2 yields $\chi^2_{(1)}$ = .68, thus not supporting a positive Head Start effect. Furthermore, the model of Table 7.7 with no Head Start effect is entirely plausible statistically, with probability level p=.53. An important feature of this model is that X_4 could be specified to have a nonzero error variance, which is a realistic feature absent from Magidson's models.

Models quite similar to those presented in Tables 7.6 and 7.7 are presented in Tables 7.8 and 7.9, which differ, as before, in the presence or

Table 7.8 Parameter Estimates for an Alternative Y_1–Y_2 Model

	Lambda X				Theta		Phi			
	ξ_1	ξ_2	ξ_3	ξ_4	Delta		ξ_1	ξ_2	ξ_3	ξ_4
X_1	.49(.09)	.60(.15)	0	0	.40(.10)	ξ_1	1.0			
X_2	.44(.09)	.42(.12)	0	0	.63(.09)	ξ_2	0	1.0		
X_3	.48(.08)	0	.27(.07)	0	.69(.07)	ξ_3	0	.24(.11)	1.0	
X_4	.31(.10)	0	.95(.05)	0	0	ξ_4	-.41(.13)	.16(.14)	-.06(.07)	1.0
Z	0	0	0	1.0	0					
Gamma	.56(.11)	0	0	.13(.10)		Psi = .38(.10)				
Lambda X			Theta Epsilon							
Y_1	1.0		.35(.03)							
Y_2	1.0		.35(.03)							

$\chi^2_{(9)}$ = 8.18

Table 7.9 Estimates of Alternate Model Y_1 and Y_2 of Table 7.8 with Gamma 4 Set to Zero

	Lambda X				Theta		Phi			
	ξ_1	ξ_2	ξ_3	ξ_4	Delta		ξ_1	ξ_2	ξ_3	ξ_4
X_1	.49(.09)	.72(.28)	0	0	.25(.40)	ξ_1	1.0			
X_2	.49(.09)	.32(.16)	0	0	.66(.10)	ξ_2	0	1.0		
X_3	.50(.08)	0	.26(.07)	0	.68(.07)	ξ_3	0	.21(.14)	1.0	
X_4	.31(.11)	0	.95(.05)	0	0	ξ_4	-.26(.08)	.02(.09)	-.10(.06)	1.0
Z	0	0	0	1.0	0					
Gamma	.48(.08)	0	0	0		Psi = .42(.08)				
Lambda Y			Theta Epsilon							
Y_1	1.0		.35(.03)							
Y_2	1.0		.35(.03)							

$\chi^2_{(10)}$ = 9.88

absence of the Head Start parameter. The models of these tables differ from the previous ones in not making the common factor underlying Y_1 and Y_2 a strict linear combination of the four Lambda X factors. Rather, a residual is allowed, as determined by the LISREL III program to be Psi=.38. As before, Beta=1.0 and, unfortunately, X_4 has to be specified as possessing no error variance for the solutions to be statistically sound. The crucial comparison, of course, is the relative fit of the models in Tables 7.8 and 7.9. We obtain $\chi^2_{(9)} = 8.18$ and $\chi^2_{(10)} = 9.88$ for Tables 7.8 and 7.9, respectively, so that we have $\chi^2_{(1)} = 1.70$, not significantly greater than any plausible value of α-level χ^2. Again, there is no statistically sound evidence for any positive effect of Head Start participation, and the model with no Head Start effect adequately describes the data, with p=.45.

CONCLUSION

In spite of Magidson's creative application of Jöreskog's LISREL model to one of the most difficult program evaluation data sets, a careful application of this statistical methodology unfortunately provides no support for the conclusion that Head Start had a positive impact on its participants. It is, of course, possible that similar analyses undertaken on alternative data sets would find Head Start to have a statistically reliable effect on cognitive measures, but this remains to be demonstrated in the future.

Although there is no question that the use of causal modeling has a proper place in the evaluation of social programs, the Head Start example makes it clear that this new research tool must be used with care and caution. In addition to the traditional caveats mentioned in the relevant literature (e.g., the necessity for multinormally distributed data, a condition of course not met in this instance by the experimental, binary variable), it must be noted that any comparison of models (as in the various previous comparisons involving the treatment effect) can depend upon the context of the comparison. We have accepted Magidson's model, and have developed more complex, similar models ourselves; it may be concluded that no evidence for positive Head Start effects can be demonstrated with such models on the data of Table 7.10. Nonetheless, it is certainly possible that a similar test carried out in the context of a completely different type of model might yield evidence favorable to the Head Start program. Finally, the hope may remain that a still more appropriate statistical model may yield a conclusion more favorable to the

Head Start program than we have been able to demonstrate. The current report, being consistent with Magidson's approach, focused on an analysis of the combined experimental and control group correlation matrix. A method more analogous to ANCOVA (e.g., Sörbom, 1976) would involve estimating a model to fit the two within-group covariance matrices and the two sets of means, and evaluating such effects as a possible treatment-covariate interaction. Thus, the final word on Head Start effects surely has not been written, but a belief in the positive efficacy of Head Start can clearly not rest upon Magidson's report.

REFERENCES

BARNOW, B. S. (1973) "The effects of Head Start and socioeconomic status on cognitive development of disadvantaged children." Doctoral dissertation, University of Wisconsin, Madison.

BENTLER, P. M. (1976) "Multistructure statistical model applied to factor analysis." Multivariate Behavioral Research 11: 3-25.

CICIRELLI, V. G. et al. (1969) The Impact of Head Start: An Evaluation of the Effects of Head Start on Children's Cognitive and Affective Development (Vols. 1 and 2). Athens, OH: Ohio University and Westinghouse Learning Corporation.

JÖRESKOG, K. G. (1973) "A general method for estimating a linear structural equation system," pp. 85-112 in A. S. Goldberger and O. D. Duncan (eds.) Structural Equation Models in the Social Sciences. New York: Seminar Press.

--- (1976) Structural Equation Models in the Social Sciences: Specification, Estimation, and Testing. Uppsala, Sweden: Department of Statistics, University of Uppsala.

--- and D. SÖRBOM (1976) LISREL III: Estimation of Linear Structural Equation Systems by Maximum Likelihood Methods. Chicago: National Educational Resources.

--- (1977) "Statistical models and methods for analysis of longitudinal data," pp. 286-325 in D. J. Aigner and A. S. Goldberger (eds.) Latent Variables in Socio-Economic Models. Amsterdam: North-Holland.

MAGIDSON, J. (1977) "Toward a causal model approach for adjusting for preexisting differences in the nonequivalent control group situation: a general alternative to ANCOVA." Evaluation Quarterly 1: 399-420.

SÖRBOM, D. (1976) A Statistical Model for the Analysis of Covariance with Fallible Covariates. Uppsala, Sweden: Department of Statistics, University of Uppsala.

WHEATON, B., B. MUTHEN, D. F. ALWIN, and G. F. SUMMERS (1977) "Assessing reliability and stability in panel models, pp. 84-136 in D. R. Heise (ed.) Sociological Methodology. San Francisco: Jossey-Bass.

APPENDIX

Jöreskog (1976) proposed that the observed random vectors y and x of order (px1) and (qx1) can be represented by factor analytic measurement structures

$$y = \Lambda_y \eta + \varepsilon$$
$$x = \Lambda_x \xi + \delta, \qquad [1]$$

where Λ_y and Λ_x are (pxm) and (qxn) matrices of parameters. The latent random vectors η and ξ are related by the structural equation

$$B\eta = \Gamma\xi + \zeta, \qquad [2]$$

where B and Γ are (mxm) and (mxn) matrices of parameters. Using typical assumptions regarding the pairwise orthogonality of (η,ε), (ξ,δ), and (ξ,ζ), one obtains the covariance structure

$$\Sigma = \begin{matrix} \Sigma_{yy} & \Sigma_{yx} \\ \Sigma_{xy} & \Sigma_{xx}, \end{matrix} \qquad [3]$$

where $\Sigma_{xx}=\Lambda_x\phi\Lambda_x'+\theta_\delta$, $\Sigma_{yx}=\Lambda_y B^{-1}\Gamma\phi\Lambda_x'$, and $\Sigma_{yy}=\Lambda_y B^{-1}(\Gamma\phi\Gamma'+\Psi)B'^{-1}\Lambda_y'+\theta_\varepsilon$, and where ϕ(nxn), Ψ(mxm),θ_ε, and θ_δ are the covariance matrices of ξ, ζ, ε, and δ, respectively. The notation of Tables 2-9 of the current paper represents the structure. This structural equation model is a special case of Bentler's (1976) general statistical model for a random vector z, which may be written in this context as

$$z = \Lambda_1\Lambda_2\Lambda_3\Lambda_4\lambda_4 + \Lambda_1\Lambda_2\Lambda_3\lambda_3 + \Lambda_1\Lambda_2\lambda_2 + \Lambda_1\lambda_1, \qquad [4]$$

where Λ_1, Λ_2, Λ_3, and Λ_4 are parameter matrices and λ_1, λ_2, λ_3, and λ_4 are random vectors that are independent of each other. A specialization of this model yields the LISREL model. This can be verified by equating $z'=[y', x']$, $\lambda_1'=[\varepsilon', \delta']$, $\lambda_2=0$, $\lambda_3'=[\zeta', 0]$, $\lambda_4=\xi$, $\Lambda_1=I$, $\Lambda_4'=[\Gamma', I]$, and

$$\Lambda_2 = \begin{matrix} \Lambda_y & 0 \\ 0 & \Lambda_x \end{matrix} \text{ and } \Lambda_3 = \begin{matrix} B^{-1} & 0 \\ 0 & I \end{matrix}. \qquad [5]$$

8

DON'T THEY ALL MEASURE THE SAME THING?

Consequences of Standardized Test Selection

Robert E. Floden, Andrew C. Porter,
William H. Schmidt, and Donald J. Freeman

INTRODUCTION

Several authors have recently called attention to the match between the content of instruction and the content of tests used to assess instruction (e.g., Walker and Schaffarzick, 1974; Wiley, this volume; Porter et al., 1977). If the test content does not match the instructional content, then the test results may provide a distorted picture of the instructional effects. A great number of tests, for example, cover only a fraction of the content presented in many elementary classrooms. Since the major standardized

AUTHORS' NOTE: The work reported herein is sponsored by the Institute for Research on Teaching, College of Education, Michigan State University. The Institute for Research on Teaching is funded primarily by the Teaching Division of the National Institute of Education, United States Department of Health, Education and Welfare. The opinions expressed in this publication do not necessarily reflect the position, policy, or endorsement of the National Institute of Education (Contract No. 400-76-0073).

achievement tests for elementary schools focus on basic skills, the test scores reflect only achievement in basic skills, rather than achievement in the total instructional content that was presented in the classroom.

Although many people acknowledge that instruction in content outside of the basic skills is not reflected in test scores, it has seldom been recognized that the definition of basic skills may vary across the standardized tests. Despite prevailing opinion to the contrary (e.g., Cooley and Lohnes, 1976), the tests do not all measure the same content knowledge. To ensure that the test results reflect achievement on the content considered important in a local school district, therefore, particular attention should be paid to the content of the tests chosen.

While the effect of test content on test scores has been acknowledged, the effect of test content on instruction has received little attention. Although some people believe that the initiation of a testing program may have global effects on instruction, perhaps leading to greater emphasis on the basic skills, investigation on the subtler shifts in instructional content dependent on the particular test chosen has only recently begun. These and other influences on a teacher's selection of instructional content deserve careful investigation.

DISTRICT TEST USE

School district administrators are often concerned with raising student achievement in the basic skills. Administrative policies reflecting this concern include constructing lists of objectives, meeting with teachers in workshops to discuss goals and methods, rewarding school building administrators for improved performance in their schools, and testing student progress on a regular basis. Although these actions are frequently coupled with the development of criterion-referenced tests, nearly all districts continue to administer norm-referenced standardized achievement tests to assess improvement within the district and to compare their district's performance to national norms.

Little is known about the criteria used to choose a test series. The factors considered probably include cost, ease of administration, ease of scoring, and reporting format. But the specific content covered by each subtest is a criterion that is given insufficient attention.

School personnel have been led to believe that the major test series differ little in topics tested, at least for subtests with similar titles. The high correlations among the tests, together with the apparent unidimensionality of each subtest, have suggested that the tests all measure the same thing. If that were the case, then the variance of content among tests would be negligible, and content covered by the test could not be a test selection criterion. Selection would then have to be done on the basis of criteria like those suggested above.

In this paper, we argue that the major tests do differ in content covered, and that the differences have consequences, not only for appropriateness of the procedures for assessing district progress, but also for the content of classroom instruction in the district.

TEST ANALYSES

Four test series dominate the market in elementary reading and mathematics. These series are: the Stanford Tests of Basic Skills (SAT), the Iowa Test of Basic Skills (ITBS), the Metropolitan Achievement Tests (MAT), and the CTB/McGraw-Hill Comprehensive Tests of Basic Skills (CTBS). Each series is composed of tests designed for specific levels of achievement, roughly corresponding to grade levels. Within each level, a test is composed of several subtests, broadly grouped into areas such as mathematics applications, computation, and concepts.

In our recent work, we compared the content coverage of the four test series in fourth grade mathematics. An iterative process of analysis and classification of items on the SAT was used to develop a taxonomy for describing these standardized tests of fourth-grade mathematics. The taxonomy was used to reliably describe the tests. A complete presentation of the taxonomy is given in Figure 8.1. Each cell in the classification matrix corresponds to a topic that a teacher might elect to cover. The process of test analysis has been described elsewhere in greater detail (Porter et al., 1977; Schmidt et al., 1978). Comparisons of the four tests are detailed in Table 8.1.

Although it can be seen that the tests are quite similar in some respects, striking differences are also evident. For example, on the "operations" dimension, the tests were quite similar in the percentages of items involving subtraction without borrowing (6-8%), adding, or subtracting fractions without a common denominator (0-2%), and dividing with remainder (1%). For the rest of the levels there were modest to strong differences among the tests. For example, 21% of the items on the MAT involved addition, which was about 8 percentage points more than the other tests.

MODE OF PRESENTATION

Nature of the Material/Operation		Graphs, Figures, Tables or Physical Objects												Operation(s) Specified												Operation(s) Not Specified (Story Problems)											
		1	2	3	4	5	6	7	8	9	10	11	12	1	2	3	4	5	6	7	8	9	10	11	12	1	2	3	4	5	6	7	8	9	10	11	12
Whole Numbers	Single digits																																				
	Single digits and Multiple digits																																				
	Multiple digits																																				
Fractions	Single																																				
	Multiple																																				
Decimals																																					
Percents																																					
Alternate Number System																																					
Place Value																																					
Sentences[b]	Number																																				
	Algebraic																																				
[c]Essential Units of Measurement																																					
Geometric Figures																																					
Other																																					

Operations:

1. Add
2. Subtract without borrowing
3. Subtract with borrowing
4. Add or Subtract Fractions
5. Multiply
6. Divide without remainder
7. Divide with remainder
8. Combination
9. Grouping
10. Identify Equivalents
11. Identify Rule (Order)
12. Identify Terms*

* Be sure to identify specifics on attached page.

Figure 8.1: Operations:

Table 8.1 Item Distribution for Each Factor Across Tests[a]: Fourth-Grade Level

	IOWA	MAT	SAT	CTBS
I. Mode of Presentation				
--graphs, figures, tables, etc.	43	15	21	19
--operation(s) specified	29	52	53	59
--operation(s) not specified	29	32	27	22
	(N=84)	(N=115)	(N=116)	(N=113)
II. Nature of Material				
--single digits	12	15	20	2
--single and multiple digits	12	20	23	18
--multiple digits	24	19	22	19
--total: whole numbers	47	54	66	39
--single fraction	6	4	5	7
--multiple fractions	5	3	--	7
--decimals	6	5	4	10
--percents	--	--	1	6
--alternate number systems	--	2	1	--
--place value	8	3	5	4
--number sentences	6	1	2	--
--algebraic sentences	8	10	8	12
--essential units of measurement	10	15	7	11
--geometric figures	2	3	3	2
--other	1	1	--	2
III. Operations				
--add	12	21	13	14
--subtract without borrowing	8	8	6	8
--subtract with borrowing	11	11	6	5
--add or subtract fractions without common denominator	1	--	--	2
--multiply	11	19	16	17
--divide without remainder	6	9	15	14
--divide with remainder	1	1	1	1
--combination	8	6	7	7
--grouping	2	--	5	--
--identify equivalents	20	18	16	15
--identify rule (order)	11	3	5	12
--identify terms	8	5	6	4

a. Entries are percentages.

The ITBS had at least 5 percentage points fewer multiplication items than did the other tests. Grouping was tested by the SAT but not at all by either the MAT or the CTBS.

With respect to the nature of the material, while there were more similarities than differences, the differences may be quite important. Six percent of the items on the CTBS, for example, involved percentage, while the ITBS and MAT have no such items. The MAT and SAT both have items on alternative number systems, while the ITBS and the CTBS do not.

These statements are perhaps more meaningful when one considers that success on a single item on the SAT math subtest can add approximately .2 to a student's grade equivalent score, if he is near the middle of the norm distribution. The importance of variation in that coverage is increased by the usual small size of any differences in educational achievement produced by changes in instruction. Since improvements of a fraction of a grade level are generally considered important, it seems likely that the differences among tests could lead to score differences that would also be considered important.

Although the analysis of mathematics tests may be open to criticism, it serves as a good illustration of the differences which can exist among the standardized tests, tests that are often believed to be virtually interchangeable. For a school district that valued progress in learning to work with percentages in fourth grade, the ITBS would give a distorted picture of achievement going on during the school year. Alternatively, a district in which percents were not taught until the sixth grade would be inappropriately discouraged by the results of the CTBS.

Other authors have identified differences in supposedly equivalent tests. A change in test forms can lead to substantially different grade equivalent scores for low-achieving children (Linn and Slinde, 1977). Even when tests have been empirically equated, the choice of test can greatly influence the estimate of program effects (Linn, this volume). Neither of these studies attempts to explain the cause of discrepancy in results.

Differences in test content may partially explain the discrepancy. The discrepancy in content may result, not from the test publishers' failure to include the appropriate content, but from a general lack of agreement on the definition of basic skills.

In mathematics, for example, considerable attention was given during the nineteen-sixties to the question of whether or not material such as elementary set theory was part of the mathematical basic skills. The question of the composition of the basic mathematical skills was never answered, however, as evidenced by proceedings of a National Institute of Education Conference in October 1975, directed at the question, "What *are* basic mathematical skills and learning?" (NIE, 1975).

> It is proposed here that the determination of what mathematics is most worth learning is a task that will require careful and systematic

> study from the perspectives of several interest groups (Helms and Graeber, 1975: 70).
>
> The challenge to describe basic skills and learning in school mathematics is an assignment full of pitfalls. In the past five years, hundreds of mathematics educators, school systems, professional groups and the National Assessment have been busily composing taxonomies of fundamental objectives for mathematics instruction at various grade levels. With few exceptions, these efforts to establish a reasonable list of basic skills have been failures. There has been no general agreement among the competing groups. Moreover, the implementation of the various lists of curriculum guidelines threatens to produce fragmented mathematics programs that resemble occupational training more than they resemble education in mathematical methods and understandings likely to be of long range value (Fey, 1975: 51).

These mathematics educators may have exaggerated the differences of opinion concerning composition of the basic skills, but it cannot be assumed without argument that some set of skills has general sanction.

EMPIRICAL UNIDIMENSIONALITY

Empirical studies of the four tests cited seem to contradict the findings of our content analysis. The high internal consistency reported for virtually all subtests seems to indicate that the test developers have been successful in constructing unidimensional tests. For example, the mathematics subtests of concepts, computation, and applications on the SAT Intermediate Level 1, Form A, are reported to have internal consistency reliabilities of .87, .91, and .93, respectively, when given to beginning fifth graders. Evidence of internal consistency has been taken as evidence that all items measure a single trait and so brings into question the utility of identifying subsets of items (e.g., Goolsby, 1966). There are at least two reasons why evidence of empirical unidimensionality of a test may be misleading. The first reason stems from the definition of empirical unidimensionality; the second is a function of the ways in which unidimensionality is estimated.

The empirical definition of unidimensionality calls for a large first factor on the item intercorrelation matrix. Thus, empirical unidimensionality is a static concept specific to the time of test administration and to the population of respondents. Consider a population of respondents and sets of items that yield an item intercorrelation matrix with equal off-diagonal elements. Let half the items require division with remainder and half the items require multiplication of three digit numbers. An intervention focused exclusively on multiplication of three digit numbers might uniformly reduce the difficulty of half the items. The intervention's only effect on the item intercorrelation matrix would be to create a difficulty factor. Yet, despite empirical unidimensionality, both prior to and after the intervention, it is clear that there is a useful distinction between the two subsets of items. It is of interest, therefore, to ask whether a test is unidimensional relative to differences in instruction, i.e., does all fourth-grade mathematics instruction affect all item difficulties equally? Searching for differential effects across items is analogous to searching for aptitude by treatment interactions, ATIs, and might be called the search for item by treatment interactions, ITIs.

Most test data, however, are not confined to people receiving uniform instruction. Different students receive different educational experiences and these experiences may have different effects across items. If a test is comprised of sets of items defined by concepts such that within each set the effect of an intervention is constant, and if the effects of interventions vary with less than perfect correlation across sets of items, the sets of items should be reflected in the pattern of item intercorrelations; the intervention effects contribute to both the covariance and variance of items within a set but not to the covariance of items in different sets.

Estimates of internal consistency based on data from norm groups of standardized tests seem to challenge the importance of ITIs. The apparent unidimensionality of standardized tests, however, may provide evidence only for the existence of a strong single dimension, not for the absence of content factors. The Spearman-Brown prophecy formula implies that the more concepts included, the stronger the general factor. Furthermore, the fewer items per concept, the less clearly defined will be the second-order concept factors. Evidence of an internally consistent test should not be misconstrued as indicating a lack of utility to searching for ITIs in evaluations using that test.

EFFECTS ON CLASSROOM INSTRUCTION

In considerations of test selection, while little attention has been given to alterations in test scores, even less attention has been given to the possible effects on classroom instruction. Critics of testing have shown concern with the global effects of testing programs, but no one has reflected on the differential effects of using one test rather than another. Even the broader considerations of the effects of testing on classroom instruction have seldom been supported by empirical evidence.

It is generally believed that testing programs have some influence on the content teachers present. The prevailing opinion is that teachers will be apt to "teach to the test," that is, to present content that closely follows the content of the test (see, e.g., Cooley and Lohnes, 1976: Ch. 4). Those who believe that the tests represent only a fraction of the content important for that grade level consider this phenomenon undesirable, as do those who believe that teachers should exercise their own judgment in determining instructional content. On the other hand, those who believe that the content of instruction should be uniform across classrooms, perhaps focusing on the basic skills, may see testing programs as a valuable tool for determining classroom instructional content. Both groups base part of their assessment of tests on the assumption that teachers "teach to the test," but neither group can provide much empirical evidence to support that assumption.

It may be that the institution of a testing program leads teachers to spend more time on the material in the general area of test coverage, without any ties to the specific items covered by the test. Teachers might pay attention to the titles of the subtests, but use preconceived ideas about the content to cover. Alternatively, teachers might consider the testing program an unwarranted imposition and pay no attention to the test. In short, while plausible, it is far from certain that teachers would teach to the specific content covered by the test.

The likelihood of teaching to the test seems even smaller when one considers the other factors that might influence teacher content choice. A frequently mentioned alternative influence is the textbook supplied to the teacher. Schutz (this volume) has indicated that while teachers may initially claim that they choose their content by considering abstract goals of instruction, when pressed for detail, they often admit that they teach whatever material is covered in the textbook used by their students. Lists of objectives issued by the school district are another likely source of influence. The objectives are generally intended to influence, if not determine, content choice, and hence they act as a strong competitor to a testing program's influence. It is not difficult to add to the list of possible influences. Additional possible categories of influence include teacher conceptions of subject matter, teacher assessment of student achievement, and student interest in subject matter. Once alternative partial determinants of content are suggested, the assumption that teachers will teach to the test seems much less reasonable.

Research is needed to sort out the mechanisms through which teachers respond to the multitude of pressures to choose content for instruction. A first attempt at investigating this area is now underway at the Institute for Research on Teaching. In two parallel studies, the relative influences of six factors are being studied: a testing program, a set of objectives, textbooks, pressure from parents, pressure from other teachers, and pressure from the principal. In one study, teachers are asked to indicate how they think they would react to these pressures in a hypothetical situation. In the second study, associations between the content covered and the existence of a similar set of factors will be determined in a number of school districts (Porter, 1978; Schmidt, 1978; Freeman, 1978). Both studies are restricted to the content of mathematics presented in the fourth grade. While these studies should give some clues about the ways in which content choices are determined, the process is surely complex and will require prolonged study before being well understood.

ADVICE TO SCHOOL DISTRICTS

The discussion above offers immediate suggestions to guide school districts in their selection of standardized tests. These considerations apply to the decision about whether any testing should be conducted only insofar as they may help determine the likely impact of existing tests. The recommendations made are general; more specific recommendations must await the results of research in the area suggested above.

First, the multitude of possible influences on content choice implies a minimal requirement for district controls over instructional content in the classroom—consistency. If district administrators want specific content presented throughout the district, they are well advised to ensure that the tools at their disposal are used toward the same end. If textbook selection, test selection, and lists of objectives all are determined at the district level, then the administrator should make choices that lead to a consistent pressure to teach the desired content. To avoid losing the ground gained with a carefully chosen test through choosing a textbook covering different material, careful examination must be made of tests, texts, and objectives. Furthermore, the administrator should use whatever control he has over possible influences such as parent pressure and principal pressure, to make sure that all factors that are in any way controllable emphasize the same desired content.

Second, even if tests are found to have little specific influence on instructional content, it is still important that the contents covered by the test match the contents of most concern to those using the test results. The tests do not all measure achievement in the same content areas, and the use of a test that assesses progress on some less relevant content may be misleading.

CONCLUSION

The effects of test selection, both on the interpretation of results and on the content of instruction, have been oversimplified, denied, or ignored. Yet an examination of four major tests has shown that the prevalent belief that all these tests measure the same achievement is questionable. If such a widely held assumption does not stand up well to scrutiny, there is ample reason to question other assumptions about the effects of test selection.

Consideration of the effects of tests on content leads immediately to a broader area much in need of study—the manner in which teachers choose instructional content. The folklore about the decision process ranges from assertions that teachers draw on their practical wisdom in making the choices to the claim that teachers will teach whatever content is presented in the text materials they are given.

The importance of the content covered for student achievement is generally acknowledged. If content is so important, then the means by which teachers select content, and by which administrators can influence that choice must be better understood. Such understanding could be the key to the much sought increase in student performance. Test selection on the basis of content coverage may provide immediate benefits, and can serve as a starting point for the investigation of the relationships between testing, achievement, and content coverage.

REFERENCES

COOLEY, W. W. and P. R. LOHNES (1976) Evaluation Research in Education. New York: Irvington.

FEY, J. T. (1975) "Remarks on basic skills and learning in mathematics," in The NIE

Conference on Basic Mathematical Skills and Learning Volume 1: Contributed Position Papers. Washington, DC: National Institute of Education.

FREEMAN, D. J. (1978) "Conceptual issues in the content/strategy distinction." Presented at the Annual Meeting of the American Educational Research Association, Toronto, March.

GOOLSBY, T. M. (1966) "Differentiating between measures of different outcomes in the social studies." Journal of Educational Measurement 3: 219-222.

HELMS, D. and A. GRAEBER (1975) "Problems related to children's acquisition of basic skills and learning of mathematics and some suggested R&D options for NIE support," in The NIE Conference on Basic Mathematical Skills and Learning. Volume 1: Contributed Position Papers. Washington, DC: National Institute of Education.

LINN, R. L. and J. A. SLINDE (1977) "The determination of the significance of change between pre and postesting periods." Review of Educational Research 47: 121-150.

National Institute of Education. (1975) The NIE Conference on Basic Mathematical Skills and Learning. Volume 1: Contributed Position Papers. Washington, DC: National Institute of Education.

PORTER, A. C. (1978) "Factors affecting teachers' decisions about content." Presented at the Annual Meeting of the American Educational Research Association, Toronto, March.

---, W. H. SCHMIDT, R. E. FLODEN, and D. J. FREEMAN (1977) "Impact on what? the importance of the content covered." Presented at the 1977 meeting of the Evaluation Research Society, Washington, DC, October.

SCHMIDT, W. H. (1978) "Measuring the content of instruction." Paper presented at the Annual Meeting of the American Educational Research Association, Toronto, March.

---, A. C. PORTER, R. E. FLODEN, and D. J. FREEMAN (1978) "Training manual for the classification of the content of fourth grade mathematics" (Research Series No. 4). East Lansing, Michigan: Michigan State University, Institute for Research on Teaching.

WALKER, D. F. and J. SCHAFFARZICK (1974) "Comparing curricula." Review of Educational Research 44: 83-111.

9

EVALUATION OF TITLE I VIA THE RMC MODELS:

A Critical Review

Robert L. Linn

Three evaluation "models" are described by Tallmadge and Wood (1976) in a report entitled "User's Guide: ESEA Title I Evaluation and Reporting System." The models were developed under U.S. Office of Education Contract at the RMC Research Corporation. The work was initiated by USOE in response to a congressional directive to the U.S. Commissioner of Education which called for the development and dissemination of acceptable evaluation models for federally supported education projects.

Although not mandatory at this time, the RMC models are recommended by USOE for Title I evaluations. In addition to the Tallmadge and Wood "User's Guide," other publications are available from USOE that deal with the RMC models. For example, the first two publications in the recently inaugurated USOE *Series of Monographs on Evaluation in Education* describe the RMC models and some of their applications (Horst et al., 1975; Tallmadge and Horst, 1976). Presumably, the RMC models will be further disseminated by the recently established Technical Assistance Centers.

Given the USOE endorsement of the RMC models, it seems likely that these models will receive considerable use whether or not they eventually are mandated for use in the evaluation of federally funded education projects. Hence, it is important that these models be subjected to careful scrutiny and criticism. The purpose of this paper is to provide a critical analysis primarily of one of the three models.

SOME PRELIMINARIES

This paper is primarily focused on limitations of the RMC models, especially "Model A," the norm-referenced model. It is important, however, that the criticism be put into perspective. There are a number of aspects of the models and work related to them that I would evaluate very positively. In many instances, the recommendations are substantial improvements over common practice. Furthermore, Model A, which is critiqued in most detail, is the one that is acknowledged by the developers to be "the least rigorous of the three models" (Tallmadge and Wood, 1976: 37).

The reasons for devoting special attention to the weakest of the three models will be discussed below. A few comments about some of the strengths of the proposed models, however, should be made. They will be kept brief because the positive aspects of the models have already been emphasized in the USOE publications and because the focus of this paper is on limitations.

Among the strengths of the proposed models, I think the following deserve special mention.

(1) The recommendation that, if possible, the same level of a test be used for the pretest and the posttest is sound. This practice avoids the serious biases that can result from changes in test level because of inadequate vertical equating (see, e.g., Barker and Pelavin, 1975; Slinde and Linn, 1977).

(2) Also beneficial is the requirement that normative interpretations of test results be based on administration dates that are close to actual dates of obtaining data. This practice avoids the problems caused by extensive interpolations based upon assumed growth rates.

(3) The recommended Normal Curve Equivalents (NCEs) are apt to be an improvement over the commonly used Grade Equivalent Scores that they are meant to replace. Like many others, I have argued against the use of Grade Equivalent Scores (Linn and Slinde, 1977), so it is not surprising that I would view positively the strong rejection of Grade Equivalent Scores in the publications describing the RMC models.

(4) Models B and C, the "control group design" and the "special regression design" are based on sound principles, although they are based on strong assumptions that will rarely be met in practice.

Each of the above features of the models and reasons for considering them to be strengths could be elaborated and, indeed, other strengths could be added. But that elaboration would call for another paper. For the present purpose, critical analysis of the three models, I will now turn to a brief description of the RMC models followed by an analysis of some of their limitations.

A DESCRIPTION OF THE RMC MODELS

"The focus of all the models is to obtain as clear and unambiguous an answer as possible to the question, 'How much more did pupils learn by participation in the Title I project than they would have learned without it?' " (Tallmadge and Wood, 1976: 2). In attempting to answer this question, each model would require the comparison of the observed performance of students following a period of participation in a Title I program with "an estimate of what that performance would have been without the Title I project" (p. 2). As stated, the problem sounds much like a standard research problem where the goal is the estimation of a "treatment effect." The tricks, of course, are (1) deciding how to measure the performance, (2) determining what the treatment is and when it is implemented, and (3) obtaining the estimate of what the performance would have been without the treatment.

The main concern addressed by the RMC models is the generation of the "no-treatment expectation." Virtually no attention is given to the sticky, but important, concern of treatment definition, and only little attention is given to the concern about how performance should be measured. The measurement of performance does serve as the basis for distinguishing two forms of each model depending on whether performance is measured by a normed achievement test (Models A1, B1, and C1) or by a nonnormed achievement test (Models A2, B2, and C2). Special booklets have also been prepared so as to provide guidance regarding the selection of a norm-referenced test (Fagan and Horst, 1975) and the use of a criterion-referenced test in a Title I evaluation (Tallmadge, 1976). But the main emphasis of the RMC models is clearly on ways of generating the no-treatment expectation.

MODEL A

Under Model A, the no-treatment expectation is obtained from normative data. The underlying assumption on which the expectation is based is that, in the absence of Title I, the group mean would be at the same percentile at the time of the posttest as it was at the time of the pretest. If a nationally normed test is used, Model A1 would require that a test form be administered on a date closely corresponding to an administration date used in the norming. The same test form and level or an alternate form at the same level would be readministered as a posttest following participation in a Title I project. The date of the posttest administration would also need to correspond closely to a normative sample administration date.

Given the pre- and post-test scores, project impact would then be determined by comparing observed mean posttest performance to the expected no-treatment mean posttest performance. The percentile of the pretest mean would be used to compute the no-treatment expectation. The norms appropriate to the pretest date would be used to determine the percentile equivalent of the pretest mean. The no-treatment expectation would be the same percentile but in the norms appropriate to the date of the posttest. A positive (negative) impact would be indicated by an observed mean performance with a percentile equivalent greater (less) than the no-treatment expectation.

For purposes of statistical analysis and agregation of data at the state and national level, the observed and expected no-treatment posttest scores would be expressed in normal-curve equivalents (NCEs). The NCEs are simply normalized standard scores with a mean of 50 and a standard deviation of 21.06. They range from 1.0, which is the NCE corresponding to a percentile of 1.0, to 99.0, which is the NCE corresponding to a percentile of 99.0. In comparison with percentiles, NCEs are more spread out toward the middle of the distribution and less spread out at the extremes and have equal numerical values at 1, 50, and 99.

As previously indicated, I think that NCE scores provide a preferable metric to the commonly used grade equivalent units. It must be recognized, however, that the NCEs offer no panacea. They are obviously dependent on the norms data, and strong assumptions are needed to support the equal interval claim that has been made for them. In essence, NCEs are simply a refinement of the stanine score; they share the same strengths and weaknesses of other normalized standard score scales such as T-scores.

The actual comparison of the observed and expected no-treatment posttest scores may be made in terms of local or national norms. National norms are required, however, to permit the NCEs to be used for aggregation purposes. The locally normed test could be used as the pre- and post-test with the no-treatment expectation derived from the local norms. A test with national norms would also have to be administered, however. The nationally normed test would be used solely to convert the results based on the locally normed test to NCE units for purposes of aggregation.

Model A2, a variation on the above process, is intended to allow the use of a nonnormed test. This test would be administered as pre- and post-test. At pretest time, however, it would also be necessary to administer a nationally normed test. No-treatment expectations would be based on the results on an equi-percentile equating of the normed and nonnormed results at the time of the pretest. The median pretest score on the normed test would be used to determine the percentile needed to find the expected no-treatment score. The median for the nonnormed tests at the time of the posttest would be converted to its normed "equivalent" using the results of the equi-percentile equating of the pretest. Norms corresponding to the time of the posttest would then be used to obtain a percentile which would then be considered the observed posttreatment performance, which, if higher than the percentile of the median pretest score, would be taken as an indication of positive impact.

MODEL B

Model B, the control group design, comes directly from notions of basic experimental design. The idealized, albeit seldom realized, application of model B would involve random assignment of children to "treatment" and control groups. Both groups would be administered a pretest and a posttest. The tests could be normed (model B1) or nonnormed (B2), but in the case of the latter a normed test would also be needed so that the results of the nonnormed tests could be converted to the NCEs required for aggregation purposes.

In view of the fact that random assignment of children can seldom be realized in practice, randomization is not presented as a requirement of model B. Rather, it is only required that the preexisting "treatment" and "control" groups either be "enough alike to be considered random samples from a single population" (Tallmadge and Wood, 1976: 6) or, failing that, the preexisting differences be "small." In the former case, analysis of covariance would be used to estimate treatment effect. In the latter case, adjustments would be made using "the principal-axis or standardized-gain-score method" (p. 6).

Wisely, Tallmadge and Wood do not present precise rules for determining when differences are small enough to make model B appropriate. Model B is the clearly preferred model where a "good" control can be formed. The guiding principle would be to switch from model B to Model C or A only when one of those models is likely to yield a more accurate no-treatment expectation than model B. That determination is admittedly a difficult one which requires "good judgment." As a rule of thumb, however, Tallmadge and Wood suggest that model C or model A may be preferable to model B if the treatment and control groups differ on the pretest by more than a fifth of a national norm group standard deviation (1976: 25).

MODEL C

The last model is the "special regression design." Where feasible, it is considered preferable to model A but less desirable than model B. The special requirement of model C is that assignment to a Title I project be based exclusively on the pretest. All children below a cutoff would be assigned to the Title I project; all those above the cutoff would not participate in the project but would be retained as a comparison group. In other words, model C is what Campbell and Stanley (1963) described as "regression-discontinuity analysis."

As with the other models, model C may be used with normed or nonnormed tests. With nonnormed tests a normed test would also need to be administered to obtain NCEs, however.

CRITIQUE

I suspect that for many people the first area of concern with the RMC models would be the lack of attention to some important evaluation issues. As previously noted, little attention is given to the problems of treatment definition and description. Nor is much attention given to the type or breadth of measures that are used to measure performance. Standardized achievement tests in reading and math are seemingly accepted as sufficient.

The need for greater attention to the description of the instructional activities being evaluated, the need to attend to the context in which the activities take place, and the desirability of considering a variety of outcomes in addition to student achievement as measured by existing standardized tests are all arguable points. But while these are important issues, they go beyond the confines of what the RMC models are purported to do, namely to answer, in a fairly narrow sense, the control question, " 'How much more did pupils learn by participating in the Title I project than they would have learned without it?' " (Tallmadge and Wood, 1976: 2).

Although the question, as it is stated, may avoid the issue of considering outcomes other than achievement, its narrow focus on one or two outcome measures is still questionable. There has been considerable debate on the suitability of standardized, norm-referenced achievement tests for evaluating compensatory education programs. Certainly, greater justification of the narrow focus of the RMC models would seem to be called for in view of the range of curricula and objectives found in various Title I projects. I will not dwell on this issue, however. Rather, the remainder of my comments will be directed to how well the control question may be answered within the confines of the RMC models, which imply only a limited array of outcome measures.

THE NEED FOR ADJUSTMENTS

The researcher's paradigm can seldom be imposed upon a school system. Random assignment of children, in addition to causing operational problems, is also apt to be opposed on philosophical grounds. A positive answer to the impact questions is generally assumed in advance of the evaluation, and it is considered unethical to deny the advantage to some of the most needy solely for purposes of the evaluation. But even if random assignment were possible, it is not likely that an evaluator could control the treatments as closely as is required by the research paradigm. Thus, the distinctions between the "treatment" and "control" groups are apt to be blurred.

In the absence of random assignment the key questions are: (1) How comparable are the groups? and (2) How should adjustments be made for preexisting differences? In the RMC models the pretest would be used to reach a conclusion regarding comparability. This use of the pretest is certainly reasonable because it would almost surely be more highly related to the posttest than almost any other variable. It is, of course, conceivable that while two groups are comparable on pretest scores, they could differ on some other characteristics which, in the absence of a treatment effect, could result in differences on the posttest. This possibility is probably of more theoretical than practical concern, however. With essentially equivalent pretest distributions, an explanation of observed posttest differences in terms of other hypothesized preexisting differences is not apt to be very plausible.

Of course, by the very nature of Title I programs, there generally will be differences between "treatment" and "control" groups on pretest scores as well as on a variety of other variables. Under those conditions there is no guarantee that an adjustment is the right adjustment. Although much has been written on this problem (e.g., Campbell and Erlebacher, 1970; Cronbach et al., 1977; Lord, 1967; Rubin, 1974), there are no foolproof solutions.

Under specialized assumptions, analysis of convariance or analysis of covariance with adjustments for errors of measurement on the covariate, are appropriate (Goldberger, 1972, Kenny, 1975; Rubin, 1977). Cronbach et al. (1977) have demonstrated that in general only what they call the "complete covariate" or the most predictive composite within groups will result in an unbiased estimate of the effect. The complete covariate is a theoretical variable, an optimum combination of all conceivable variables on which the groups differ. Thus, in practice, the proper adjustment is unknown and can only be approximated to an uncertain degree of accuracy.

THE FAN-SPREAD HYPOTHESIS

The adjustment method suggested in the RMC model in the case of preexisting differences between the groups is the "principal-axis or standardized-gain-score adjustment method." This adjustment procedure is similar to an analysis of covariance where the within-group correlation between pretest and posttest is assumed to be an equal to 1.0. The adjustment may be accomplished either by the use of the principal axis of the pretest-posttest scatter plot or by standardizing the pretest and the posttest scores and computing standardized gain scores.

The principal axis adjustment method is consistent with the type of assumptions used for model A. It is also consistent with Campbell's (1967) fan-spread hypothesis. Kenny (1975) has argued that this adjustment procedure is the most appropriate one given the fan-spread hypothesis and that the basis for assignment to groups is unknown.

In essence, the fan-spread hypothesis is that in the absence of treatment effects, groups will maintain their same average percentile rank or standard score position within the distribution of individual scores. Groups are expected to fan out over time on commonly used scales such as the ubiquitous grade-equivalent scale. But in standard score terms, the expectation is a constant value over time. It should be clear that this expectation is based on a rather strong assumption. Linn and Werts (1977) have shown that this standardized-gain-score method can lead to biased estimates, if the fan-spread hypothesis is false.

The fan-spread hypothesis is difficult to evaluate because it would require the availability of data where there were no differential treatment effects. Of course, different groups are experiencing different educational experiences, so we lack an ideal basis on which to test the hypothesis. It can be evaluated in a more limited sense, however, by asking whether the current state of affairs is for groups to maintain roughly constant percentile ranks or standard score positions. If that were found to be the case, then the hypothesis could be used as the basis for determining if new programs alter the status quo. This is basically the idea behind the use of standardized-gain-scores in model B and is clearly the basis for obtaining the expectation in model A.

Some support for the fan-spread hypothesis seems to be provided by Coleman and Karweit (1970) who argue that percentile rank may be a reasonable basis for determining the direction, though not the amount, of change. Certainly the expectation of a constant percentile rank is sounder than the initial level (Linn and Slinde, 1977). If a constant percentile is a reasonable expectation of a gain of one grade equivalent, regardless of the basis for evaluating the direction of change, so too is a constant NCE, which also has more desirable properties for evaluating the amount. But is a constant NCE the right no-treatment effect expectation for all groups? An unequivocal answer to this question is probably beyond our reach. Some results that are relevant to the question are available, however.

Van Hove et al. (1970) summarized achievement tests results for two grade levels in New York, Los Angeles, Chicago, Philadelphia, Detroit, and Baltimore. Test results for these cities were available in grade 6 and either grade 3 or grade 4 on one of three standardized achievement test batteries. Schools were categorized by percentage of minority students in the school. Unweighted average percentile ranks were then obtained for groups of schools categorized by percentage minority. As a global summary, the average percentile ranks over parts of the same test battery were calculated and reported for schools where students were almost entirely minority group members and for schools with enrollments of primarily majority group students.

I have converted the global results reported by Van Hove et al. to NCE scores. The resulting NCEs are reported in Table 9.1 for "earlier grade," which is either grade 3 or grade 4, and for "later grade," which is grade 6 in all instances. The difference between the NCE of the later and earlier grade is also reported for each category of schools and each city and test combination. With the exception of city A, the later grade NCE is lower than the earlier grade NCE for the nearly all-minority schools in all cities. The later grade NCEs are also lower than the earlier grade NCEs in 5 of the 7 instances for the nearly all-majority schools. The decline for the nearly all-majority schools is generally less than that for the all-minority schools, however.

The data on which the results in Table 9.1 are based are not completely satisfactory for our purposes. For instance, they are cross-sectional rather than longitudinal, the level of the test is not constant across grades, and averaging of percentile ranks across parts of a battery may conceal interesting trends in parts of a battery. Nonetheless, they are sufficient to raise some doubts about the universal applicability of the constant NCE score as the expected no-treatment effect. The unweighted average of the difference in NCEs for the nearly all-minority schools in Table 9.1 is -2.8 and ranges from -7.7 to +4.4. It seems debatable that a zero NCE difference is the right no-treatment effect expectation.

Even if the limitations of the data in Table 9.1 are deemed too great to give them much weight for evaluating the adequacy of the no-treatment effect expectation, they raise doubts about another aspect of model A—the option of using either local or national norms. Consider the choice from the perspective of a director of a project in city E, for example. Based on the results in Table 9.1, local norms would be expected to make

Table 9.1 NCE Scores at Two Grades for Nearly All-Minority Schools and Nearly All-Majority Schools in Several Cities[a]

		Nearly All Minority			Nearly All Majority		
City	Test[b]	Earlier Grade	Later Grade	Diff.	Earlier Grade	Later Grade	Diff.
A	1	30.7	35.1	4.4	41.9	45.8	3.9
B	1	33.0	29.9	-3.1	44.7	43.6	-1.1
C	1	29.9	26.3	-3.6	44.7	45.2	.5
D	1	33.0	25.3	-7.7	51.6	51.1	- .5
D	2	34.4	33.7	- .7	57.0	54.2	-2.8
E	2	40.1	33.7	-6.4	55.3	50.5	-4.8
F	3	23.0	20.4	-2.6	50.0	46.3	-3.7

a. Based on average percentile ranks over parts of the same test battery as reported by Van Hove, Coleman, Rabben and Karweit, 1970.

b. The tests are (1) Iowa Tests of Basic Skills, (2) Metropolitan Achievement Test, and (3) Stanford Achievement Tests.

the project appear better with the use of test 2 than would national norms. In cities where the test results tend to fall behind the national norms over increasing grades, the local norms are sure to seem preferable from the perspective of the project director.

A more recent and comprehensive evaluation of the constant NCE as a no-treatment effect expectation is provided by Kaskowitz and Norwood (1977). They compared the empirical posttest and pretest scores to equipercentile expectations using a longitudinal sample on the Metropolitan Achievement Tests (MAT). The data were obtained as part of the norming and have previously been discussed by Beck (1975).

Kaskowitz and Norwood found some differences between the longitudinal and cross-sectional norms. The differences were not consistently in one direction nor were they judged to be very large. The pretest and posttest NCE scores corresponding to the pretest and posttest percentiles reported by Kaskowitz and Norwood are shown in Table 9.2. The pretest NCE is equal to the no-treatment expectation that would be obtained using model A1. Thus, the differences between posttest and pretest NCEs, which are reported in the last column of Table 9.2, show the degree of systematic error in the model A1 estimates for this longitudinal sample when cross-sectional norms are used.

Table 9.2 Pretest and Posttest NCE Scores for the Longitudinal Norms Sample on the Metropolitan Achievement Tests[a]

Test	Grade	Sample Size	Pretest NCE	Posttest NCE	Difference in NCE's
Total	2	2854	54.0	56.1	2.1
Reading	3	1638	51.9	54.0	2.1
	4	2175	51.7	51.5	- .2
	5	2624	50.6	51.6	1.0
	6	2732	53.0	53.4	.4
	7	2154	49.6	52.5	2.9
	8	2030	50.6	51.8	1.2
	2	2853	50.8	56.3	5.5
	3	1609	53.1	51.9	-1.2
	4	2130	50.3	50.0	- .3
	5	2595	51.9	53.6	1.7
	6	2699	54.5	54.2	- .3
	7	2120	51.7	52.8	1.1
	8	2002	50.7	52.0	1.3

a. Based on percentiles reported by Kaskowitz and Norwood, 1977

The differences, though often statistically significant due to the large samples, are generally quite small. Even a systematic error of 2 NCE units may be of concern, however, if the size of effects to be detected are quite small. But of greater concern is the finding by Kaskowitz and Norwood (1977) that the relatively good approximation for scores in the midrange does not hold up as well toward the extremes.

Kaskowitz and Norwood found a consistent tendency for the empirical average posttest scores to be above the constant NCE expectation for very low pretest scores. The opposite tendency was found for high pretest scores. Since Title I projects are specifically aimed at the population of students who would be expected to have low pretest scores, the lack of fit between the constant NCE expectation and the empirical posttest results in that region is serious.

In another analysis, Kaskowitz and Norwood compared the empirical posttest on pretest regressions for minority and for majority students. Based on these analyses, they concluded that the constant percentile expectation based on the standardization group norms would lead to a no-treatment expectation that is too high for minority students. This tendency is opposite in effect to the results reported above for the MAT longitudinal norms sample. "Depending on the distribution of children on pretest scores, then, the equal percentile assumption could lead either to the conclusion that a program did have an impact when in fact it did not or to the conclusion that the program did not have an impact when in fact it did" (Kaskowitz and Norwood, 1977: 55).

These results underscore the tenuous nature of the key assumption on which model A is based. That is the assumption that in the absence of an effect due to special treatment, the achievement level of the group would maintain a constant NCE as defined by the norm group. This assumption was acknowledged as a weakness of model A by Horst et al. (1975), who noted that "empirical support for this assumption is minimal" (p. 72). They went on to argue that the assumption is most plausible "when the norm group is like the treatment group" (p. 72). By definition, however, the samples used to develop national norms on standardized tests are not like the specially defined subpopulations to which compensatory education programs are directed. A simple regression effect would lead one to expect that program gains would be underestimated. Differences between norm groups and program groups might lead to either an over- or an underestimate of gains. The key point is simply that there is not an adequate basis for using a constant percentile as the no-treatment expectation.

CHOICE OF TEST

For purposes of aggregation, the NCE results are treated as equivalent regardless of test. Jaeger (n.d.) has thoroughly analyzed the question of equivalence using the Anchor Test Study (ATS) data (Loret et al., 1972). Jaeger concluded that:

> Strictly speaking, NCE conversion does not make the tests used in the ATS equivalent any more than would some other, more widely recognized derived score. NCE scores do not reflect a common metric. Nor would selection of a test for evaluation be a point of total indifference to a knowledgeable project manager (n.d.: 24).

Jaeger considered hypothetical differences between pretest and posttest for 5, 10, or 15 percentile ranks as defined by ATS norms. The differences were then converted to NCE units using the publisher's norms for each of the eight reading comprehension tests included in the ATS. For example, at grade 4 an ATS percentile rank of 10 corresponds to a percentile rank of 6.93 and an NCE of 18.83 on the norms of the Gates-MacGinite Reading Tests (GMT). An ATS percentile rank of 15, also at grade 4, concerts to a GMT percentile rank of 10.9 and an NCE of 24.10. An observed gain of this magnitude would thus yield an observed NCE posttest that was 5.27 (i.e., 24.10-18.83) NCE units above the no-treatment expectation. That same increase from the 10th to 15th percentile in terms of ATS norms would translate to a 2.59 NCE difference on the Stanford Achievement Tests at grade 4.

After a detailed comparison of the differences in the gains in NCE scores on various tests corresponding to constant percentile gains on the ATS, Jaeger (n.d.) concluded "that the mean NCE gains likely to be realized on a variety of widely used standardized tests are not comparable, and that such mean gains should not be aggregated across projects that employ different achievement tests" (p. 58).

From the perspective of the local Title I project, Jaeger's tables provide a project director with a guide to the reading comprehension test that could be expected to make the local project look best. For example, suppose it is known that the grade 4 pretest performance is at the 10th percentile on the ATS norms. Increases corresponding to gains of 5, 10, and 15 ATS percentile points would translate to the NCE gains shown in Table 9.3 for the various tests. From an inspection of Table 9.3 it is clear that the choice of a reading comprehension test would not be a matter of indifference to my hypothetical project director. The changes for registering an impressive gain appear much better on the ITBS than on the SAT.

Table 9.3 Means Gains in NCE Units on Eight Reading Comprehension Tests Corresponding to Constant-Percentile-Rank Increases on the ATS Norms for Students in Grade 4[a]

ATS Percentile-Rank Increase	ATS Gain in NCE Units	Mean Gain in NCE Units on the Test Indicated							
		GMT[b]	ITBS	MAT	SAT	CAT	CTBS	SRA	STEP
10-15	5.2	5.27	8.43	4.17	2.59	4.75	4.75	6.32	5.80
10-20	9.3	9.27	12.64	8.43	5.79	8.54	7.75	9.72	9.59
10-25	12.8	12.67	15.58	12.67	8.66	12.12	11.28	12.63	13.38

a. Based on Jaeger (1977, Tables 9, 12 and 15).

b. GMT = Reading Comprehension Subtest of the Gates-MacGinitie Reading Tests
ITBS = Reading Comprehension Subtest of Iowa Tests of Basic Skills
MAT = Reading Subtest of the Metropolitan of Achievement Test
SAT = Paragraph Meaning Subtest of the Stanford Achievement Tests
CAT = Reading Comprehension Subtest of the California Achievement Tests
CTBS = Reading Comprehension Subtest of the Comprehensive Tests of Basic Skills
SRA = Reading Comprehension Subtest of the SRA Achievement Series
STEP = Reading Comprehension Subtest of the Sequential Tests of Educational Progress

The cautious project director might also be concerned about the appearance of losses and so might want to look at an ATS percentile decrease from 10 to 5. But, the choice of a test clearly seems important.

It could be argued that the differences such as those displayed in Table 9.3 and the many others analyzed by Jaeger are not very large. They do represent constant errors, and whether they are considered small or large is a matter of judgment. That judgment should take into consideration the likely size of project effects as registered on these instruments. If project effects of, say 10 NCE units, i.e., almost a half of a standard deviation for the norm group, were routinely anticipated, then constant errors of even 3 or 4 points might be tolerated. That is, with a strong signal more noise can be tolerated. On the other hand, if the signal is weak, even small amounts of noise can be serious. In view of the experience that has accumulated from numerous evaluations over the past decade it is hard to be sanguine about the prospect of large effects. In my opinion, the effects are apt to be small, and the level of noise found by Jaeger to be introduced by combining results for different tests is unfortunately large by comparison.

THE USE OF NONNORMED TESTS IN MODEL A2

The problems of comparability for purposes of aggregation are apt to be exacerbated in model A2. The use of nonnormed tests will be welcomed by critics who view existing normed tests as insensitive to educational effects. Their enthusiasm may be dampened by the requirement that a normed test also be administered and used as the basis of NCE scores via an equi-percentile equating with the nonnormed test. But, if a specially constructed test or an available criterion- or domain-referenced test is judged to be more sensitive to educational effects, model A2 might still be considered an improvement over model A1.

As in model A1, the no-treatment expectation for model A2 is based on the assumption that the project participants would maintain the same percentile rank over time in the absence of any project effect. In addition, however, model A2 depends on the adequacy of the equating of the normed and non-normed tests using pretest data and an assumption that the equating would be the same at posttest. These assumptions are all questionable. This is recognized by Tallmadge and Wood (1976) who note, that model A2 "is less rigorous than any of the other models including model A1 and should only be used when it is not possible to have a control or a comparison group, and when the testing instrument for the evaluation has neither national nor local norms" (p. 43).

Unfortunately, as has previously been argued, adequate control groups will be unavailable for many Title I projects. Thus, the first condition for using model A2 will often be met. The second condition is really a matter of choice, and people who believe that specially constructed tests or other nonnormed tests will be more sensitive than a normed test would naturally prefer model A2.

Recognizing that model A2 is the least rigorous model is not sufficient. Judgments need to be made as to whether the model is good enough to make the tie to norms to create NCEs and the aggregation of data worthwhile. From the local perspective, a judgment is needed regarding possible systematic errors that may result from use of the model and whether these errors are apt to be large enough to invalidate the results. People will surely differ in their judgments on these issues. As I will try to show below, however, large systematic errors may occur in the use of model A2. They are potentially too large, in my opinion, to justify aggregating the data or to put much credence in the results.

One of the rules of implementation for model A2 is that the "normed and non-normed tests should measure approximately the same ability" (Tallmadge and Wood, 1976: 45). The tests must be highly correlated. The minimum correlation mentioned by Tallmadge and Wood is .6, but they presumably would want considerably higher correlations if possible. Nonetheless, this standard is much too lenient.

The tests equated in the Anchor Test Study (Loret et al., 1974) had intercorrelations substantially higher than .6, yet even that equating would result in noticeable errors if used as in model A2. To illustrate this, ATS results for the Sequential Tests of Educational Progress (STEP) and the California Achievement Tests (CAT) were used. Suppose that the STEP Reading Comprehension Test was administered at grade 4, and the median raw score was 10. This raw score corresponds to a percentile rank of 28 and an NCE of 37.7. If the STEP was to be administered in grade 5 for the posttest then the expected no-treatment outcome would be a median raw score of 11.8, which is the raw score corresponding to an NCE of 37.7 in the 5th grade norms.

Now suppose that STEP was a nonnormed test. To use it in model A2, the CAT reading comprehension subtest would be administered at the pretest time in grade 4 along with the STEP reading comprehension subject. The procedure for using model A2 would then be based on the equating of the STEP and CAT grade 4 raw scores. The CAT norms for grades 4 and 5 would be used to define the no-treatment expectation. I have simulated this process using the ATS grade 4 equating results and the

ATS norms for the CAT in grades 4 and 5. The procedure and the data source for each step is outlined in Table 9.4.

The results of the simulation are shown in the bottom half of Table 5. As can be seen, the no-treatment expectation is a STEP raw score of 13.0. This may be compared to the corresponding value of 11.8 that would have been obtained under model A1 (see the top half of Table 9.5).

Table 9.4 Procedure for Simulating A2 Results Using the Anchor Test Study Data

Step	Procedure	Data Source
1	Obtain CAT grade 4 mean raw score equivalent of STEP grade 4 mean raw score.	ATS grade 4 equating table
2	Convert CAT grade 4 raw score to percentile rank.	ATS grade 4 norms table
3	Convert CAT average percentile rank to no-treatment expected grade 5 CAT raw score.	ATS grade 5 norms table
4	Obtain STEP no-treatment expected grade 5 raw score.	ATS grade 4 equating table

Table 9.5 Hypothetical No-Treatment Expectations for the STEP Reading Comprehension Subtest Based on Models A1 and A2[a]

Test	Type of Score	Grade 4 Mean	Grade 5 No-Treatment Expectation
		Model A1	
STEP	RAW	10.0	11.8
	NCE	37.7	37.7
		Model A2	
STEP	RAW	10.0	13.0
	RAW	17.0	21.0
	NCE	37.7	37.7

a. The NCE's and the raw score equating of STEP and CAT are based on Anchor Test Study results (Loret et al., 1974).

The STEP raw score no-treatment expectation of 11.8 is the value that would be obtained using model A1. The value of 13 is the result of the simulated application of model A2. In terms of NCE units these two expected no-treatment outcomes are 37.7 and 41.3 respectively. A difference of 3.6 NCE units may seem large to some but acceptably small to others. I will not argue that issue but merely note that even under equating conditions much better than can generally be expected for model A2 applications, systematic errors may be introduced simply due to the equating.

The correlation of the STEP and CAT reading comprehension subtests in grade 4 was .76 for the ATS sample. Correlations even lower than this may be expected when nonnormed tests are correlated with normed tests in model A2. Jaeger (n.d.), for example, noted that Athey and O'Reilly had found predictive validities of a criterion-referenced test with the CAT Total Reading Subscore ranging from .37 to .69. Grandy et al. (1977) reported correlations of .73 and .70 between the Georgia Criterion Referenced Tests in reading and the Total Reading Score on the Iowa Tests of Basic Skills at grades 4 and 8, respectively. The corresponding figures for math were .71 and .76.

How disparate might the results of model A2 be from these based on an actual norming of the nonnormed tests with a correlation of only about .7 between the normed and nonnormed tests? Although I know of no data that directly answer this question, I have used data reported in the CAT manuals (Tiegs and Clark, 1970, 1972) to simulate the type of results that might realistically be obtained.

The correlation between the Math Computation Subtest and The Math Concepts and Problem Subtest on Form A, Level 2 of the CAT was reported to be .70 for the grade 2.6 normative group (Tiegs and Clark, 1972). The correlation is at the desired level for the simulation. The two subtests are also of interest for my purposes because, although they are both part of the Total Math Subscore, they might be expected to be differentially sensitive to instruction between grades 2.6 and 3.6. Indeed, the CAT item data show large increases in proportion passing on the computation items between grades 2.6 and 3.6, particularly on the multiplication items. The corresponding increases for the concepts and problems items are smaller.

For purposes of my simulation, I assumed that the Concepts and Problems Subtest was the normed test and the Computation Subtest was the nonnormed test. My imaginary project director presumably opted for the nonnormed test because it contained those items on which large gains were expected as the result of the instructional program. For percentiles of 15 through 50 in steps of 5 percentile points the grade 2.6 Computation Scores were used to obtain two no-treatment expected NCE scores at grade 3.6. First, the actual grade 3.6 Computation norms were used. In other words the percentiles were simply converted to NCE scores. Second, the posttest expected NCEs under no-treatment effect assumptions were obtained as they would be in model A2. That is, the grade 2.6 Computation and Concepts Problems scores were equated, the grade 3.6 Concepts and Problems NCE was then used to identify the corresponding raw score, which in turn was used in the grade 2.6 equating to obtain the equivalent Computation raw score. Finally, the Computation raw score was converted to an NCE using the grade 3.6 Computation Subtest Norms. Normally this last step would be impossible since the test in model A2 is nonnormed.

The resulting expected no-treatment effect NCE scores are shown in Table 9.4. The difference between actual NCE and the "equated" NCE that would result from model A2 is also shown. These differences are of the order of a third to a half of a norm group standard deviation. Differences of this magnitude surely would be considered too large to tolerate by any standards. See Table 9.6.

Table 9.6 Expected No-Treatment Effect Posttest Scores Based on Actual Computation Subtest Norms and Based on Equi-Percentile Equating with the Concepts and Problems Subtest[a]

	Expected NCE		
Percentile	Actual Norms	"Equated" Results	Difference Actual Minus "Equated"
15	28.2	21.8	6.4
20	32.3	24.8	7.5
25	35.8	27.5	8.3
30	39.0	29.6	9.4
35	41.9	32.3	9.6
40	44.7	34.7	10.0
45	47.4	36.5	10.9
50	50.0	38.1	11.9

a. Based on Tiegs and Clark (1970, 1972). The subtests are parts of the California Achievement Tests.

CONCLUSION

The RMC models are intended to deal with a very difficult problem. The models were selected because they were considered "feasible to implement in actual school settings" (Tallmadge and Wood, 1976: 2). The models are also expected to yield "valid, comparable, and interpretable results" (Tallmadge and Wood, 1976: 2). There is of course a tension between the goal of feasibility, which includes consideration of cost, level of disruption, and skill requirements for conducting the evaluation, and the goal of obtaining sound results.

Model B is high on one dimension, but will often be low in terms of feasibility. Actually, feasibility considerations lead to compromises in the application of model B. "Comparison" groups that differ from treatment groups in small but systematic ways are accepted in place of control groups. As a result, model B applications are faced with the old but difficult problem of adjusting for preexisting differences.

Model A is high on the feasibility dimension but low in terms of its ability to provide "valid, comparable, and interpretable results." It shares some of the notable features of its automotive namesake. It is very simple. It requires neither exotic statistical techniques nor expensive and typically unfeasible control groups. On the other hand, I doubt that model A can live up to its automotive namesake's reputation of dependability.

It would be nice to end this paper on an optimistic note. The RMC models were developed in response to a real need. They represent, despite the limitations that I have emphasized, responsible efforts by able professionals. As indicated early in this paper, the recommendations in a number of areas would represent improvements over current practice. Yet in my judgment, they are apt to fall short of providing "valid, comparable, and interpretable results."

I do not have the "solution" to the problem. But I do have two minor suggestions to make. First, I think that the enterprise of educational evaluation is far too immature to be ready for a fixation on any small set of "models." The second suggestion is that we might benefit by moving away from the notion that each year's evaluations should stand on their own. The development and systematic use of historical data may in many instances provide a better basis for comparison than can be provided by constructing "control groups" or using national norms.

REFERENCES

BARKER, P. and S. PELEVIN (1975) "Concerning scores and scale transformations in standardized achievement tests, their accuracy and dependability for individual and aggregation: The case of MAT 70. A working note prepared for the National Institute of Education, WN-9161-NIE." Santa Monica: RAND Corporation, September.

BECK, M. D. (1975) "Development of empirical "growth expectancies" for the Metropolitan Achievement Tests." Presented at the Annual Meeting of the National Council on Measurement in Education, Washington, DC, March.

CAMPBELL, D. T. (1967) "The effects of college on students: proposing a quasi-experimental approach." Research Report. Evanston, IL: Northwestern University.

--- and A. ERLEBACHER (1970) "Reply to the replies," pp. 221-225 in J. Hellmuth (ed.) Compensatory Education: A National Debate. Vol. 3: Disadvantaged Child. New York: Brunner/Mazel.

CAMPBELL, D. T. and J. C. STANLEY (1963) "Experimental and quasi-experimental designs for research on teaching," in N. L. Gage (ed.) Handbook for Research on Teaching. Chicago: Rand McNally.

COLEMAN, J. S. and N. L. KARWEIT (1970) "Measures of school performance." Santa Monica: Rand Corporation, R-488-RC, July.

CRONBACH, L. J., D. R. ROGOSA, R. E. FLODEN, and G. G. PRICE (1977) "Analysis of covariance in nonramdomized experiments: parameters affecting bias." Occasional Paper, Stanford Evaluation Consortium, Stanford University.

FAGAN, B. M. and D. P. HORST (1975) "Selecting a norm-referenced test: ESEA Title I evaluation and reporting system." Technical Paper No. R. Mountain View, CA: RMC Research Corporation, October.

GOLDBERGER, A. S. (1972) "Selection bias in evaluating treatment effects: some formal illustrations." Madison, WI: Institute for Research on Poverty, University of Wisconsin.

GRANDY, J., C. WERTS, and W. SCHABACKER (1977) "Equating of ITBS and Georgia CRT Reading and Mathematics Tests in the eighth and fourth grades." Princeton, NJ: Educational Testing Service, September.

HORST, D. P., G. K. TALLMADGE, and C. T. WOOD (1975) A Practical Guide to Measuring Project Impact on Student Achievement. Number 1 in a series of monographs on evaluation in education. Washington, DC: U.S. Department of Health, Education and Welfare.

JAEGER, R. M. (n.d.) "On combining achievement test data through NCE scaled scores." Draft report prepared for Research Triangle Institute, Research Triangle Park, North Carolina (USOE Contract No. 300-76-0095).

KASKOWITZ, D. H. and C. R. NORWOOD (1977) "A study of the norm-referenced procedure for evaluating project effectiveness as applied in the evaluation of project information packages." Research memorandum. Menlo Park, CA: Stanford Research Institute, January.

KENNY, D. A. (1975) "A quasi-experimental approach to assessing treatment effects in the nonequivalent control design." Psychological Bulletin 82: 345-362.

LINN, R. L. and J. A. SLINDE (1977) "The determination of the significance of change between pre and posttesting periods." Review of Educational Research 47: 121-150.

LINN, R. L. and C. E. WERTS (1977) "Analysis implications of the choice of a structural model in the nonequivalent control group design." Psychological Bulletin 84: 229-234.

LORD, F. M. (1967) "A paradox in the interpretation of group comparisons." Psychological Bulletin 68: 304-305.

LORET, P. G., A. SADER, J. C. BIANCHINI, and C. A. VALE (1974) Anchor Test Study: Equivalence and Norms Tables for Selected Reading Achievement Tests (Grades 4, 5, and 6). Washington, DC: U.S. Government Printing Office.

--- (1972) Anchor Test Study: Final Report. Berkeley, CA: Educational Testing Service.

RUBIN, D. B. (1977) "Assignment to treatment group on the basis of a covariate." Journal of Educational Statistics 2: 1-26.

--- (1974) "Estimating causal effects of treatments in randomized and non-randomized studies." Journal of Educational Psychology 66: 688-701.

SLINDE, J. A., and R. L. LINN (1977) "Vertically equated tests: fact or phantom?" Journal of Educational Measurement 14: 23-32.

TALLMADGE, G. K. (1976) "Criterion-referenced tests: ESEA Title I evaluation and reporting system." Technical Paper No. 11. Mountain View, CA: RMC Research Corporation, October.

--- and D. P. HORST (1976) A Procedural Guide for Validating Achievement Gains in Educational Projects. Number 2 in a series of monographs on evaluation in education. Washington, DC: U.S. Department of Health, Education and Welfare.

TALLMADGE, G. K. and C. T. WOOD (1976) User's Guide: ESEA Title I Evaluation and Reporting System. Mountain View, CA: RMC Research Corporation, October.

TIEGS, E. W. and W. W. CLARK (1972) Bulletin of Technical Data Number 2: California Achievement Tests, 1970 Edition. Monterey, CA: CTB/McGraw Hill.

--- (1970) Examiner's Manual California Achievement Tests 1970 Edition Level II, Form A. Monterey, CA: CTB/McGraw Hill.

VAN HOVE, E., J. S. COLEMAN, K. RABBEN, and N. KARWEIT (1970) "Schools performance: New York, Los Angeles, Chicago, Philadelphia, Detroit, Baltimore." Unpublished manuscript, Baltimore, October.

10

PREDICTION ANALYSIS AND THE RELIABILITY OF A MASTERY TEST

Rand R. Wilcox

INTRODUCTION

The purpose of this paper is to examine the problems of estimating a binomial probability function based on a relatively small number of observations. To motivate this study, a current measurement problem is first described.

In various educational settings an examinee is given a mastery or criterion-referenced test which determines whether the student is advanced to the next level of instruction within a particular program of study. Typically the test consists of n dichotomously scored test items which represent the behavioral objectives that are being addressed by the course. If x, the examinee's observed (number correct) score is greater than or equal to a specified passing score, x_0, a mastery decision is made and the examinee is advanced to the next level of instruction; otherwise he is given remedial work. For a recent review of this area of measurement, the reader is referred to Hambleton et al. (1978).

One of the fundamental problems associated with mastery tests is finding an index that characterizes the test in some meaningful way. Several indices have been proposed (see, for example, Hambleton and Novick, 1973; Swaminathan et al., 1974; Harris, 1974; Brennan and Kane, 1977; Wilcox, 1977). Conceptually, the simplest index is the proportion of agreement which, for a single examinee, is the probability of making a mastery/mastery or nonmastery/nonmastery decision on two randomly parallel tests. Regardless of the merits of the other indices, at a minimum we want the proportion of agreement to have a value close to one.

Recently, Subkoviak (1976) proposed a single administration estimate of the proportion of agreement which may be described as follows: Suppose that for a given true score p, the distribution of observed scores for a single examinee is given by

$$f(x \mid p) = \binom{n}{x} p^x (1-p)^{n-x}, \qquad [1.1]$$

the binomial probability function. In other words, Subkoviak is adopting the binomial error model (Lord and Novick, 1968: Ch. 23) which is frequently used to describe a mastery test. The parameter p is referred to as the percent correct true score of the examinee. Further, suppose that the random variable y is the examinee's observed score on an n-item randomly parallel test. This means that

$$f(y \mid p) = \binom{n}{y} p^y (1-p)^{n-y}. \qquad [1.2]$$

The proportion of agreement, as defined by Subkoviak, is

$$P = \Pr(x \geqslant x_0, y \geqslant x_0) + \Pr(x < x_0, y < x_0).$$

He assumes x and y are (conditionally) independent which means that

$$P = \Pr(x \geqslant x_0)\Pr(y \geqslant x_0) + \Pr(x < x_0)\Pr(y < x_0) \qquad [1.3]$$

$$= \left(\sum_{y=x_0}^{n} f(y \mid p)\right)^2 + \left(\sum_{y=0}^{x_0-1} f(y \mid p)\right)^2.$$

Thus, any estimate of (1.2) using the observed score x yields an estimate of P. The classical estimate of (1.2) is to replace p with x/n (Aitchison and Dunsmore, 1975) although other approaches such as the one used by Subkoviak might be used.

Recent results in the statistical literature suggest two alternatives to the classical estimate of a binomial probability function. This paper describes and compares these two alternative techniques with emphasis on estimating the proportion of agreement. Only the case in which "reliability" (the proportion of agreement) is defined in terms of a single examinee will be considered.

ESTIMATES OF $f(y \mid p)$

We let $q(y \mid x)$ represent an estimate of $f(y \mid p)$. In the context of a mastery test we have two n-item randomly parallel tests, an examinee takes the first test, gets x items correct and so $q(y \mid x)$ is our estimate of the probability that he will get y items correct if he takes the second n-item test. For notational convenience, we write the classical estimate of $f(y \mid p)$ as

$$q_1(y \mid x) = \binom{n}{y} (x/n)^y (1 - x/n)^{n-y}.$$

For a Bayesian estimate of $f(y \mid p)$ the reader is referred to Aitchison and Dunsmore (1975: Chs. 2 and 3; see also Aitchison, 1975; Huynh, 1976).

Our first alternative estimate of $f(y \mid p)$ views p as arising from some prior distribution but no assumption is made about the form of the prior as is done in the typical Bayesian approach. For any distribution, Dunsmore (1976) suggests

$$q_2(y \mid x) = f(y \mid p = \hat{p}) + \frac{1}{2} (nC(\hat{p}))^{-1} \frac{\partial^2 f(y \mid p = \hat{p})}{\partial p^2} \qquad [2.1]$$

as an estimate of $f(y \mid p)$ where

$$C(p) = - \frac{\partial^2 \ln(f(y \mid p))}{n \partial p^2}$$

and $\hat{p}$ is a maximum likelihood estimate of p. Dunsmore refers to (2.1) as an asymptotic approach to estimating $f(y \mid p)$. By this it is meant that if we assume that $\hat{p}$ is the true value of p, (2.1) approaches the usual Bayesian solution as n gets large. Thus, in the asymptotic case, (2.1) has the optimal properties described by Aitchison (1975). Immediately one might object to this solution since the number of items on a mastery test is typically small. However, little is known about q_2 as an estimate of $f(y \mid p)$ and so dismissing (2.1) on the grounds that it has asymptotically optimal properties is a bit premature. The important point is that the value of n, if any, for which q_2 is to be preferred over q_1 remains to be determined. It may be that (2.1) gives more satisfactory results even for n small.

For the binomial distribution

$$C(p) = n^{-1} y p^{-2} + n^{-1}(n - y)(1 - p)^{-2} \qquad [2.2]$$

and

$$\frac{\partial^2 f(y \mid p)}{\partial p^2} = \binom{N}{y} \Big[y(y-1)p^{y-2}(1-p)^{N-y} - 2y(N-y)p^{y-1}(1-p)^{N-y-1} + (N-y)(N-y-1)p^{y}(1-p)^{N-y-2} \Big]. \qquad [2.3]$$

For the binomial case, there are several technical difficulties with Dunsmore's estimation procedure. First, it assumes that the posterior distribution $f(p \mid x)$ is asymptotically normal with mean $\hat{p}$ and variance $(nC(\hat{p}))^{-1}$. In order for this result to hold for the present case, it is necessary to assume that p is bounded away from zero and one so that certain regularity conditions are satisfied (Johnson, 1970).

Dunsmore also assumes that a maximum likelihood estimate of p is used. However, the sample mean is no longer a maximum likelihood estimate of p when (2.4) is assumed. This problem can be circumvented by assuming

$$.01 \leqslant p \leqslant .99 \qquad [2.4]$$

and estimating p with

$$\hat{p} = \begin{cases} .01, & x/n \leqslant .01 \\ .99, & x/n \geqslant .99 \\ x/n, & \text{otherwise} \end{cases}$$

Expression (2.4) is arbitrary and so there may be situations where some other closed interval containing p is believed to be more appropriate. Finally, Dunsmore's procedure approaches the Bayesian estimate of a probability function in the sense described above and so q_2 approaches a distribution (i.e., a function that integrates to one) in the asymptotic case. However, for n small, q_2 is not a probability function. In other words,

$$\sum_{y=0}^{n} q_2(y|x) \neq 1.$$

This last difficulty can be corrected by rescaling the estimate of $f(y \mid p)$ so that it sums to one. As is typically done, we accomplish this rescaling by replacing q_2 with

$$q_3(y|x) = q_2(y|x)/t(x),$$

where

$$t(x) = \sum_{y=0}^{n} q_2(y|x).$$

Our second alternative estimate of the binomial probability function stems from results reported by Murray (1977) on estimating a multivariate normal distribution. Using a common measure of information, it is shown that Bayesian techniques based on vague prior information always produce better results than the classical solution which simply estimates the vector of means and the variance-covariance matrix in the usual way and substitutes the results in the appropriate expression. The implication is that a non-Bayesian might want to use the Bayesian solution even if he objects to the concept of a prior distribution.

For the binomial case, a vague beta prior occurs when both parameters of the beta distribution approach zero. However, the beta distribution is defined only when both parameters are greater than zero and so, to overcome this difficulty, we take the values of both parameters of the assumed beta prior to be one. This corresponds to the uniform distribution which is often used to represent vague prior information. The Bayesian estimate of $f(y|p)$ is

$$q_4(y|x) = \binom{n}{y} \frac{B(x+y+r,\ 2n-x-y+s)}{B(x+r,\ s+n-x)},$$

where r and s are the parameters of the beta prior (see Aitchison and Dunsmore, 1975, Ch. 2) and where B is the usual beta function. For a vague prior ($r = s = 1$) this becomes

$$q_4(y|x) = \binom{n}{y} \frac{(n+1)!}{x!\,(n-x)!} \frac{(x+y)!\,(2n-x-y)!}{(2n+1)!}. \qquad [2.5]$$

COMPARISONS OF q_1, q_3, AND q_4

In this section, comparisons of q_1, q_3, and q_4 are made using three criteria. Although the alternative estimation procedures described above are derived from a Bayesian framework, only classical statistical techniques will be used henceforth. We also restrict our attention to situations where n is small since the number of items on a mastery test is typically less than or equal to 25 and because it is already known, as indicated above, that both alternative estimation procedures have certain optimal properties in the asymptotic case.

RESULTS USING AN ENSEMBLE SQUARED ERROR LOSS FUNCTION

We first examine

$$R(p) = E \sum_{y} (f(y|p) - q(y|x))^2 \qquad [3.1]$$

as a measure of the accuracy of $q(y|x)$ as an estimate of $f(y|p)$. We write (3.1) as $R(p)$ to emphasize that the accuracy of any statistic $q(y|x)$ depends on the unknown value of p. Our reason for considering this criterion is that it is frequently used in density estimation (see, for example, Wegman, 1972; Ott and Kronmal, 1976) and because it allows reasonably general comparisons among q_1, q_3, and q_4.

We first note that the probability function of the statistics q_1, q_3, and q_4 are a function of $f(x|p)$. More specifically, for a given y, there are $n+1$ possible estimates of $f(y|p)$ (values of q_1, q_2, and q_3) corresponding to $n+1$ possible values of x. For a given value of p and y, the probability of predicting $q_1(y|x)$ or $q_3(y|x)$ or $q_4(y|x)$ is $\binom{n}{x} p^x (1-p)^{n-x}$, the probability of getting x correct on the first test. That is, we know the probabilities corresponding to the $n+1$ values of the statistics q_1, q_3, and q_4 for fixed y and p.

Since we know the probability function of q_1, q_3, and q_4, we can evaluate (3.1) for any p. Letting q represent any one of our proposed estimates of $f(y \mid p)$, we have that

$$R(p) = \sum_x \sum_y (f(y \mid p) - q(y \mid x))^2 \binom{n}{x} p^x (1-p)^{n-x}. \qquad [3.2]$$

We evaluated (3.2) for $n = 4(1)25$ and $p = .01\ (.01).99$. Plots of the results are shown in Figures 10.1, 10.2, and 10.3 for the special cases $n = 4, 10, 25$. As can be seen, q_1 performs better than q_3 for all three values of n. As for q_4, we get improvement over q_1 and q_3 for nearly all values of p. For $n = 4$, q_4 is better than q_1 for $.06 \leqslant p \leqslant .94$. For $n = 10$ the range is $.03 \leqslant p \leqslant .97$, and for $n = 25$ we get improvement for $.02 \leqslant p \leqslant .98$. Moreover, the amount by which q_4 reduces R(p) may be substantial, particularly for n small. For $p = .5$, $n = 4$ we have $R(.5) = .2267$ for q_1 while for q_4, $R(.5) = .0927$. The interval $(p_0, 1 - p_0)$ over which q_4 is superior to q_1 is summarized in Table 10.1 for $n = 4(1)25$.

ESTIMATING $\sum_{y=x_0}^{n} f(y \mid p)$

We now consider the estimation of

$$v = \sum_{y=x_0}^{N} f(y \mid p)$$

and

$$w = \sum_{y=0}^{x_0-1} f(y \mid p).$$

Let

$$\hat{v}_i = \sum_{y=x_0}^{N} q_i(y \mid x), \quad i=1, 2, 4$$

$$\hat{w}_i = \sum_{y=0}^{x_0-1} q_i(y \mid x), \quad i=1, 2, 4.$$

text continues p. 156

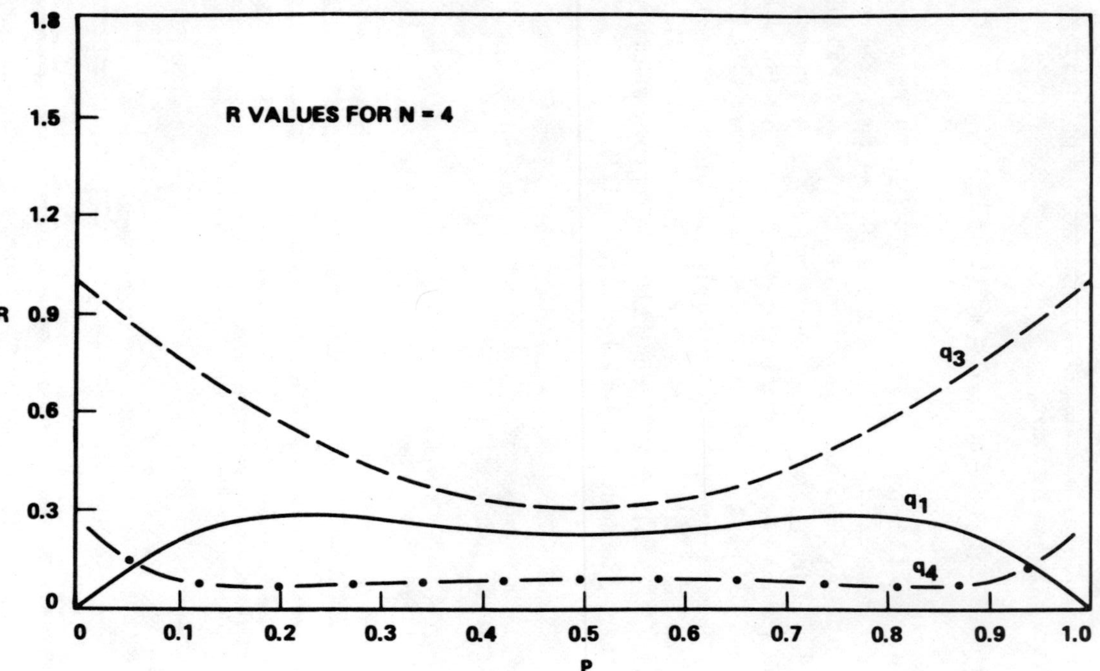
R VALUES FOR N = 4
R
1.8
1.5
1.2
0.9
0.6
0.3
0
0.1
0.2
0.3
0.4
0.5
0.6
0.7
0.8
0.9
1.0
P
q3
q1
q4

Figure 10.1a

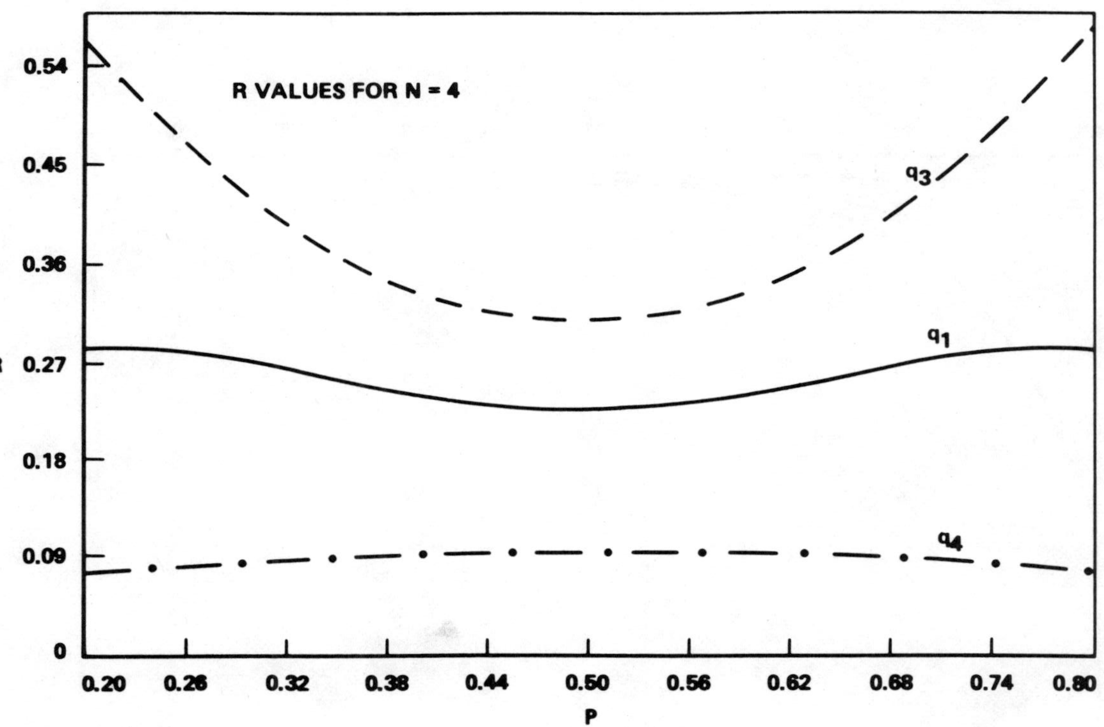
R VALUES FOR N = 4
q3
q1
q4
0.54
0.45
0.36
R 0.27
0.18
0.09
0
0.20
0.26
0.32
0.38
0.44
0.50
0.56
0.62
0.68
0.74
0.80
P

Figure 10.1b

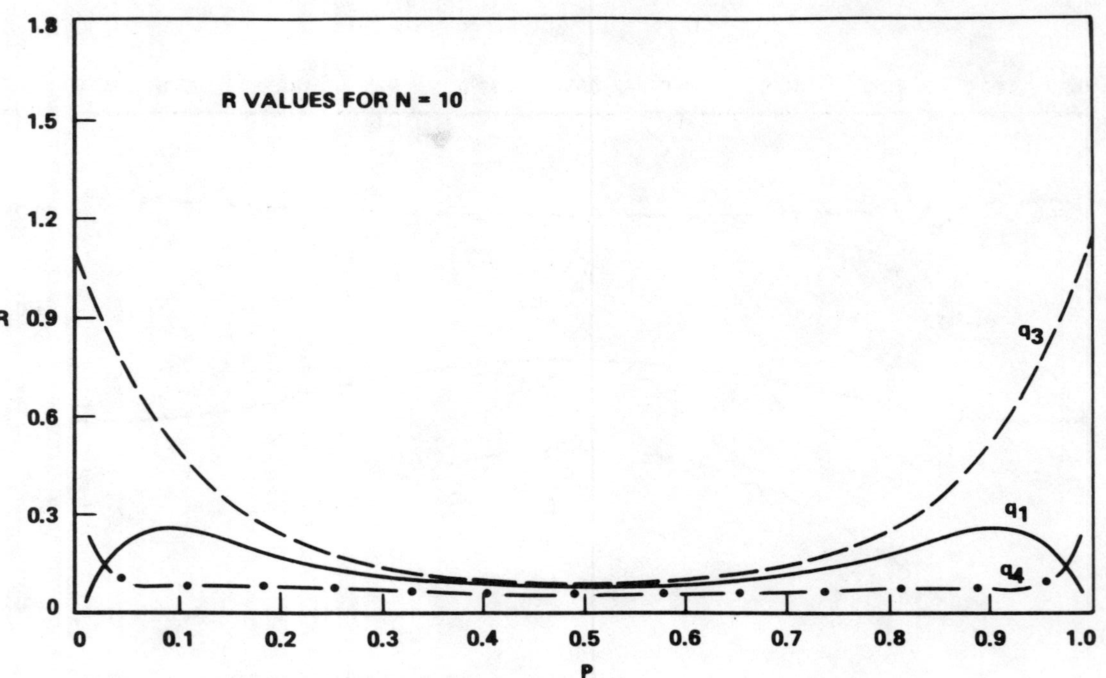
R VALUES FOR N = 10
R
1.8
1.5
1.2
0.9
0.6
0.3
0
0.1
0.2
0.3
0.4
0.5
0.6
0.7
0.8
0.9
1.0
P
q3
q1
q4

Figure 10.2a

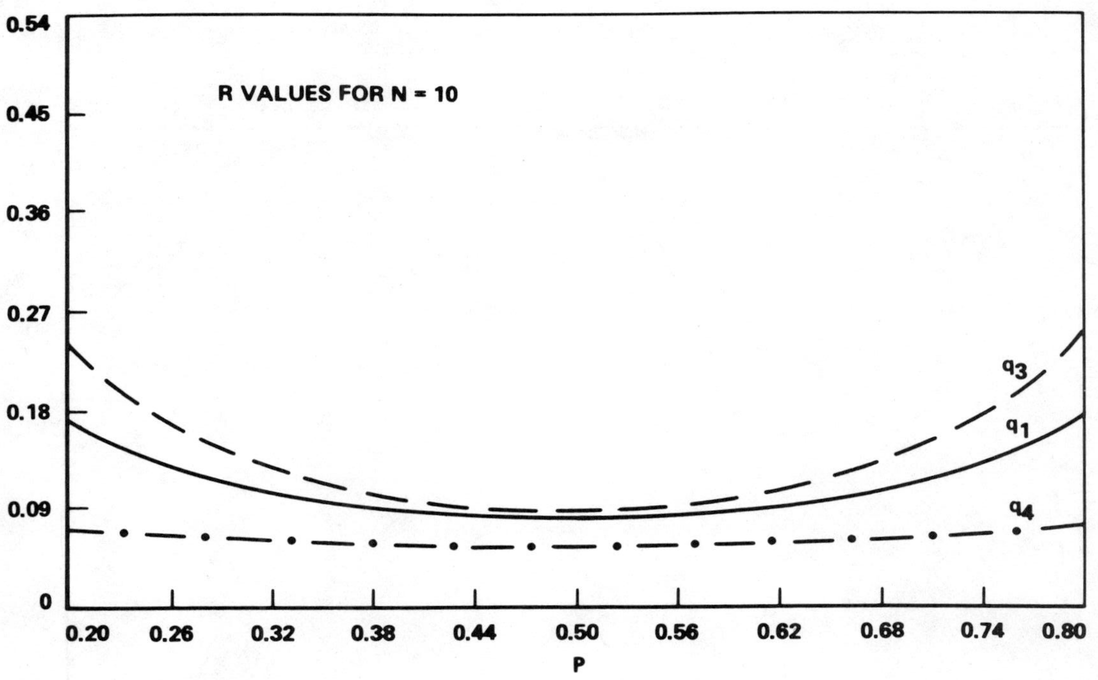
R VALUES FOR N = 10
0.54
0.45
0.36
R 0.27
0.18
0.09
0
0.20
0.26
0.32
0.38
0.44
0.50
0.56
0.62
0.68
0.74
0.80
P
q3
q1
q4

Figure 10.2b

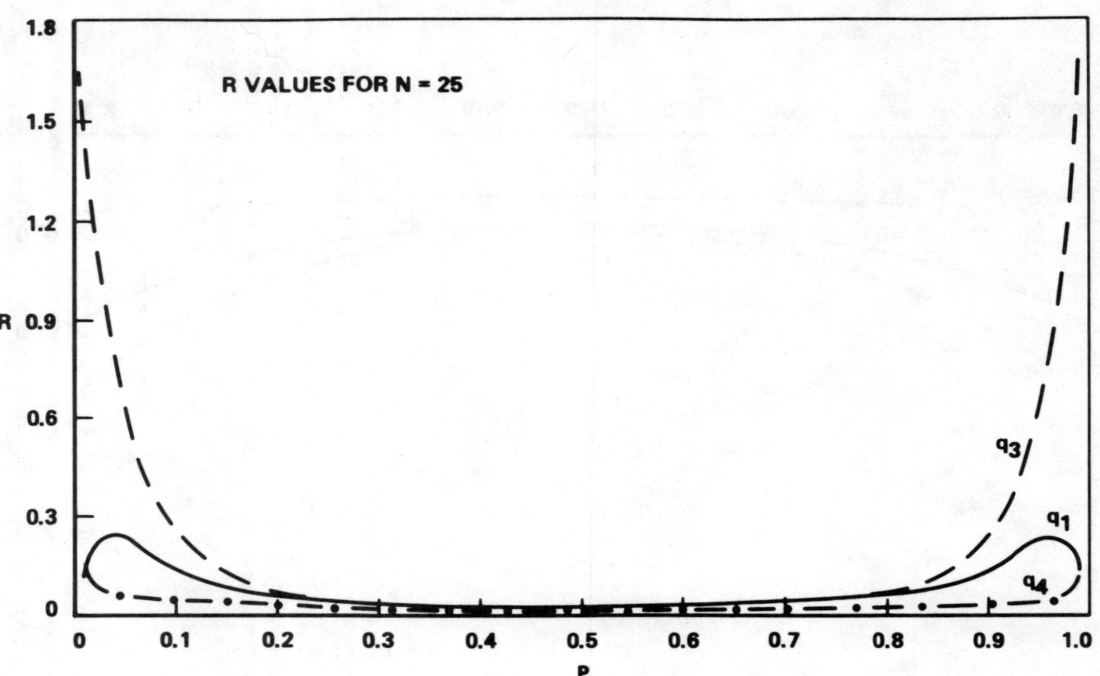
R VALUES FOR N = 25
R
1.8
1.5
1.2
0.9
0.6
0.3
0
P
0
0.1
0.2
0.3
0.4
0.5
0.6
0.7
0.8
0.9
1.0
q3
q1
q4

Figure 10.3a

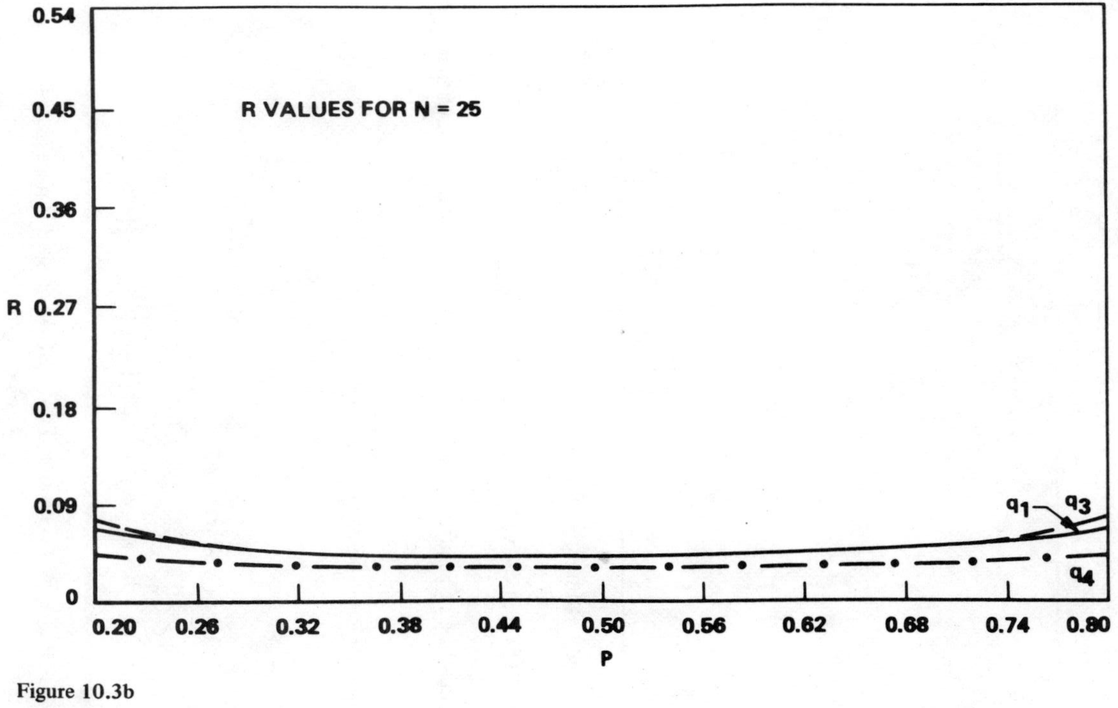
R VALUES FOR N = 25
0.54
0.45
0.36
R 0.27
0.18
0.09
0
0.20
0.26
0.32
0.38
0.44
0.50
0.56
0.62
0.68
0.74
0.80
P
q1
q3
q4

Figure 10.3b

Table 10.1 The Interval (p_o, $1-p_o$) for Which q_4 Is Superior to q_1 in Terms of (3.2)

n	p_0	n	p_0
4	.06	15	.02
5	.05	16	.02
6	.05	17	.02
7	.04	18	.02
8	.04	19	.02
9	.03	20	.02
10	.03	21	.02
11	.03	22	.02
12	.03	23	.02
13	.03	24	.02
14	.02	25	.02

For any estimate $\hat{v}$ of v we use

$$S(p) = E(v - \hat{v})^2 \tag{3.3}$$

as a measure of accuracy. Assuming $f(y \mid p)$ is binomial, we have that

$$S(p) = \sum_{x=0}^{n} (v - \hat{v})^2 \binom{n}{x} p^x (1-p)^{n-x}.$$

As for w, we use

$$T(p) = E(w - \hat{w})^2$$

$$= \sum_{x=0}^{n} (w - \hat{w})^2 \binom{n}{x} p^x (1-p)^{n-x}.$$

Since $w = 1 - v$, we see that $T(p) = S(p)$ and so it is necessary to consider only $T(p)$.

To give some indication of how the three estimation procedures compare, we evaluated $T(p)$ for $n = 4$ ($x_0 = 3$), $n = 10$ ($x_0 = 6, 7, 8, 9, 10$), $n = 25$ ($x_0 = 16(1)22$) and for $p = .01(.01).99$. Table 10.2 gives the interval (p_1, p_2) for which q_3 and q_4 are superior to q_1. More n values are considered in section 4.

For values of p close to zero we found the improvement of q_1 and q_3 and q_4 to be negligible since the values of T(p) for all three estimators were usually very small. If, however, the investigator has a priori information that p is reasonably close to one, q_1 may give a more accurate estimate of v and w.

To give some indication of the magnitude of T for the various estimation techniques, we present Table 10.3 as a typical case which gives the value of T for $n = 10$, $x_0 = 7$, $p = .05(.05).95$. As can be seen, q_4 improves on q_1 where it does the most good, that is, where the values of T are largest for q_1. For values of p close to zero or one, we see that the value of T becomes relatively small which is, of course, to be expected for q_1.

Table 10.2 Approximate Intervals for Which q_3 and q_4 Are Superior to q_1

		q_3		q_4	
n	x_0	p_1	p_2	p_1	p_2
4	3	.33	.72	.26	.83
10	6	.38	.72	.34	.71
10	7	.49	.82	.40	.77
10	8	.60	.80	.44	.83
10	9	--	--	.47	.90
10	10	--	--	.43	.97
25	16	.52	.72	.49	.71
25	17	.56	.76	.50	.73
25	18	.60	.80	.54	.77
25	19	.65	.84	.57	.80
25	20	.69	.87	.57	.83
25	21	.74	.88	.63	.87
25	22	.79	.90	.61	.90

A MINIMAX CRITERION FOR ESTIMATING v AND w

In many situations the examiner might not have a priori information regarding the unknown value of p and so it might be difficult to choose a particular estimation procedure based on the methods and results given above. One possible approach is to guard against the worst possible case. That is, we choose the estimator which minimizes the maximum possible

Table 10.3 Values of T for q_1, q_3, q_4, n=10, x_o=7, p=.05(.05).95

p	q_1	q_3	q_4
.05	0.000	0.000	0.000
.10	0.000	0.000	0.000
.15	0.001	0.002	0.002
.20	0.002	0.006	0.005
.25	0.005	0.013	0.011
.30	0.013	0.024	0.018
.35	0.024	0.038	0.028
.40	0.039	0.052	0.039
.45	0.056	0.064	0.047
.50	0.072	0.069	0.051
.55	0.085	0.067	0.051
.60	0.091	0.060	0.050
.65	0.091	0.054	0.051
.70	0.085	0.052	0.056
.75	0.073	0.052	0.062
.80	0.055	0.049	0.063
.85	0.033	0.038	0.052
.90	0.014	0.022	0.033
.95	0.002	0.007	0.013

error. We may write this criterion more formally as follows: Let $T(p; q_i)$ be the value of $T(p)$ using q_i, i = 1, 2, 3. Let $\tilde{T}_i = \sup T(p; q_i)$, where sup means supremum or least upper bound. We choose the estimator which yields the smallest value for $\tilde{T}_i$ (i = 1, 3, 4). This criterion is similar to using a minimax estimation technique. It is also somewhat similar to using a Tchebycheff norm (see Prenter, 1975: Ch. 1).

In practice it may be inconvenient to determine the exact value of $\tilde{T}_i$. However, a useful approximation to it can be obtained by evaluating $T(p; q_i)$ for p = .01(.01).99 and setting $\tilde{T}_i = T(p; q_i)$ for the value of p which maximizes $T(p; q_i)$.

As an illustration, consider the case n = 10, x_0 = 7. Evaluating $T(p; q_1)$ for p = .01, .02, . . . , 99 we found that its maximum value occurred at p = .62 with a value of .0915. Thus, $\tilde{T}_1 \doteq .0915$. Proceeding in a similar manner for q_3 and q_4, we have that $\tilde{T}_3 \doteq .0686$ and $T_4 \doteq .0637$. Hence, we would choose q_4 to estimate v and w.

In nearly all cases considered, q_4 was superior to q_1 and q_3 in terms of $\tilde{T}$. The only exception occurred for n = 10, x_0 = 10. In this case, $\tilde{T}_1 \doteq .167$, and $\tilde{T}_4 \doteq .171$.

THE SINGLE ADMINISTRATION ESTIMATE OF THE PROPORTION OF AGREEMENT

In this section we consider the estimation of P, the proportion of agreement. Substituting $(q_i(y|x)$ for $f(y|p)$ in expression (1.3) yields an estimate of P which we write as

$$\hat{P}_i(x) = \left(\sum_{y=x_0}^{n} q_i(y|x)\right)^2 + \left(\sum_{y=0}^{x_0-1} q_i(y|x)\right)^2, \quad i=1, 2, 4. \qquad [4.1]$$

Since

$$E(P - P_i(x))^2 = \sum_{y=0}^{n} (P - \hat{P}_i(x))^2 \binom{n}{x} p^x (1-p)^{n-x} \qquad [4.2]$$

we can evaluate the expected squared error loss for any p. We did this for n = 4(1)16, x_0 = n/2, . . . , n for n even and x_0 = (n + 1)/2, . . . , n for n odd. Larger values of n were not considered because the number of items on a mastery test is usually very small.

The estimate of P using q_4 nearly always gives better results than q_3 for the cases considered. Thus, the use of q_3 is contraindicated when squared error loss is believed to be appropriate and when n is small. However, the choice between q_1 and q_4 is not always clear, particularly when x_0 is close to n/2. Figures 10.4 and 10.5 show plots of the values of (4.2) as a function of p for the special cases n = 10, x_0 = 7 and n = x_0 = 10. These results are typical of what we found to be true for other values of n. More specifically, the interval over p for which $\hat{P}_4(x)$ improves on $\hat{P}_1(x)$ tends to be centered around p = .5 when x_0 = n/2. As x_0 approaches n, the midpoint of this interval moves toward p = 1. Another noteworthy result is that for x_0 close to n, there is relatively little advantage in using one statistic over another for small or moderate values of p.

Although there are no situations for which one estimation procedure gives consistently better results than the other, it would seem preferable to use $\hat{P}_4(x)$ when x_0 is close to n since it might be considerably more

text continues p. 162

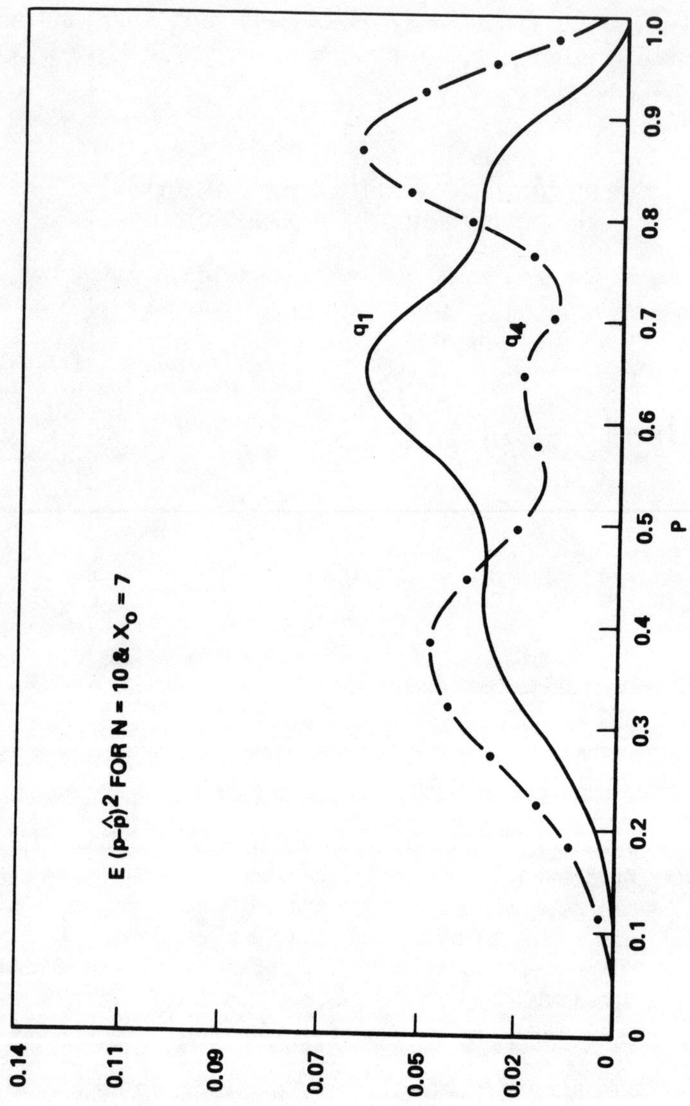

E (p−p̂)² FOR N = 10 & X₀ = 7
0.14
0.11
0.09
0.07
0.05
0.02
0
0
0.1
0.2
0.3
0.4
0.5
0.6
0.7
0.8
0.9
1.0
P
q1
q4

Figure 10.4

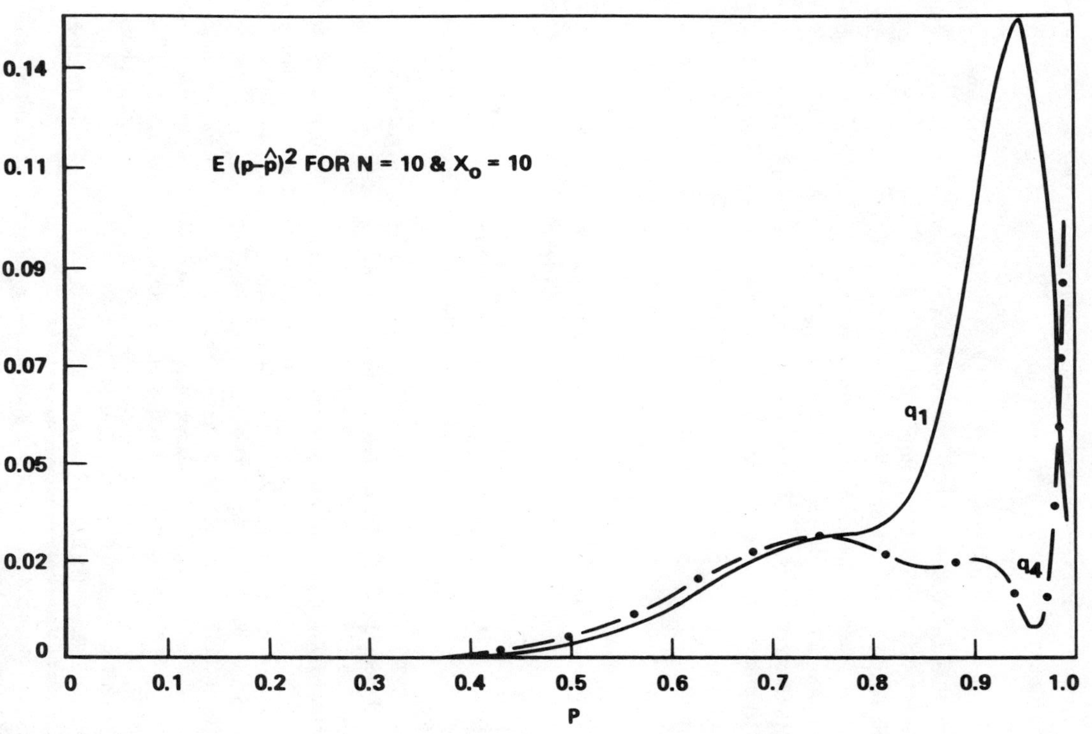
E $(p-\hat{p})^2$ FOR N = 10 & X_o = 10
0.14
0.11
0.09
0.07
0.05
0.02
0
0
0.1
0.2
0.3
0.4
0.5
0.6
0.7
0.8
0.9
1.0
P
q_1
q_4

Figure 10.5

accurate than $\hat{P}_1(x)$ while the reverse is seldom true. One interesting observation is that even for x_0 close to n/2, the maximum value of $E(P - \hat{P}_4(x))^2 - E(P - \hat{P}_1(x))^2$ over all possible values of p tends to be larger than the maximum value of $E(P - \hat{P}_1(x))^2 - E(P - \hat{P}_4(x))^2$, which suggests that $\hat{P}_4(x)$ is to be preferred over $\hat{P}_1(x)$. However, one might argue in favor of $\hat{P}_1(x)$ on the grounds that the length of the interval over p for which $\hat{P}_4(x)$ improves on $P_1(x)$ is shorter than the sum of the lengths of the two intervals for which $\hat{P}_1(x)$ improves on $\hat{P}_4(x)$. Nevertheless, Figures 10.4 and 10.5 would seem to suggest that $\hat{P}_4(x)$ is preferable to $\hat{P}_1(x)$, particularly when x_0 is close to n. Even for x close to n/2 one might use $\hat{P}_4(x)$ unless there is a priori information that p is close to one.

REFERENCES

AITCHISON, J. (1975) "Goodness of prediction fit." Biometrika 62: 547-554.

--- and I. R. DUNSMORE (1975) Statistical Prediction Analysis. New York: Cambridge Univ. Press.

BRENNAN, R. L. and M. T. KANE (1977) "An index of dependability for mastery tests." Journal of Educational Measurement 14: 277-289.

DUNSMORE, I. R. (1976) "Asymptotic prediction analysis." Biometrika 63: 627-630.

HAMBLETON, R. K. and M. R. NOVICK (1973) "Toward an integration of theory and method for criterion-referenced tests." Journal of Educational Measurement 10: 159-170.

HAMBLETON, R. K., H. SWAMINATHAN, J. ALGINA, and D. B. COULSON (1978) "Criterion-referenced testing and measurement: a review of technical issues and developments." Review of Educational Research 48: 1-47.

HARRIS, C. W. (1974) "Some technical characteristics of mastery tests," in C. W. Harris, M. C. Alkin, and W. J. Popham (eds.) Problems in Criterion-Referenced Measurement. CSE Monograph Series in Evaluation, No. 3. Los Angeles: Center for the Study of Evaluation, University of California.

HUYNH, H. (1976) "On the reliability of decisions in domain-referenced testing." Journal of Educational Measurement 13: 253-264.

JOHNSON, R. A. (1970) "An asymptotic expansion for posterior distributions." Annals of Mathematical Statistics 41: 851-864.

LORD, F. M. and M. R. NOVICK (1968) Statistical Theories of Mental Test Scores. Reading, MA: Addison-Wesley.

MURRAY, G. D. (1977) "A note on the estimation of probability density functions." Biometrika 64: 150-151.

OTT, J. and R. A. KRONMAL (1976) "Some classification procedures for multivariate binary data using orthogonal functions." Journal of the American Statistical Association 71: 391-399.

PRENTER, P. M. (1975) Splines and Variational Methods. New York: John Wiley.

SUBKOVIAK, M. J. (1976) "Estimating reliability from a single administration of a criterion-referenced test." Journal of Educational Measurement 13: 265-276.

SWAMINATHAN, H., R. K. HAMBLETON, and J. ALGINA (1974) "Reliability of criterion-referenced tests: a decision-theoretic formulation." Journal of Educational Measurement 11: 263-267.

WEGMAN, E. J. (1972) "Nonparametric probability density estimation: I. a summary of available methods." Technometrics 14: 533-546.

WILCOX, R. R. (1977) "Estimating the likelihood of a false-positive or false-negative decision with a mastery test: an empirical Bayes approach." Journal of Educational Statistics 2: 289-307.

11

AN ACHIEVEMENT-TEST ITEM MODEL

Chester W. Harris

I wish to describe an achievement-test item model that I believe is appropriate for providing new evidence about the effectiveness or ineffectiveness of an instructional program. This new evidence consists of separating the conventional "difficulty" (proportion of students who correctly answer the item) into the product of a term that describes their success with the generalized task of which the item is a sample and a term that describes their success with the particulars of the item itself. For example, we can conceive of a domain of items involving column addition of, say, four two-digit numbers, and we can generate any and all such items, using ideas presented by Wells Hively and his associates (1973). We can then administer to students a random sample of these items to gain, for each student, an estimate of the proportion of the universe of such items that he or she can handle successfully. Presumably, by administering different samples of items during the days or weeks of instruction in column addition, one could track the progress of each student, and of the group of students as well. The item model that I wish to describe recognizes that it is the combination of the difficulty of the task (e.g., column addition) and the difficulty of the particular number combinations appearing in that item that determine the overall difficulty of the item for the group, and thus the overall success of the group with this type of task.

Early work of Lazarsfeld and Kendall, reported by Goodman and Kruskal in their series of articles in the *Journal of the American Statistical Association,* provides the basis for this model. Work by Wilcox (1977) is also relevant. What I call the "primitive" model is given in Figure 11.1, which specifies the relationship (in a two-by-two table) of an undefined latent trait with performance of an item for which there is no successful guessing; completion or production items seem to fit this restriction. The parameter k represents the proportion of a population of students who are in the + category on the latent trait. The parameter x represents the conditional probability that a student in the + category on the latent trait will fail the item. The difficulty of the item is then seen to be k(l - x), which is a marginal in Figure 11.1.

If we accept this primitive model, then we can write in terms of k and x the two-by-two table representing the relationship between performance on the same item administered twice with no intervening learning; this I call a stability measure. Figure 11.2 gives this two-by-two table in terms of the parameters k and x. Note that the difficulty of the item is assumed to be the same on the two repeated administrations, since we assume that no fundamental change in performance has taken place. It should be emphasized that Figure 11.2 describes parameters, and not observations; it is obvious that an actual experiment using a sample of students is likely to give at least slightly different sample difficulty values for the item on the two administrations.

		Latent Trait +	Latent Trait -	
Item	+	k(1-x)	0	k(1-x)
	-	kx	1-k	1-k + kx
		k	1-k	1

Figure 11.1

		Administration Two +	Administration Two -	
Administration One	+	$k(1-x)^2$	kx(1-x)	k(1-x)
	-	kx(1-x)	$1-k+kx^2$	1-k + kx
		k(1-x)	1-k + kx	1

Figure 11.2

We now can move to the equivalence situation. We now assume two different items drawn from the same domain, administered to a population of students resulting in a two-by-two table given as Figure 11.3. We designate these as items a and b, and consequently specify x_a and x_b as the (probably) different parameters for the two items. Note, however, that k has a single value; in other words, we assume that the two items drawn from the same task domain are "equivalent in k," but different in x. The difficulties of the two items are not allowed to be different ($k(1 - x_a)$ versus $k(1 - x_b)$), but each difficulty is still a product of two parameters.

Finally we develop Figure 11.4 to represent the two-by-two table describing performance when learning of the task takes place (k_1 changes to k_2) and the specific difficulty of the item or items also changes (x_1 changes to x_2). Note that if we take $k_1 = k_2$, Figure 11.4 reduces to Figure 11.3.

We have begun an investigation of this achievement-test item model. We know some things that are generally true, such as what the product-moment correlation between items must be when the model holds, and how the model relates to latent class theory and to the Spearman conception of a single general factor. We can also relate the model to one type of

		Item b +	Item b −	
Item a	+	$k(1-x_a)(1-x_b)$	$k(1-x_a)x_b$	$k(1-x_a)$
Item a	−	$kx_a(1-x_b)$	$1-k+kx_ax_b$	$1-k+kx_a$
		$k(1-x_b)$	$1-k+kx_b$	1

Figure 11.3

		After Instruction (2) +	After Instruction (2) −	
Before Instruction (1)	+	$k_1(1-x_1)(1-x_2)$	$k_1x_2(1-x_1)$	$k_1(1-x_1)$
Before Instruction (1)	−	$k_1x_1 - k_1x_1x_2 + (k_2-k_1)(1-x_2)$	$k_1x_1x_2 + 1-k_2 + (k_2-k_1)x_2$	$1-k_1+k_1x_1$
		$k_2(1-x_2)$	$1-k_2+k_2x_2$	1

Figure 11.4

item characteristic curve, and we at least understand, though we perhaps have not solved completely, the problem of estimating the parameters involved. We have also begun to collect data for several types of completion items and have a fairly extensive example of one method of estimating the parameters k and x. These empirical results indicate that for samples of items drawn from a well-defined domain, estimates of k and x based on the responses of elementary school students reproduce the observed difficulties of the items quite well. A report of these results is scheduled for publication in the *Journal of Educational Statistics.*

REFERENCES

GOODMAN, L. A. and W. H. KRUSKAL (1959) "Measures of association for cross classifications II: further discussion and references." Journal of the American Statistical Association 54: 123-163.

HARRIS, C. W., A. PASTORAK, and R. WILCOX (1977) Achievement Test Items: Methods of Study. CSE Monograph Series in Evaluation, No. 6. Los Angeles: Center for the Study of Evaluation, University of California.

HIVELY, W., G. MAXWELL, G. RABEHL, D. SONSEAR, and S. LUNDEN (1973) Domain-Referenced Curriculum Evaluation: A Technical Handbook and a Case Study from the MINNEMAST Project. CSE Monograph Series in Evaluation, No. 1. Los Angeles: Center for the Study of Evaluation, University of California.

PART III

EVALUATION AND TESTING POLICY

INTRODUCTION

When one considers the relationship of tests and evaluation to public policy, the reflection can rest on any one of a number of facets. First, we can attempt to describe what the policy regarding tests and evaluation is and, as a corollary, where it came from. A second level might be how the use of technologies, such as evaluation and testing, influences educational policy. Third, we could muse regarding the alternative policy roles of different forms of testing and evaluation. Let's dispatch the first level relatively quickly, not on the basis of import but rather on the present reality. Policy on testing and evaluation can be gleaned from formal statements, legislative and judicial mandate, and from organizational arrangements and financial allocation. Formal statements regarding ,the policy of the United States on educational evaluation and testing are aperiodic in their release and rather negative in their intent. Policy statements at the national level have claimed that no national achievement test policy is intended, a statement most recently reaffirmed by former Secretary of Health, Education, and Welfare, Califano, at the 1978 Conference on Achievement Testing in the Basic Skills.

On a national legislative level, however, the mandated evaluations attached to social and educational programs in the 1960s and continued in the 1978 amendments to the Elementary and Secondary Act generate a good deal of the attention to evaluation and testing as part of program compliance. At the state level, the wave of legislative requirements for state assessment, essentially temperature taking of academic achievement in the aggregate, and competency and proficiency testing, the certification of individuals' accomplishments related to school programs, have both been increasing. Recent judicial decisions in Florida have upheld the states' general authority to require such tests for high school certification. In addition, such rulings have identified the need for stronger methodological safeguards surrounding the preparation of the tests and the corresponding instructional program, before individual "rights" may be abridged by consequences of performance on such a test. The force of such decisions is likely to increase the scrutiny directed to tests of all types. Other litigation, undertaken to clarify policy related to testing, involves the right of the public to have full access to such tests. In addition, policy statements, on the national level, have been issued by school organizations, with the National Education Association, which represents a large segment of teachers in public education, holding that the use of standardized achievement testing should be restricted. Thus, there is no clear national consensus on whether tests, and the evaluation intents which they support, are desirable or undesirable. As with most practices, a division of opinion exists.

Organizationally, testing and evaluation account for a significant amount of resources in the educational sector. Private and nonprofit agencies have sprung up in the last ten years, and many of these multimillion dollar concerns derive their support exclusively from contracts issued by the federal and state governments for the evaluation of educational programs. Public school districts have established units devoted exclusively to developing evaluation and testing programs to meet federal, state, and local requirements for accountability. The use of tests purchased from the large private and nonprofit corporations devoted to the development of school-related measures is well known. Various estimates of the purchasing cost of such tests, exclusive of scoring, interpretation, and administrative expenditures, have run in the range of a half a billion dollars annually.

Thus, by inspecting the reality of testing and evaluation in education alone, it is clear that formalized statements are not necessary: testing and evaluation absorb increasing amounts of public attention and dollars. We have policy on testing and evaluation—we are to do it. What we do not have is a policy which allocates effort and systematically sets expectations for what all this activity will contribute to public education.

Without apology, the pieces included in this section related to policy do not raise the issue at the first level discussed. Glass and Popham discuss the policy implications of a testing procedure and take opposite sides in arguing for the utility of competency testing as it is currently implemented. Wiley's chapter reminds us that our methodology is too insensitive to detect what our common sense tells us are significant changes in educational resources available to schools. Thus, his point is that educational policy is not being influenced by evaluation. It may be argued that evaluation, when it is insensitive, operates in a way to promote the faddism and waves of "solutions" which seem to characterize educational practice. In his 1977 paper, Henry Aaron, then Assistant Secretary for Planning and Evaluation, Department of Health, Education and Welfare, noted that our methodology, based as it is on social science research paradigms, is inherently conservative. Differences in effects of new programs and conventional practice show up infrequently, and the new programs rarely have a chance to develop the kind of support necessary to allow their potential benefits to accrue.

In this section, we have also included comments by Richard Schutz and Jason Millman pertinent to the presentations made. These comments are provided partly to give a better sense of the issues which are raised by the scholarly community at large. This section is thin, a fact which testifies in part to the scholars' reluctance to jump into the field. Policy and politics share a common root, and politically inexperienced scholars have been burned repeatedly by unexpected political flares.

Without doubt, the policy role of testing and evaluation will continue to be probed. It is hoped that the problem can be addressed, if not as whole on a systematic level, at least in fraction, and that the best minds in the field will see their role as contributors to the growing debate.

–Eva L. Baker

12

POLICY-RESPONSIVE EDUCATIONAL EVALUATION: Conceptions and Suggestions

David E. Wiley

I would like to share with you some thoughts that have evolved over the last four or five years, but for which I don't have what might be called a "bang" at the end. Perhaps it's more of a whimper. In this paper, then, I aim to stimulate thought, but I will not conclude with a cohesive set of positive recommendations about current practices. Specifically, I would like to lay out a conceptual framework for educational evaluations related to my understanding of what goes on in American schools. And I believe that I have a somewhat different perspective concerning the major factors controlling the consequences of schooling than that which is implicit in the practice of current evaluations.

Let me start with my political orientation.[1] I think of education as inherently goal-oriented and instrumental. However, there have been a number of developments in evaluation which have deemphasized these instrumental aspects of education. Robert Stake, for example, has said much that leads me to conclude that he believes the educative consequences of learning and schooling activities are not their primary and most important feature. His belief, as I see it, is that the experiences of the participants are perhaps more important than the instrumental values of education.

I wish to clearly state my view at the beginning, because later I will discuss the extreme difficulty of interpreting test-based evaluations, and I do not want to be confused with those who disvalue an instrumental view of education.

I fully believe that education is inherently instrumental; that we wish to develop the individual in ways that go beyond his immediate educative experience; that we are interested in making changes in individuals, and that these changes should be and are pervasive and lasting and contribute to their later life.

Further, I also want to express the view that within education the determination of goals must be a political rather than a personal activity, and surely not a technical one. Especially among those of us who have been involved in the kinds of technical activities that underlie much of educational research, there has been a regrettable tendency to view education as a technical activity and thus assume that most of the problems that need to be solved are "scientific." I strongly believe that the most important issues are inherently political. They are not technical, although they may be technically informed.

In addition, educational goals are never fully articulated. When goals are set and give rise to educational activities, the resulting goal statements never fully express all of the intentions inherent in that activity. One of the main reasons for this is that it requires too many resources to specify goals in great detail and to incorporate them into statements which are fully reflective of the intentions of curricular activity.

Finally, all educative activities have multiple goals and multiple consequences. Together, these four propositions imply that evaluation as an activity is inevitably political and that the evaluator is a political actor and cannot merely retreat into a solely technical role. I have highlighted these views so that what I say later can be traced to my basic orientation toward evaluation as a political activity, toward education as an instrumental activity, and to my noncynical view of politics as a meaningful activity in society.

In this paper I will limit myself to a discussion of evaluative activities within a particular rather than a universal framework. My own experience over the past three or four years has been mainly with evaluations and studies of schooling which have two characteristics. They have been oriented primarily toward elementary schooling, and their intent has been to inform national policy with respect to federally funded education programs. This surely colors my experience and perhaps makes some of it less relevant to evaluations conducted in other settings.

I do believe that the federal setting has implications for almost any of the contexts within which evaluations are conducted, but I would like to focus my remarks and make them somewhat more concrete by emphasizing curriculum and program evaluations on a relatively large scale and with an elementary school focus. My orientation is toward evaluations of the following kinds of programs: the "new math" as represented by the School Mathematics Study Group (SMSG) curriculum, the Emergency School Aid Act (ESAA) program, the Follow Through Curricula, or Title I. I will also talk about the evaluation of curricula or programs that are implemented in real or "natural" settings, that is, evaluation in public school settings where a curriculum is embedded into an ongoing system rather than a more focused evaluation where particular components are isolated for study and improvement.

I include experimental studies as well as quasi- or non-experimental ones in my domain of discussion. One of my most recent experiences was serving on the advisory panel for the evaluation of the Emergency School Aid Act; and that evaluation was undertaken as a "true" field experiment with random assignment of treatment conditions to schools, even though the evaluation was fully embedded in a real school setting. Thus, I want to construct my domain broadly enough to include experimental field trials, quasi-experimental, and more "naturalistic" circumstances.

My major thesis is that most of what passes for curricular or instructional innovation within these kinds of large-scale, heterogeneous programs consists of modifying the goals and/or the resources for schooling and implementing these modifications in customary ways. That is, the content of instruction is modified, or the level of intensity with which instruction takes place is changed. This statement may seem either to be prosaic or mystical; let me be more concrete. Over the last several years, I have come to believe that most of the achievement-relevant consequences of curricular and instructional innovation have not to do with the efficiency with which new curricula operate but with the effects of changes (1) in the goals or intended consequences of the curriculum and (2) in the resource levels that are provided for their implementation.

When a curricular or instructional innovation is implemented in a school setting, it replaces what's already there. If one implements a new reading program in the school system, one typically replaces the old program with a new program. (Title I might be an exception in that federal regulations require that funds supplement rather than supplant other instruction.) One of the major events that typically occurs, and that is usually the major motivation for changing curricula, is a goal change. A good example, historically, is the "new math." When the SMSG curriculum was implemented in a school, it would replace and not supplement the "old math" curricula; thus, there was a redistribution of goals. In that particular case, the conventional wisdom, and some empirical study, support the notion that the change resulted in the teacher spending more time, i.e., placing stronger emphasis, on what might be called "conceptual mathematics." And concommitantly, computational aspects of mathematics were emphasized to a lesser degree than before. Thus, one of the major changes that occurred was clearly in the area of goals.

Of the changes accompanying a new program, I believe that modification of curricular emphasis typically has the largest single effect on achievement and on achievement test scores. This point was strongly made by Walker and Schaffarzick (1974). They concluded that when a curricular innovation was evaluated, the achievement tests oriented toward the new goals generally showed positive effects, and the results of tests which were oriented toward the more traditional goals declined. These differences in curricular emphasis are extraordinarily underemphasized sources of variations in educational achievement. It may well be that the majority of school-to-school differences in achievement could be accounted for by these differences in emphasis. I believe that the effects of these differences account for most achievement-test derived differences in educational evaluations.

To summarize, most curricular innovations tend to involve significant changes in goals and, therefore, significant changes in *what* is learned; and these "qualitative" changes invalidate quantitative inferences concerning how much is learned. I believe, therefore, that conclusions concerning the relative effectiveness of alternative programs cannot be drawn using current methods.

Changes in resource levels are the second most important cause of differences in educational achievement. This is surely not the conventional wisdom in the sense that most evaluation studies show little or no effect from variations in resource levels. But I believe that the primary effects of Title I are resource-based. In reviewing what happens when districts receive Title I funds, I have concluded that the effects on curricular goals are not as large as those in most curricular innovations. Title I does tend to reorient instruction to some degree in terms of the amounts of time allocated to basic skills; however, such reorientation is relatively small in comparison to resource effects. The typical uses of Title funds are three: (1) reducing class size–and that's surely a resource change in the sense that if the size of a class is reduced by half, the cost is about twice as much, since the vast majority of all costs in education take the form of teachers' salaries; (2) acquiring teacher aides and other such assistants thereby increasing the total number of adults who can engage in classroom instruction; and (3) hiring specialist teachers, especially those who engage in "pullout" instruction. These three uses appear to take up the majority of Title I instructional funds.

The critical question then is: Do these resource intensifications have an effect? I think that they do, and I will attempt a little later in the paper to describe the kinds of effects they have and why the effects are so difficult to detect with current evaluation ideology and methodology.

Let me provide an example of an innovation for which I have quantitative data. The Follow Through Program is an innovation which involved increases in resource level and considerable change in curricular orientation. Recently, my colleagues and I performed some fairly primitive secondary analyses of the observational data collected by Jane Stallings and her colleagues (1974) in their process evaluation of Project Follow Through. We found some extraordinary differences among curricular approaches both in resource levels and in curricular emphasis.[2]

I have picked out four of the Follow Through curricula for illustration: the *EDC Open Education Program,* the *Bank Street College of Education Approach,* the *Behavior Analysis Approach–University of Kansas,* and the *Englemann-Becker Model for Direct Instruction–University of Oregon.* The data from these curricula are based on adequate sample size, and therefore the differences to be exhibited are reliable. While first- and third-grade data have identical patterns, I will use only the first-grade data for illustration. The programs using EDC and Bank Street curricula each spent 14% of their total time on mathematics, while Kansas devoted 22% and Oregon 27% of their totals to that topic. Since the time available was essentially the same for each curriculum, it is noteworthy that Oregon pupils spent almost twice as much time on mathematics as did EDC pupils. This pattern is repeated for reading and language: EDC spent 29% of their time on these areas, Bank Street spent 40%, Kansas spent 59% and Oregon spent 54%. Looking at the total time spent in these basic skills areas, we see that it ranges from 43% for EDC to 81% for Kansas and Oregon. These are very striking differences in curricular emphasis.

Based on Stalling's classroom observations, we can get a picture of the actual resource levels used in the implementation of these curricula. For example, we can analyze the pupil/adult ratios in these programs. EDC, Bank Street, and Oregon–with 8.6, 8.0, and 8.0 pupils per adult–were highly resourced compared to ordinary first-grade classrooms; but Kansas, with a ratio of 6.2, consumed 39% more personnel resources than EDC. Like the differences in curricular emphasis, these are striking differences in resource levels. Yet even if these resources have powerful effects on achievement, these effects will be masked. The differences in curricular emphasis will overshadow anything else in assessing the achievement outcomes of these programs. The variations are so wide that any evaluation aspirations that one might have for comparative achievement testing are surely doomed from the beginning.

Let me comment further on the issue of curricular emphasis before discussing resources and their consequences for learning. Other things being equal, a change in curricular emphasis will result in roughly corresponding changes in achievement. That is, there is a rough but strong causal relationship between curricular emphasis and achievement. This proposition is supported by Walker and Schaffarzick (1974) and others in the literature as well as by our own work. Let me explain what I mean by "rough." Typically, the large differences we see in content emphasis when we compare curricula are *relatively smaller* than existing variations in content emphasis found among classrooms. At the class level, the differences are *huge.* Let me give some examples.

In two studies that we conducted over the last two or three years,[3] we found that in elementary school reading, in samples of eight or ten classrooms, the typical range of time variation in content emphasis is three or four to one. These class-to-class variations in the amounts of time allocated to reading instruction are enormous. The corresponding variations in areas such as mathematics are also shocking but not quite as large. Teachers have, under the current social organization of schooling, an enormous amount of latitude on how they organize their instruction, and they seem to have large differences in preferences or priorities for basic skills subjects.

If you believe as I do, then, that these variations in curricular emphasis will result in correspondingly large variations in achievement, then the task of the evaluator is practically hopeless. Even if programs using different curricula spend an equal and fairly average amount of their time on a content area, it becomes very difficult to detect differences in effectiveness, because these differences are superimposed over large and idiosyncratic variations among classes. Even with the vast differences in time allocations to basic skills which exist among the Follow Through curricula, it may be difficult to detect differences using test scores because of the enormous natural variation in the preferences and activities of teachers and classrooms.

But there are still further problems. In some of the work that we have been doing with existing achievement tests and their content subdividions, it has become clear that in trying to trace the effects of curricular coverage on test scores, there are large ceiling and floor effects which vary from class to class in those item clusters that bear upon the instruction. When these are aggregated over a heterogenous test, they greatly attenuate inherently strong relations of coverage and achievement. Thus, it is extremely difficult to detect even the grossest effects of curricula on achievement using the kinds of standard methodologies that have evolved for carrying out educational evaluations.

Let me address, now, the effects of changes in resource levels. I indicated earlier that after curricular emphasis, differences in resource levels are the second major cause of acheivement differences in educational programs. That is, resource increases are effective in improving, perhaps substantially, the achievements of children; small class sizes, teacher aides, pullout programs, and other costly ways of intensifying education probably have profound effects on how much children learn.

But no one has ever been able to find such effects, and I consider that to be one of the major failings of educational research. It is a clear symptom of the problem we have in producing meaningful knowledge for improving education; if we cannot detect the effect of relatively sizable changes in resources, then we probably cannot detect the effect of very much at all. Surely one major reason that we cannot detect the effect of resource level changes is that they are associated with curricular goal changes. In view of what I have said about changes in curricular goals, corresponding systematic changes in curricular emphasis, and the enormous idiosyncratic variation in such emphasis in existing classrooms, the resource level changes are in many cases completely overlaid with these goal differences, and thus it is extremely difficult to detect anything.

There are other reasons why the effects of resources are difficult to detect. Let us address the issue of class size, for example. Suppose one teacher has a class of thirty children. There are many ways in which that teacher could organize instruction in a given curricular area. He or she could devote all of the time to whole-class instruction in that curricular area. Or he or she could divide the class into two groups of fifteen children each and spend 50% of the time with one group and 50% with the other group. When the first group of fifteen were being taught by the teacher, the other fifteen could be doing something that is ordinarily called "seat work." And when the second group of children were being taught by the teacher, the first group would then be engaged in "seat work."

The teacher might also split the class into three or four subgroups and spend one-third or one-fourth of the time with each of these subgroups.

While one subgroup was being taught, the other children would spend two-thirds or three-quarters of their time by themselves using curricular materials intended to facilitate unsupervised individual work.

Finally, the teacher could engage totally in tutorial instruction; he or she would spend one-thirtieth of the time tutoring each child, and consequently every child would spend twenty-nine-thirtieths of the time not interacting with the teacher.

These are a few different instructional strategies which a teacher could use with a class of thirty children. If the teacher had a class of fifteen, then he or she could engage in the same general kinds of strategies, but whole-class instruction would, of course, mean teaching a group of 15 children full time with no seat work. Splitting the class would result in correspondingly smaller groups, but equal allocations of seat work.

It seems clear to me that there should be a systematic relationship between the group size in which an individual is taught and his learning rate, i.e., his rate of progression through the curriculum. I think there is fairly convincing evidence of this relationship at the extremes. Tutoring is a group size of one. Surely tutoring has a greater effect in terms of taking a particular child through a curricular sequence. He can proceed faster under tutoring than he could in that same sequence if he were taught in a group of thirty children.

But the problem is that the relationship between group size and achievement will be highly nonlinear. Surely if we believe that current practices are at all rational, it would be much more difficult to teach reading in primary schools with thirty children in a single group than by using subgrouping. Therefore, the amount of learning per unit of time ought to be sufficiently greater in subgroup instruction to compensate for the lower learning rate during seat work. We have very little quantitative knowledge about these effects, but they must surely be sizable.

These effects also differ from one curricular area to another. The relationship between group size and achievement must be considerably different for science than it is for reading. Otherwise, it would not be reasonable that with available instructional materials, most teachers use whole-class instruction for science and small groups for reading.

Therefore, even though the effects are complex, if we cut the class size from thirty to fifteen there ought to be an increase in achievement. Perhaps a teacher may fail to take advantage of additional resources and may still be lecturing to fifteen pupils just as he or she was with thirty. Increases in resources, then, may not always result in useful changes in teaching strategy, and thus the potentialities may not be realized. But surely they are realized in enough cases so that there *is* a strong, real, and systematic relationship between resource allocation and achievement.

We have not been able to find these relations because we have oversimplified the problem. We are faced with large masking variations in curricular emphasis, a large but systematic array of alternative teaching strategies, and likely sizable nonlinearities and subject-matter interactions. The most "creative" strategy to date has been correlation and regression analyses of class (not group) sizes and achievement. With such little thought and imagination, it is no wonder that educational researchers never find anything.

As I indicated at the beginning, I believe that the largest effect of curricular innovation is on goals and thence, upon curricular emphasis, and that this effect accounts for the largest amount of difference in classroom and school achievement test scores. The second largest effect is on resources; it is a major failure of educational research that we have not detected any of the differences resulting from these effects. Certainly curricular and instructional innovations have effects other than changes in goals and curricular emphasis, and there are effects of new educational programs which are not solely resource-based. The research and development resources that have been devoted to curricular construction in NIE-supported laboratories and centers and efforts supported by the National Science Foundation do not represent wasted money. We can create more efficient ways of communicating curricular content, and we can improve instruction.

But these worthwhile effects are small in comparison to effects resulting from differences in curricular emphasis and variations in resource levels, and that makes these kinds of (efficiency) changes almost impossible to detect in large-scale field studies using current methods of data collection and analysis. I think they are detectable in closely controlled experimental studies that are close to laboratory settings, but they are almost impossible to detect with the methodologies we currently use for investigating the effects of implemented curricula.

A solution to the problem is possible. That solution must explicitly take into account variations in curricular emphasis, and it must embody more sensible approaches to looking at the allocations of resources before we will be able to strip off these effects and detect more subtle ones.

NOTES

1. The words "politics" and "political" currently have strong negative connotations among large portions of the populace and particularly among academics. My use

of these terms carries no such connotations; I view politics as any social activity which attempts to resolve conflicts. Within our society, conflicts arise because of differences in values or interests and these differences are (hopefully) resolved through the political activities of groups. In education, as with other social concerns, conflicts arise over resource allocation and use, and thus our politics relate to goals and funds and the ways they are aligned to persons and groups.

2. The analyses of resource variations are described in DeVault et al. (1977a) and the variations in curricular emphasis are presented in Wiley and Harnischfeger (1975). We are grateful to Jane Stallings for giving us access to these data.

3. These studies are reported in Harnischfeger et al. (1976) and DeVault et al. (1977b).

REFERENCES

DeVAULT, M. L., A. HARNISCHFEGER, and D. E. WILEY (1977a) Curricula, Personnel Resources, and Grouping Strategies. Chicago: CEMREL.

--- (1977b) Schooling and Learning Opportunity. Chicago: CEMREL.

HARNISCHFEGER, A., R. E. PIFER, N. J. SUTTON, and D. E. WILEY (1976) Instructional Time Allocation in Fifth Grade Reading. San Francisco: Far West Laboratory for Educational Research and Development.

STALLINGS, J. A. and D. H. KASKOWITZ (1974) Follow-Through Classroom Observation Evaluation–1972/73. Menlo Park, CA: SRI.

WALKER, D. F. and J. SCHAFFARZICK (1974) "Comparing curricula." Review of Educational Research 44: 83-111.

WILEY, D. E. and A. HARNISCHFEGER (1975) "Time allocation as an accounting scheme for process evaluation in education." A presentation to the Working Group in Educational Evaluation (May 12 Group), October.

13

WHEN EDUCATORS SET STANDARDS

Gene V Glass

Quoting oneself could be either the height of narcissism or simple laziness. I feel slightly guilty of both and am unwilling to resist the impulse. In the fall of 1976, I wrote a paper on the problems of setting standards, criteria, or cutoff scores on criterion-referenced tests for purposes of determining "mastery" or "competence." The gist of my remarks is captured in the following passages:

> I have read the writings of those who claim the ability to make the determination of mastery or competence in statistical or psychological ways. They can't. At least, they cannot determine "criterion levels" or standards other than arbitrarily. The consequences of the arbitrary decisions are so varied that it is necessary either to reduce the arbitrariness, and hence the unpredictability of the consequences of applying the standards, or to abandon the search for criterion levels altogether in favor of ways of using test data that are less arbitrary and, hence, safer.

After describing in detail Robert F. Mager's (1962) recommendations on stating a standard for every behavioral objective (e.g.,"The student must be able to spell correctly at least 80% of the words called out to him during an examination period.") I wrote:

> This language of performance standards is pseudoquantification, a meaningless application of numbers to a question not prepared for quantitative analysis. A teacher, or psychologist, or linguist simply cannot set meaningful standards of performance for activities as imprecisely defined as "spelling correctly words called out during an examination period." And, little headway is made toward a solution to the problem by specifying greater detail about how the questions, tasks or exercises will be constructed.

I went on in the paper "Standards and Criteria" to examine a half-dozen classes of method for establishing mastery levels, standards, or cutoff scores; each proved to yield arbitrary and potentially dangerous results. This language may sound theatrically portentous; it will, in the end, I think, be justified. I concluded the paper with the following remarks:

> Perhaps the only criterion that is safe and convincing in education is change. Increases in cognitive performance are generally regarded as good, decreases as bad. Although one cannot make satisfactory absolute judgments of performance (Is this level of reading performance good or masterful?), one can readily judge an improvement in performance as good and a decline as bad. My position on this matter is justified by appeal to a more general methodological question in evaluation. Is all meaningful evaluation comparative? Or do there exist absolute standards of value? I feel that in education there are virtually no absolute standards of value. "Goodness" and "badness" must be replaced by the essentially comparative concepts of "better" and "worse." Absolute evaluation in education—as reflected in such endeavors as school accreditation and professional licensing—has been capricious and authoritarian. On the other hand, the value judgment based on comparative evidence impress me as cogent and fair. Data from comparative experiments, norm-referenced tests and longitudinal assessments of change are comparative evidence, and thus enjoy a presumptive superiority over non-comparative evidence. To my knowledge, every attempt to derive a criterion score is either blatantly arbitrary or derives from a set of arbitrary premises. But arbitrariness is no bogeyman, and one ought not to shrink from a necessary task because it involves arbitrary decisions. However, arbitrary decisions often entail substantial risks of disruption and dislocation. Less arbitrariness is safer.

In a paper entitled "Mathew Arnold and Minimal Competence," delivered in June 1977 in Boulder, I railed against the minimal competence movement in education and its partnership with criterion-referenced testing:

Teachers and their consultants attempting to define "competencies" and writing test items intended to reflect minimal levels of acquisition are engaged in a bootless and potentially embarrasing endeavor. They are likely to construct a competency-based test for graduation that, perhaps, only half of the seniors can pass; then they will be forced to back off and be accused publicly of either not knowing what students ought to know or else not teaching students what they ought to learn. They are, in fact, guilty on neither count. No one knows how well a person must read to succeed in life or what percent of the graduating class ought to be able to calculate compound interest payments.

I have imposed these quotations upon your kind attention partly to establish an evidentiary fact. My rather grim and pointed criticisms of the criterion-referenced testing technique and its part in the minimal competence testing movement were delivered six months and one year ago, each several months before the incident I am about to relate. Prediction remains the litmus test of understanding, even when one moves out of the laboratory into the complex world beyond. The incident in question concerns the State of Florida competence-based high school graduation testing program. What happened there and what has ensued can only be described as "dislocating and disruptive," what is yet to be made of it cannot fail to embarrass the principal actors involved.

The December 12, 1977, issue of *Time* carried the following item:

FORIDA FLUNKS

A scandal for schools

Last October Florida's 120,000 high school juniors sat down to take a new exam: a Functional Literacy Test ordered by the state legislature to determine whether, as critics had charged, state schools had been graduating as many as 10,000 virtually illiterate seniors each year. The three-hour exam, divided into math and verbal sections, focused on students' ability to cope with such simple tasks as filling out job applications and reading labels on canned goods. The exam, said the state testing director, Thomas Fisher, was "very, very basic."

Yet when the results began to filter out last week, they proved truly alarming. In Duval County, which includes Jacksonville, 45% of the juniors failed the math section and 14% could not handle the reading and grammar part. Only 6% of the juniors at Jacksonville's overwhelmingly black Stanton High School passed the math section.

> Those who failed will be placed in remedial classes, paid for by a $10 million grant from the legislature. The remedial students will be given two more tries. Some school officials fear that a lot of the flunkers will never pass. A number of Florida juniors apparently agree: they have fled to high schools in Georgia, which does not require students to pass a minimal competency test to graduate.

I spent two weeks after reading this item on the phone interviewing people in Florida and New Jersey who were involved in the incident, reading documentation, and listening to tape recordings of meetings. The facts beyond the news item are these.

In 1976, the Florida legislature enacted an accountability law that required high school students to pass an examination in basic skills and functional literacy–the House bill specified "basic skills," the Senate specified "functional literacy," the conference committee resolved the matter by requiring both. Students who failed (three times in a row) would be issued a "Certificate of Attendance" instead of a diploma. Just where the booby prize would leave a student applying for a job or college is not known.

The Florida Department of Education (DOE) was directed to construct the test and determine a passing standard, which local districts could raise but not lower–none raised it. The DOE had the objectives already drawn up from previous assessment projects; they contracted with ETS-Princeton to write the test items. The DOE constituted a Committee on Minimal Performance Standards. Standards were set, and the tests were administered in October 1977. In mid-December, it appeared from early returns that about 35% of the students failed the math exam and about 10% failed the communications (reading and writing) exam. These students will come up for graduation in the spring of 1979. The Florida legislature has appropriated $10 million for remedial programs; the DOE feels that $26 million would be more appropriate, considering the epidemic of failure. Most of the remedial funds will be allocated to math instruction. "After all, that's where the kids will have to work to pass the test," said one DOE official. This same official felt that the general public favored the program four-to-one; and in spite of the high failure rate and the jeopardy in which it places 40,000 students, one hears time and again that the students like the program, respect it, and praise their elders for finally setting a standard for them to shoot at. (What well of masochism and guilt the affair taps in this generation is unfathomable to me.)

I am principally concerned with the technical decisions that led to this extraordinary state of affairs. Three interviews cast light on the technical foundations of the program: interviews with an employee of the DOE testing division, with the chairman of the Committee on Minimal Performance Standards, and with the director of the ETS item development contract.

The Florida DOE test specialist talked openly about the minimal competence graduation testing program. His department had monitored the ETS item development contract; the test was secure, he couldn't send me a copy. He was happy to send me lists of objectives and copies of the legislation. All my questions were answered calmly and confidently, until I inquired as to who set the passing cutoff score and how it was done. The test specialist laughed nervously and asked whether my tape recorder was running; I assured him it wasn't. "The criteria were set by a department committee, the Committee on Minimal Performance Standards," he reported. "We were grinding and gnashing our teeth about it. We wanted to do something more scientific."

The DOE chairman of the Committee on Minimal Performance Standards was expansive and quite willing to talk; his phone was busy most of the time, and he answered my questions with lengthy paragraphs apparently polished by frequent repetition.

Q: How did you go about setting the pass-fail cutoffs?

A: Our standards were developed by DOE staff and local school people meeting in workshops around the state.

Q: Did you take ETS-developed items out for them to study and judge?

A: No. We didn't look at the ETS items. We had the objectives that we sent to ETS. And each objective was broken down into two skills and then we knew there would be five items for each skill.

Q: How did you finally decide what score was passing?

A: Well, we worked with people at Florida State and Iowa City, and we spent a lot of time in workshops with local curriculum people. Of course, it's always going to be subjective; but we had to have political credibility in the state. We finally defined "mastery" as 70% of the items correct. We found that the vast majority of the schools in Florida regard 70% as passing. Of course, it's somewhat subjective.*

*If our dialogue had had an interlocutor, he would have interrupted here to make a point that might escape some laymen. The Florida committee's techniques and justification are the kind of reasoning that makes psychometricians gag, and which they felt had been obliterated from the earth years ago by dint of their tireless teachings. One cannot reliably know whether the germ of this misconception has lain dormant for the last twenty years and was revived in the favorable environment created by criterion-referenced testers or whether the idea has been always with us.

Q: How are the schools responding to the 35% failure rate in math versus the 10% failure rate in reading-writing?

A: I've heard schools say, "If we've got four remedial teachers, we'll put three of them in math." We're going to ask them to look closely at their basic programs. The math skills on the test were O.K.; it's the reasoning and applications where they really fall down. They've got to start doing more with problem solving and that sort of thing.

Q: Are you at all concerned that someone who writes an item can write it either hard or easy and they might look the same? Do you think ETS might have just written harder math items than reading items? Or do you think you've got a real math emergency in your state?

A: Oh, I don't see any math emergency. It could be that it's just a harder test; but we held workshops after we got the ETS items, and threw out all the racially biased ones and that sort of thing. I think maybe there was a tendency for ETS to write items at the top of skill in math but not for reading and writing where the objectives were broader and vaguer.

Bemused as to how someone could recognize the arbitrariness of the difference in difficulty between the math and reading tests and at the same time advise schools on the basis of the scores to get to work on remedial math programs where the problems lie, I hung up the phone expecting to have my confusion dispelled by a quick call to ETS-Princeton. I easily reached the gentlemen who had directed ETS work on the Florida contract. Almost immediately he sensed my motives, having read the "Standards and Criteria" paper and having debated the issues in the paper with his colleagues.

GG: How did you go about constructing the items for the Florida exam?

ETS: We didn't produce items to any statistical prespecifications. That is, we weren't trying to build a test with any particular mean or variance.

GG: But how do you get around the fact that two people can look at the same objective, and one will write an easy item and the other will write a hard item?

ETS: I'm not sure I believe that. People say that, but have you done it yourself; have you actually written two items on the same objective and one turned out to be hard and the other easy?

Like a rookie lawyer, I was distracted by his truculent question and started answering instead of asking.

GG: Well, I have here two questions asked in a New Jersey assessment. They both test the objective "adding single digit numbers." But in one item the digits are arranged vertically, and the other item has the two digits arranged horizontally. Of third-grade pupils, 86% got the vertical item correct and 46% got the horizontal item correct.

And here are two items from the Stanford Reading Test that both test the objective "the pupil should be able to discriminate the grapheme combination 'vowel + r.' "

Item 1): "Mark the word 'firm.' " (And the proctor reads "firm," "form," and "farm.")

Item 2): "Mark the word 'girl.' " (And the proctor reads "goal," "girl," and "grill.")

The difficulty for examinees of Item 1 is 56%; for Item 2 it's 88%. [I fell silent, confident that I had made my point.]

ETS: Yeah, but have *you* actually written items that are that different?

GG: Well, they exist. It hardly matters who wrote them.

I finally regained the offensive and began again to ask the questions.

GG: Do you know how the results are looking from the October administration of your test?

ETS: Not exactly, but I hear that more are flunking math than communications.

GG: More than three times as many, to be exact. I've got the National Assessment data for the Southeastern United States in front of me. Florida constitutes 16% of the population of this region and I'd be surprised if its NAEP data were any different. These data show that the Southeast is between 3% and 6% below the national average across all subject areas: literature: -5%; music: -5%; social studies: -3%; science: -3%; career and occupations: -4%; reading: -5%; and math: -5%. How do these data square with the data from your test that show substantially worse performance in math than in reading?

ETS: Well, it's my experience that curriculum people in math and the sciences generally aspire higher and have higher standards than the others.

I was stunned by this blatant disciplinary chauvinism. Before I could reply that the Florida people didn't aspire higher in math than in reading-writing (they aspired 70% in each) and if anyone's aspirations were causing kids to be labeled failures in Florida it was his aspirations since he wrote the items, I heard the ETS man promise to send me a manual they had constructed for "setting standards." He predicted that I wouldn't agree with it; he was right.

The manual arrived a week later. It would be instructive to quote from it at some length, but space doesn't permit. Suffice it to say, that the authors are guilty of every non sequitur, every solecism and wrong thought that I warned against in my paper "Standards and Criteria." They recommend setting standards by the Nedelsky method, which I showed in the earlier paper to be egregiously untrustworthy, and by a maladaptive mutation of the Nedelsky method due to Angoff. Not content merely to give bad advice, the authors warn against the only hope that could ever exist for setting sensible and safe standards: "to help avoid the circularity of having the judgment (of minimally competent) based on the test score, it is a good idea to collect the judgments before the score reports are distributed."

Without question, Florida represents an educational system in the throes of disruption and dislocation. Even if hundreds of pupils are not fleeing to Georgia to escape the test, as the *Time* article alleges, one wonders how many pupils have been nudged out of school by their first encounter with the test. For how many was it the final discouragement? Allocations of remedial education funds are being based on fatuous data generated by an indefensible assessment system. The system and its use are supported by false beliefs in a certain approach to measurement and standards and minimal competence. A segment of the scholarly and professional measurement community must share some of the responsibility for boondoggles such as the Florida incident. There is a great deal of loose talk in our journals, at our meetings, and in our contracts about mastery and minimal competence and setting standards based on professional judgment or for political purposes where it is acknowledged that professionals never will be able to make such judgments. I doubt that the measurement experts will be around in Florida when the lawsuits are filed, as they inevitably will be unless the minimal competence graduation test program is quickly undone.

From a political point of view, the Florida experience is interesting as an example of how a liability has been turned to political advantage under the guise of scientific management. "Accountability" arose as a legislative movement to check nonproductive growth in the schooling industry. Now the education establishment is using the scientific findings of accountability assessments to argue for increased funding. The Florida DOE told the Florida legislature that the minimal competence tests showed matters to be so serious that its Compensatory Education appropriation should have been 250% larger. We educationists used to envy medicine its deadly scourge; we imagined that the spectre of cancer could always be invoked to extort funds from stingy legislatures. Perhaps education has found its spectre; tests are now alleged to measure the minimal levels of competence required for success in life. Educators speak darkly of minimal competence tests being measures of "survival skills."

At an October 29-30 meeting in Atlanta on "Minimal Competence" sponsored by the Education Commission of the States, a delegation of Florida teachers, school district personnel and PTA officials devised the following recommendations:

(1) That the Florida Legislature reinvestigate the purpose and validity of the Certificate of Attendance (the booby prize for the failures) and its real meaning to education;

(2) That the State of Florida delay for one year the implementation of promotion and graduation regulations on the state assessment test, even though the state should still give the test.

The following reasons are given for the postponement: The need for

(a) a study of the impact of the Certificate of Attendance;
(b) a study by each district on remediation techniques;
(c) a study of the logistics of remediation and compensatory monies;
(d) a study of the Functional Literacy Test with people who are and are not successful in life;
(e) a study of the state tests in terms of minorities.

The delegation was more timid than I would have been under the same circumstances. I would have called for an immediate suspension of the minimal competence graduation requirements program because it is based on indefensible technology. The items of the test have never been validated as measures of "survival skills," and the pass-fail standards were set mindlessly and capriciously.

I predict that the Florida minimal competence graduation assessment will be suspended before the end of the year. And to help this prophecy fulfill itself, I have sent a copy of this paper to each school superintendent in the state of Florida.

REFERENCES

GLASS, G. V (1978) "Mathew Arnold and minimal competence." Educational Forum (January): 139-144.

MAGER, R. F. (1962) Preparing Instructional Objectives. Palo Alto, CA: Fearon.

APPENDIX

Objective: "The student will be able to perform basic algebraic manipulations involving summation operators."

Item 1): The expression $a\sum_{i=1}^{2}(X_i + Y_i + 1)$ is equivalent to

a. $aX_1 + aX_2 + aY_1 + aY_2 + 2$

b. $a(X_1+X_2) + Y_1 + Y_2 + 2$

c. $a(X_1+X_2) + a(Y_1+Y_2) + 2a$

d. $a(X_1+X_2) + a(Y_1+Y_2) + 4a$

Item 2): Examine the following expressions:

A. $\sum_{i=1}^{n}(X_i + c)^2 = \sum_{i=1}^{n}X_i^2 + nc^2$

B. $\sum_{i=1}^{n}X_i^2 = (\sum_{i=1}^{n}X_i)^2$

a. A is true and B is true.
b. A is false and B is false.
c. A is true and B is false.
d. A is false and B is true.

Results:

The percentage of examinees who answered Item 1 correctly is $\frac{63}{76} = 83\%$.

The percentage of examinees who answered Item 2 correctly is $\frac{42}{76} = 55\%$.

Objective: "Given a set of data, the student will correctly calculate the value of Spearman's rank correlation coefficient."

Item 1): Calculate r_s, Spearman's rank correlation coefficient, on the following ranks:

Person	X	Y
1	3	4
2	1	2
3	2	1
4	4	3

a. .93
b. .74
c. .60
d. -.60

Item 2): Compute Spearman's rank correlation coefficient given the following test scores:

Person	Test Scores	
1	2	3
2	7	10
3	11	8
4	20	16
5	18	17

r_s equals

a. .25
b. .80.
c. -.80.
d. .75.

Results:

The percentage of examinees who answered Item 1 correctly was $\frac{91}{120}$ = 76%.

The percentage of examinees who answered Item 2 correctly was $\frac{60}{120}$ = 50%.

14

KEY STANDARD-SETTING CONSIDERATIONS FOR MINIMUM COMPETENCY TESTING PROGRAMS

W. James Popham

The minimum competency testing movement, at least for the present, appears to be displaying bona fide magnetic attributes. During the past few years an increasing number of state legislatures and boards of education have been drawn, almost like iron filings, into the enactment of programs requiring students to pass minimum competency tests in order to secure high school diplomas.

The installation of these minimum competency programs has, however, forced into the open a problem that has troubled educators ever since prehistoric teachers of hand-axe honing were faced with a pass/fail decision. Although educators have perennially been obliged to decide when a student "passed a test" or "passed a course," this obligation has characteristically been discharged in private, behind closed classroom doors.

Now, with the enactment of legislation and regulations that require students to pass minimum competency tests as a precursor to high school graduation, the issue of what it means to *pass* minimum competency tests is clearly receiving spotlight attention. But, unlike some problems which, when illuminated, become less vexing, the recent highlighting of our standard-setting shortcomings has not been accompanied by the emergence of effective solution strategies.

Putting it simply, educators have always faced decisions about whether students' performances were good enough to pass the students, but those decisions were typically made individually and privately. Now, educators are being called on to deal *openly* with the question, "How good is good enough?" Moreover, instead of setting a passing level individually, so that it affects only one set of class grades, educators are currently being asked to set passing levels collectively for large numbers of students, such as all seniors in a school district or even an entire state.

When teachers were tussling with the passing standards problem in private, we could take solace in the fact that if some students were penalized because of the too stringent standards in one teacher's class, they would most likely benefit from another teacher's fluffy grading standards. Most of us remember classes in which our final grades seemed unwarrantedly low or charitably high. Thus, educators could console themselves in the belief that grading inequities tended to cancel each other out over the long haul.

But with minimum competency testing programs, this sort of compensation is unavailable to the student. If an excessively stringent passing standard is set on a districtwide high school graduation test, then many students will be penalized irrevocably. There won't be loads of other opportunities wherein this error will be rectified because of unduly relaxed passing standards. Clearly, errors in setting an excessively high passing score on a high stakes minimum competency test can have lasting consequences for many people, not just the students who are adversely affected, but also their families and friends.

The flip side of that argument, of course, is that if we set standards too low, then society is ultimately the loser. It is generally conceded that one strong motive underlying the enactment of minimum competency testing programs was to halt, both in the public's perception and in fact, a devaluation of the high school diploma. Clearly, if standards are set too low, then the devaluation of high school diplomas will have been accelerated, not impeded.

To review, I have been attempting to point out that educators have been historically plagued with the problem of how to set defensible passing standards, but have been unsuccessful in producing sensible solution strategies. Further, because passing standards were generally established in private by individual teachers, no large-scale attention has been given to this issue. The setting of standards has been a major, but well-camouflaged educational problem for centuries. Chiefly because of the minimum competency testing movement, that problem is now decisively out of the closet.

PROFITING FROM PRIOR PROPHETS

Anyone who has taught for a number of years should be able to recount all sorts of schemes for dealing with the grade assignment problem. Procedures have been evolved ranging from the establishment of convoluted point-allocations all the way to the teacher's clandestine assignation with a ouija board. But although we must concede that teachers have not resolved the perplexities of grading, we can still benefit from the kinds of insights they have brought to the grading enterprise.

Some teachers have devised grading systems that are just about as defensible as an individual teacher can create. Let's examine the factors that such teachers incorporate in their approaches to grading. Such an examination may isolate the ingredients which could be infused into a standard-setting procedure for a large-scale minimum competency testing program.

There are two major kinds of considerations that teachers rely on when deciding on how to set grading standards. The first of them, and probably the more important of the two, is the teacher's experience-based estimates regarding the typical performance of students. The second consideration is the expectation of others, typically colleagues, regarding how well students should be performing. Let's deal briefly with each of these two factors for purposes of illustration.

Although the end-of-course grading chores are difficult, even for an experienced teacher, for a novice teacher the assignment of grades is a real nightmare. Beginning teachers have no idea of how well students should be expected to perform because they have no idea of how those students typically do perform. After a few years of teaching, however, teachers feel far more at ease when they dispense grades, since they have a better notion of how their students typically perform.

Similarly, as teachers initially form, then modify, their personal expectations regarding how well students should perform, they are often influenced by others, particularly their teacher colleagues. Sometimes this influence will be exerted in highly informal, coffee-break settings by overhearing a fellow teacher describe preferred grading standards. Sometimes the influence will be formally solicited, as when a teacher seeks out a colleague's advice regarding such end-of-term dilemmas as "Who should get *A*s and who should get *F*s?"

Both of these considerations, namely, the performance of students and the expectations of others, are typically incorporated in a teacher's judgments regarding the establishment of performance standards. It is my view that in the creation of high-stakes standard-setting procedures for minimum competency testing programs, both of these considerations should be integrally involved.

JUDGMENT AND CAPRICE

Some writers have recently alleged that the standard-setting enterprise is, by its very nature, so arbitrary and capricious that we cannot expect it to result in truly defensible standards. Such critics, however, mistakenly equate human judgment with caprice.

The judgment of human beings definitely need not be unreliable or mindless. Indeed, to demonstrate the capabilities of people to render reliable and finely tuned judgments, we need not look beyond our television screens during a major gymnastic competition. In such events an amazing degree of similarity is registered by judges awarding points to a performer's original gymnastics routine. It is apparent from such displays of judgmental consistency that different individuals can confront a set of complex and novel stimuli, yet render highly congruent judgments.

Merely because human subjectivity will be involved in setting performance standards should not send us running in terror from the standard-setting task. Human judgment, while far from a perfect tool, is still preferable to reliance on random chance. If our choices are (1) to operate minimum competency testing programs with the most defensible standards we can set, even though those standards will not be flawless, or (2) to abandon minimum competency testing programs because we cannot set flawless standards, then I opt without hesitation for the former.

In the remainder of this discussion I shall explore three key considerations which should be addressed when standards are to be set minimum competency testing enterprises. Finally, because these three considerations need to be blended into actual procedures whose efficiency is as yet untested, I'll conclude by sketching a few instances of the kinds of methodological questions which should, without delay, be addressed by educational researchers.

Throughout this analysis I am assuming that some group of individuals, whether by designation or by default, is functioning as the standard setter. In some states, the standard setters for minimum competency testing programs are local boards of education. In other states, it is the state board of education. These standard setters will, with varying degrees of defensibility, discharge their responsibility to set performance levels which students must satisfy. The following discussion deals with the kinds of factors they may wish to take into account in their standard-setting operations.

CLARITY OF TARGET COMPETENCIES

How would you respond with any kind of sense to the following question: "What level of minimal skill should we set for graduating high school seniors in mathematics?" There are, obviously, all sorts of uncertainties associated with that question which preclude a sensible answer. The most pivotal of these indeterminacies is the elusive nature of the skill for which the performance standard is actually being set, namely, "mathematics."

It is apparent, using this extreme and patently absurd example, that since you really don't have a good fix on what's involved in as broad and diffuse an entity as mathematics, it is impossible to establish minimum performance levels. There are vast differences in our expectations for learners when we shift from asking them to add pairs of integers and, instead, demand that they solve simultaneous equations.

Although not so obvious, when standard setters attempt to pick a minimal level for pupil performance on most norm-referenced (and some so-called criterion-referenced) achievement tests, they are in a similar bind. Because, for a variety of reasons (mostly economic) norm-referenced achievement tests are accompanied only by general, vague descriptive schemes, it is next to impossible to set sensible standards for student performance on such tests. The standard setter can, of course, always consult the actual items on the test itself. Even though in that event the standard is being set less for a given skill, or set of skills, than for a particular set of test items and their idiosyncratic phrasings, distractors, etc., this is preferable to attaching performance standards to the nebulous collectivities of heterogeneous test items represented by most standardized achievement tests.

For this reason, if no other, designers of minimum competency testing programs should eschew Rorschach-ridden norm-referenced tests, preferring instead criterion-referenced tests which spell out with lucidity just what they're measuring. As implied earlier, not every test that is currently masquerading as a criterion-referenced measure does, in fact, provide an unambiguous description of the skill(s) being measured. Standard setters will be obliged to review such measures with care to be sure that they end up setting standards for competencies that are unambiguous.

RELEVANT PERFORMANCE DATA

If you were asked to set a minimum performance standard for a skill which was totally foreign to your experience, you would be at a loss. Standard setters must rely on some sort of experience in deciding on expectations. For the task facing those designing minimum competency testing programs, there are several sorts of performance data which can prove useful. By performance data, I mean the test scores of examinees on the measures actually being used to assess student mastery of competencies.

Standard setters will be able to arrive at more defensible performance levels if they have access to performance data from individuals who have been (1) uninstructed, (2) just instructed, and (3) previously instructed. Data from each of these three types of populations will provide different and useful insights regarding what might constitute a defensible performance standard for the skill in question.

To illustrate how these three categories of performance data might prove illuminating as we wrestle with the standard-setting problem, let's consider the case of establishing a passing level for a high school graduation minimum competency. More specifically, let's assume we're dealing with a competency that calls for students to be able to discern the main ideas of commonly encountered reading selections. Since this illustration is fictitious, let's dress it up properly by assuming that the competency is to be measured by a marvelous criterion-referenced test, just brimming with descriptive clarity. In other words, there's no doubt in the minds of the standard setters what skill is involved. Their only task is to set a reasonable passing level that students must reach if they're going to get a high school diploma.

The Uninstructed. Since this example involves a high school competency program, we would consider as uninstructed those pupils who are entering high school. We could administer our criterion-referenced test on main idea comprehension to a sample of pupils during the first few weeks of their high school careers. Let's assume that those students average 70% correct on the test, and that less than one student in twenty scores below 50% correct. Given access to such performance data, wouldn't standard setters be reluctant to set standards *lower* than this level?

But, you may be wondering, isn't it the case that, at least regarding this particular competence, entering high school students are not totally uninstructed? Indeed, don't students receive the bulk of their instruction in reading during the early grades of elementary school, well before they troop off to high school? The answer, of course, is yes. And this illustrates a key procedural question regarding the accumulation of performance data from "uninstructed" students, namely, how uninstructed should they be? Theoretically, we could pretest infants as they're being wheeled from the delivery room, thereby being assured of a low score on most cognitive tests. But how long should we really wait? It's apparent that with respect to almost any competency that might be included in a high school graduation minimum competency test, some students will have received instruction prior to their entry into high school. That being the case, I'd recommend the gathering of performance data from samples of students at several levels, for instance, as we see in Table 14.1.

The chief purpose of gathering performance data for uninstructed learners is to aid standard setters in isolating a lower limit for their expectations. Data such as those presented above should prove useful in that regard. For instance, it seems unlikely that, on the basis of such data, standard setters would be inclined to set a high school passing level for this skill much below 50% or 60% correct.

On the other hand, let's assume we were looking at performance data such as are presented in Table 14.2. It seems more likely that lower pass rates would be seen by standard setters as at least eligible contenders.

The Just Instructed. Carrying through with our example, we'd want some performance data regarding student skills at the close of high school. It is uncommonly helpful for standard setters to see how students "really

Table 14.1 Average Test Performance of Uninstructed Students

Sample Group	n	% Correct
Beginning Fourth Graders	98	38
Beginning Seventh Graders	93	52
Beginning High School Students	104	70

Table 14.2 Average Test Performance of Uninstructed Students

Sample Group	n	% Correct
Beginning Fourth Graders	109	24
Beginning Seventh Graders	87	31
Beginning High School Students	111	42

are doing." Let's say we administered our criterion-referenced test to all, or a large sample, of a district's high school seniors during late April. Let's imagine that these students' average scores on the main idea comprehension test turned out to be 83% correct. Further, the test data were displayed as seen in Table 14.3 indicating the percentage of students who would not receive diplomas depending on where the passing level was set.

If you are a standard setter faced with the problem of pegging a passing level for our test in comprehending main ideas, wouldn't you be assisted by having access to the kind of information presented in Table 14.3?

There is a considerable danger, of course, in being so influenced by the status quo that we let present performance blunt our aspirations for students. Clearly, what *is* must not be equated with what *should be.* If there is any validity in the current spate of criticisms regarding the effectiveness of public education, then we must improve the quality of learner performance, not merely hold the line. The most likely interpretation of the Table 14.3 data is to say that the tabled percentages of pupils will be apt to fail if instruction does not improve. But it should improve. If standard setters can be realistically confident about a school system's ability to augment its effectiveness, then it would seem prudent to bump up expectations to some extent.

Table 14.3 Projected Failure Rates for High School Seniors at Varying Passing Levels Based on 427 Seniors' Test Performance

% Correct Passing Level	Probable % of Pupils Failing
90	61
85	52
80	43
75	21
70	14
65	7

The Previously Instructed. Most of the skills being isolated for minimum competency testing programs are typically thought to be significant in an individual's future life. Thus, it would also seem useful to standard setters to see how well adults, at least postschool young adults, can perform those skills. Let's imagine we had some performance data such as those presented in Table 14.4.

The performance of previously instructed groups is particularly informative as a sort of "reality check," to help standard setters discern whether their aspirations for pupil performance are in any sense consonant with the kinds of proficiency actually needed in the real world. Further, since there is typically a certain degree of decay associated with many of the skills in which we are interested, we can see how well they hold up after a student has left high school.

In review, this fictitious example was intended to illustrate the general proposition that if standard setters have access to a wealth of data regarding how various kinds of individuals can perform the skill under consideration, the standards set for these skills will tend to be more defensible. Illustrations were provided of three major categories of performance data, namely, test results from the uninstructed, just instructed, and previously instructed.

PREFERENCES OF OTHERS

In addition to performance data, a useful sort of information for standard setters is the preferences regarding standards of various concerned groups. For example, suppose the standard setters in our previous example consisted of the local board of education. Beyond the previously described performance data, perhaps they wanted to see what other people's sentiments were regarding appropriate standards for high school graduates with respect to discerning main ideas when reading. Let's say they directed the

Table 14.4 Average Test Performance of Nonstudent Groups

Group	n	% Correct
Students Graduated Two Years Earlier	114	79
Students Graduated Four Years Earlier	89	75
A Stratified Sample of Adults in Community	172	62
Members of the School Board	7	89

Table 14.5 Recommendations from Various Clienteles Regarding an Appropriate Passing Standard for Comprehending Main Ideas

Group	n	Average Preference
This Year's High School Seniors	497	71%
Graduates of Three Years Ago Who Are Now in College	94	84%
Graduates of Three Years Ago Who Are Not in College	119	65%
District Teachers	112	78%
District Administrators	32	83%
Parents of 9th, 10th, and 11th Grade Students	814	91%
Community People	119	79%
University Reading Specialists	18	75%

school district's research and evaluation office to come up with preference data such as those seen in Table 14.5.

I am persuaded that in a judgmental operation, such as the setting of performance standards, it is beneficial to have on hand the preferences of other individuals. These other individuals can be called in either because they have a special stake in the action, such as parents of the students or business officials who will be hiring the high school graduates, or because they possess special expertise, such as the district's educators or the university reading specialists.

Care must be exercised, of course, to be *guided* by such preferences, not controlled by them. It is still the standard setter's ultimate responsibility to decide how good is good enough. The standard setters must reckon with the fact that it may be in the interest of certain groups to recommend standards which are inappropriately high or low. Such biases must be recognized so that the resulting preferences of such groups can be considered in that light.

PROCEDURAL QUESTIONS

Although it's relatively easy to proffer armchair analyses regarding the raptures of preference and performance data, the tough task is to devise and try out procedural schemes which incorporate these data sources so skillfully that we can come up with performance standards in which we have some confidence.

Without delay we need to start carving out procedural variations for setting performance standards, trying out these procedures, then sharing our insights regarding what works and what doesn't.

Simultaneously, a programmatic series of investigations should be instituted to deal with such questions as the following:

(1) How do the varying types of "charges" given to standard setters influence the standards ultimately set? (For example, will standard-setting groups told to deal with "survival skills" end up with different standards than those told to deal with "minimum skills"?)
(2) How do differences in the clarity of competency descriptions influence, if at all, the nature of standards set?
(3) How does the differential prestige of preference groups influence standard setters?
(4) What kinds of standards result from standard-setting procedures which are dominantly open (as in free, face-to-face discussions) versus those which are dominantly closed (relying on anonymous, secret ballots)?
(5) To what extent can standard-setting procedures be defensibly systematized and/or quantified?
(6) What indicators, e.g., consistency, can be employed to judge the reasonableness of standards set under varying procedural conditions?

Quite obviously, these questions fail to exhaust the important procedural uncertainties facing us. Many, more complex and more important, procedural questions surely exist.

But, as stated at the outset of these observations, because the problem of how to set performance standards is out in the open for all to see, we must get cracking in trying to bring some sensible solutions to this largely unstudied topic.

15

COMMENTARY ON MINIMUM COMPETENCY TESTING

Jason Millman

Popham's position seems to make a lot of sense. I would like to add to his statement, and discuss five reasons I have identified for why people are against setting standards. I will discuss those reasons and then make a few comments about procedures for establishing standards.

The first reason used to argue against setting standards, and perhaps the only one I can agree with, is that standards are not needed when there are no decisions to be made. Why have a standard or cutoff score or passing mark unless some action is to follow? Wanting to say that someone has mastered the material is not enough. I'm not persuaded by the claim that society will be impotent if there aren't minimum standards.

A second argument against establishing standards, and one that has only a little validity, is that minimums can become maximums. It is my experience in New York state, where we have Regents Examinations with passing scores of 65%, that a great deal of attention is devoted to getting students to pass these tests. Much time is spent reviewing previous examinations and working with students likely to have the most trouble passing. While instruction for all students may be less than optimal, the regents do serve to target the instruction on the state's curriculum.

The concern that minimums can become maximums can be lessened if competency testing for high school graduation is given early and frequently. If most students pass the examinations during eighth, ninth, or tenth grade, then standards need not receive so much emphasis; time would be available to go beyond the minimums.

A third argument against setting standards, and one I don't find persuasive at all, is the claim that different methods give inconsistent results. One paper on this subject reported that 56% more students would be expected to pass a particular test if one method of setting the passing scores was used, rather than another.

I find the logic a little mystifying. It's like saying that if we were to conduct two different statistical tests on the same data and found significance using one procedure and not by the other, somehow we should not conduct statistical tests because they may give different answers.

A fourth argument, primarily against setting minimum competency standards, is that we can't really say how much students must know in order to succeed in life. A variation of this argument is that there are no essential skills. People can be successful plumbers even though they are not very good readers. There are no universal knowledges and skills.

My reply to these claims is that the standards are not necessarily meant to imply what is needed for survival or the good life. The language we use can get in our way and instead of saying "minimum competency standards," why not choose more neutral terms like "graduation requirements," "passing scores," or even "cutoff scores"? The last term emphasizes the decision-making use of the standard.

The public accepts passing scores for the written portion of a driving test even though this knowledge is unlikely to be essential for being a good driver. The 65% passing score on the New York State Regents Examinations and the passing scores on most professional examinations seem to be accepted without pretense that the knowledge measured by the tests is perfectly related to some external criterion.

Finally, a fifth argument is the claim that standard setting is arbitrary. Popham handled this argument well when he used an example to differentiate "arbitrary," which implies randomness, from "judgment" which, although subjective, does produce some agreement among raters.

It is true that all methods of establishing standards require judgment. (I might add that any time one conducts a statistical analysis of data, judgments are made. Yet most of us would not want to avoid performing statistical analyses for that reason.) Any decision requires a judgment at some stage. We can't escape the requirement for cutoffs if we are going to make decisions.

So the question to my mind is not whether we need standards but how they are to be established. More specifically: Who determines the standards? Using what measuring instruments? To reference what criteria? Under what procedures?

Popham's suggestion for setting standards is that we mix relevant performance data on criterion-referenced tests with the preference judgments of experts. The use of performance data is consistent with Glass's plea for normative information so that standard setters will know what test performance they can expect.

There is nothing inconsistent in Popham's suggestion to collect norm information on criterion-referenced tests. Although one may argue with the details of his plan, it seems reasonable and feasible.

In thinking about alternative schemes for setting standards, I believe it useful to divide the procedures, as Richard Jaeger (1976) has, into different models depending on the inference the user wishes to make from the test performance. Is the primary interest the domain of tasks from which the test is a sample, or is there some ultimate criterion, like surviving in society, to which inferences are directed? The distinction is between content and criterion validity, and like the case with establishing validity, the appropriate procedures depend upon the desired inference.

REFERENCE

JAEGER, R. M. (1976) "Measurement consequences of selected standard-setting models." Florida Journal of Educational Research 18: 22-27.

16

COMMENTARY ON POLICY

Richard E. Schutz

Since these pieces are offered by the Center for the Study of Evaluation, I think the first responsibility of the commentary is to evaluate them. I enjoyed them. On affective grounds they rate every high; and since we hear regularly that we should be more concerned with noncognitive aspects of measurement, the session should get good marks. In terms of agreement, I'd agree at about the .10 level with what both authors had to say. But on an absolute level, it seems to me they indicate that the measurement community is still far below the level of proficiency required if we were dealing adeptly with the topic, Measurement and Public Policy.

I think the papers indicate the status of the measurement community in relationship to public policy quite well. There is still a great gap between the two. Our concerns are those of the measurement and methodology community rather than those of the public and of our elected representatives. The papers say nothing about jobs for unemployed teenagers, nothing about busing, nothing about education for the handicapped, nothing about tax equalization in financing education. I could say that these are not matters that we have to concern ourselves with—they are "someone else's" problems. But that is not a tenable position if we want to be heard by persons involved with public policy. Informed communication between groups as disparate as the educational measurement community and the public policy community is a long way off. We are currently engaging in a monologue, which is perfectly legitimate and useful communication. It just should not be treated as if it were a dialogue.

The conditions necessary for a dialogue have yet to be established, but as the title of the presentation indicates, there is motivation to do so. Education today is both a politicized and a technicalized endeavor. I don't think there is any chance that it will become either depoliticized or detechnicalized. The societal integration of policy and science/technology in education is still in an early stage, but the only question appears how it will occur, not whether it will occur.

Although in these papers we are "talking shop" as educational measurement and evaluation people, the kind of "shop" that is being talked is clearly different from the statistical and theoretical matters that usually concern us and that are treated elsewhere in this volume.

It seems to me that Wiley's intuitions are accurate: If you want to evaluate what is learned, you have to look more closely at what is taught than we have done in the past. Also, if you want to find the effects of a "program," you have to look more carefully at what is actually being implemented and use indicators of effects that have more likelihood of reflecting the implementation than those we have used in the past. Those two statements sound trite, until you recognize that they are typically disregarded in current measurement and evaluation operations in education.

What Wiley needs in order to verify his conjectures is data. And here I can upgrade his whimper with a little more of a bang. The "curricula implementation" Wiley cites is really more than ten years old, coming out of the curriculum content improvement efforts supported by the federal government in the late 1950s and early 1960s. In the period since the mid-1960s, the programmatic research and development of educational laboratories and R&D centers has been generating data bases that are a good deal more substantial than those Wiley is relying upon. It takes some years to form these data bases and to get the analyses out. But all evidence indicates that when there are sensible indicators of effects to track a "program" of identifiable operational integrity, i.e., is something more than a banner slogan, consistent functional regularities can be isolated with high reliability. Thus, Wiley's conjectures actually have a good deal more verification behind them than he realizes.

I take a more optimistic view of the future than the one Glass has presented. Incidentally, I am impressed with CSE's political astuteness in arranging Glass's paper. His comments indicate clearly that in Florida, a state that does not now have a laboratory or R&D center, things are in a sad state of affairs, whereas here in California, where we have CSE, the state has avoided such disaster. The paper also questions the competence of ETS, a major CSE "competitor." I know that Glass is just "telling it like it is," and of course, I'm being facetious about these local politics. But if we intend to operate in a public policy context, we are going to have to learn that people are not insensitive to the local and personal aspects of localized and personalized technical commentary.

I do think that Glass's "stop the world and get off of minimal competency" stance is out of keeping with the times. Too many states are already into the matter of minimal competency. It's here, and the question is what do we do about it. Actually, it's going to get a lot worse before it gets better as far as Glass is concerned, because there is already momentum to initiate this same kind of activity at the elementary school level. His conclusion is akin to going out in the rain and saying, "I think it's going to rain," or "the rain is making everything very wet."

It's really very easy to second guess what the school community or the educational R&D community has done, particularly if a researcher uses the techniques of an investigative reporter. But a researcher is not an investigative reporter. If we expect to make any positive contribution to education policy, we're going to have to learn how to help the school community, not devastate it.

I'm not advocating a pollyanna stance or picking on Glass. The point is professional rather than personal. Contrary to the belief of many in the R&D community and the school community, the public holds both communities in high regard. Polls indicate that the public would like to see more funds for R&D in education, and they highly prize the schools as an institution. However, this public confidence could be eroded very easily. In operating in a public policy area, we could easily damage the overall endeavors to which we are committed. That is, we just can't run around saying that everything we stand for is bad, and then expect people to jump to support our activities. The world just doesn't operate in this fashion.

Educational measurement and evaluation matters have advanced to a point that they have entered the arena of public policy considerations. This advance brings new responsibilities to all of us in the measurement and evaluation community. I'm confident that we can learn quickly to deal effectively in this new arena. But as in any form of learning, it will require augmentation of our present proficiency. Both of the papers give us much to think upon and much to grow upon. It seems to me that's what measurement and public policy is all about now and what it will continue to be in the future.

EPILOG

As some time has gone by and psychological distance has intervened since the occasion of the Measurement and Methodology Conference, we felt the authors' contributions might well be reviewed in the light of any recent developments in the field. Thus, two pieces, one by Joan Herman and Jennie P. Yeh on test design and use, and another by David Harman on policy implications, are presented to provide some perspective to the problems identified that winter.

17

TEST USE:

A Review of the Issues

Joan Herman and Jennie Yeh

Even the casual observer realizes that tests are an omnipresent part of schooling. Great sums of public money and school time are expended on the assessment of children's achievement. The question naturally arises, "Why? What functions are tests serving?" The answers have engendered much controversy and debate. Teachers have decried the meaninglessness of current test practices, and the National Education Association (1976) has called for a moratorium on standardized testing. Advocates of testing, on the other hand, are prone to dismiss teacher complaints on the basis of ignorance or defensiveness, i.e., teachers find tests meaningless because they don't know how to use the results, or because they fear that test scores will serve only to emphasize system failures. For their part, testing proponents suggest that tests serve a variety of important purposes, among them accountability, selection and sorting, and educative and diagnostic purposes. Tests are thus given in the name of evaluation, certifying competence, and improving the sensitivity of the instructional process to individual needs. The issues discussed in this book however, raise serious questions as to whether testing practices and current methodologies can adequately and fairly serve any of these purposes.

ACCOUNTABILITY AND EVALUATION

A majority of required tests are externally imposed on schools in the name of accountability and evaluation. For example, state and district administrators want to know how well their schools are functioning; legislators and other funding agencies, as well as the general public, need information for determining whether their money is well spent and their programs effective. Wiley in his paper strongly argues that current methodologies are incapable of providing answers to such questions because these methodologies are not sensitive to variations in goals and curricular emphases between and within programs; program effects thus go undetected.

The insensitivity of current test usage in this context may be attributed to a variety of causes, among them:

- adherence to the notion that a single achievement score can adequately and fairly assess the effects of different programs;
- a failure to recognize the tenuous nature of many educational programs; and
- the insensitivity of achievement instruments commonly used in large scale assessments.

Wiley's comments are germane to the first two causes, but he does not acknowledge the third.

Wiley clearly describes the problems inherent in the assumption that a single total score is appropriate for valid assessment of program effects. Differences in goals and emphases among programs must be taken into account in viewing achievement results. This viewpoint suggests that not only is there a need for multiple achievement scores in program evaluation, but also a need for program implementation data to provide a context for viewing the results. In other words, achievement results in isolation provide an inadequate data base for sound interpretation.

The recognition that different goals and curricular emphases differentially affect achievement implies not only that a total test score is the inappropriate level of aggregation for viewing program results, but, in addition that a single test viewed as a collection of subtests may well be differentially sensitive to different programs. For example, assuming for the moment that tests are sensitive to instructional effects, Floden's discussion indicates that the tests generally in use are not uniform in the attention they accord to particular instructional goals. Therefore, a particular test is not likely to be equally responsive to the goals and emphases of two different programs, and consequent comparisons, even accounting for program differences, will be biased.

Recognition of this biasing effect suggests that sensitivity might require separate test collections for different programs, so that goals and curricular emphases are fairly reflected. However, this approach, though program fair, would render impossible direct between-program comparisons. As Linn explains in his paper, there are severe technical problems in equating tests that are assumed to measure the same skills; equating tests that address explicitly varying content is clearly beyond the technology.

One alternative would be to construct a single test collection that equally represents the most important goals and emphases of all programs under study. The relative performance of students in each program, in conjunction with the intended goals of each, could then provide a rich array of information for making sound, albeit complex, decisions. Suppose, for example, that Program A emphasizes goals 1, 2, and 3, while Program B emphasizes goals 3, 4, and 5; assume also that all goals have merit. If students from Program A outperform those from Program B on goals 1, 2, and 3, and perform the same or better on goals 3, 4, and 5, then the decision as to which program is better is straightforward. If however, students from each program score better on their respective mutually exclusive goals, and score similarly on the one shared goal, then decisions on relative effectiveness become quite complex. Decisions would have to take account of explicit judgments on the importance and difficulty of the goals, relative costs and time spent, etc.

Accounting for the complexity of between-program differences, however, is only one problem inhibiting the current methodology. As Wiley points out, within-program differences in goals and curricular emphases produce another and larger source of error in interpreting achievement results. This source of error may be derived from the nature of educational programs, which often tend to have diffuse and poorly articulated goals. As a result, program goals are difficult to specify precisely, and the interpretation of those goals are likely to vary greatly among program participants. For example, educational programs are typically disseminated through bureaucratic channels, e.g., from the district to the school, to the classroom; and each successive level of program interpretation is likely to produce additional sources of variation. Unless programs are more carefully specified (a feature which conflicts with traditional notions of plurality and diversity), high levels of within-program variance will greatly attenuate the possibility of statistically detecting between-program differences in achievement.

Even with random assignment to experimental and control groups, the problems introduced by within-program variation render quite weak comparative designs. With the more common occurrence of nonrandom assignment, the problems preventing the discovery of valid between-program differences with current methodology appear insurmountable. As an alternative to weak posttest only comparative designs, it seems reasonable, as Linn implies, to consider repeated measures designs and to examine achievement results longitudinally. In other words, since we cannot adequately determine whether Program A is better than Program B, or a control group, we perhaps should focus our attention on the simpler question, "Is Program A associated with improvement in student achievement?" Within-program variation will still diminish the probability of detecting program effects, but accepting the statistical limits and looking for trends are likely to produce sounder answers than result from present practice.

Presumably, most district- and state-level yearly assessments are designed to detect fluctuations in student achievement from one year to the next and are appropriate for examining student achievement longitudinally. Since the total populations are assessed, statistical inferences are unnecessary, and problems of within-program variations are largely bypassed. The soundness of this approach, however, rests on the assumption that current tests are sensitive to instructional programs and actually measure student learning. Unfortunately, there is reason to believe that this assumption is untenable, a problem that overshadows the problems previously discussed. A 1976 report by the General Accounting Office (HRD-113-76) indicated that 90% of sampled respondents from local educational agencies used norm-referenced standardized tests to assess the effects of school programs. Yet, as many have pointed out, these types of tests are developed on the basis of vague content specifications to maximize discrimination between subjects and to spread scores along a continuum. Thus they may well be inappropriate for detecting instructional effects (see, for example, Tyler, 1977; Popham and Husek, 1969; Baker, 1976). In addition, even if we uncritically are willing to assume instructional sensitivity, a review of commercially available tests points to severe limitations in their technical excellence (Hoepfner, 1971). The validity of using the results of these measures for purposes of accountability or evaluation, then, is quite suspect.

Alternative forms of achievement testing that more fairly reflect instructional effects have, of course, been advocated. Criterion-referenced tests, such as the PVS system developed by the Southwest Regional

Laboratory and described in this book by Schutz, have been developed to assess specific instructional goals. However, SWRL's efforts aside, a recent review of available criterion-referenced tests indicates that these measures are also characterized by disappointing quality (CSE, 1979a). Among the problems in these measures is the paucity of accepted technology for determining test quality. Baker in her paper suggests that there is currently no acceptable means for determining item quality, and others have discussed the limits of applying classical test theory to determine the reliability and validity of criterion-referenced instruments (see, for example, Tyler, 1977; Linn, 1979). Although Wilcox's work describes one of several approaches to the problem of reliability, there is little consensus on the best technique. Thus, while criterion-referenced testing offers some promise for the future, current technology and practice presently cannot meet the need for valid and reliable assessment of program effects.

EDUCATIVE PURPOSES

Tests that cannot validly and reliably detect program effects clearly have quite limited utility for educative and diagnostic purposes. Standardized norm-referenced tests, which are built on imprecise content specifications, offer little concrete guidance for diagnosing specific learner difficulties and strengths.

Baker, in her presentation, discusses some of the present problems in developing newer criterion-referenced tests that reflect precisely circumscribed skill domains. Such tests, of course, are intended to describe the extent to which learners have achieved specific skills, and thus a priori should have more power for instructional decision-making. A major problem, as Baker indicates, is the arbitrariness of the process of skill delimitation. Whereas in norm-referenced tests, arbitrariness resides in the hands of the item writer, in criterion-referenced testing, arbitrariness resides in the hands of the domain specifier. That is, the domain specification defines a particular skill by providing rules for generating tests items with regard to admissible and inadmissible content and response attributes as well as format. Yet, the state of knowledge is such that the domain specifier may have little basis for generating such rules.

Take, for example, the task of specifying a domain for literal comprehension that is to be assessed by multiple choice test items. A preliminary problem is defining in general terms what constitutes the skill, for there exists no single, generally accepted definition. Does it, for instance, include simple transformation, paraphrasing, sequencing, etc.? Next, the task is to define the stimulus attributes of the test item. A few of the questions the specifier faces are: Should the stimulus comprise a single sentence, several sentences, a paragraph, several paragraphs? What syntax, vocabulary, etc. is appropriate for inclusion? The problems of specification continue in defining response attributes, e.g., how many distractors, what types of distractor represent common errors that would be helpful for diagnostic purposes? The point is that there are a multitude of decisions made in specifying skill domains that have little empirical or theory based support. This problem is somewhat lessened when the task is to construct a domain to reflect a particular curriculum or instructional program. It is enormous when the task is to define skills that will generalize across programs. The best solution available at the current time, as Baker indicates, is consensual arbitrariness, or in more positive terms, qualitative judgments.

Definitions of skill domains are clearly dependent on an understanding of the structure of knowledge and skill development. Baker, as well as Chi and Glaser and Frase, agree that knowledge about the organization of cognitive processes is a necessary prerequisite to effective measurement of achievement. Chi and Glaser, for example, suggest that research on the nature of competence development can provide a theoretical and empirical basis for structuring learning and assessment tasks. Shulman concurs that knowledge of the distinctions between the skill performance of the novice and that of the expert can furnish a more valid basis for measurement and instruction than reliance on traditional curriculum organization. Frase's discussion suggests that cognitive processing demands need to be considered systematically in defining skill domains, and in addition, may in themselves represent a significant domain for assessment. The thinking of these authors clearly suggests that criterion-referenced testing can and should move beyond the present state of arbitrariness toward the systematic measurement of complex skills.

It is clear that the research being advocated here for extending the state of the art of test design is tied to research on learning. That is, testing has ceased to be considered as a separate concern, but rather, as Schutz states, an integral part of an instructional system that contributes to skill development. Much of the research that serves instruction is likely also to serve test design. For example, work on learning hierarchies, e.g., White and Clark, 1973, contributes to the design of optimal instructional sequences, as well as being pertinent to the design of testing strategies that can efficiently detect areas of learner weakness. This line of research, as well as that suggested by the Chi and Glaser paper, furthers our knowledge of skill development and is a necessary prerequisite to theoretically and empirically based mastery learning and mastery testing models.

MINIMUM COMPETENCY TESTING

The limits of our understanding of skill performance and the variables affecting it, and the consequent capriciousness of current test design practices necessarily constrain both the confidence with which we can interpret individual test scores and the utility of the results for diagnostic and prescriptive purposes. Such constraints seem particularly serious in the context of minimum competency testing, where judgment based on test scores can affect a student's future, and, as Glass points out in his paper, produce political, legal, and social problems of great magnitude.

The recent surge of minimum competency testing may be viewed as the public's answer to concern over declining achievement test scores and the problems of low achievement in general. A basic premise underlying this movement is that automatic educational promotion has resulted in a deterioration in learning for many students. In response to this trend, it was felt necessary to impose an objective quality control process on the education system to insure both that students were learning essential skills and that schools were doing their part in responding to individual problems, i.e., to insure that the education system was producing "competent" products.

Testing, then, in this context has been identified as a primary tool for educational quality control. The utility of tests for serving such a purpose, however, rests on a number of shaky assumptions:

(1) There exists a common and identifiable set of knowledge and skills that all students must possess in order to function adequately;
(2) tests can be designed to assess validly and reliably the extent to which a student possesses the identified knowledge and skills;
(3) standards can be set to accurately classify students into various proficiency categories, i.e., competent and not competent.

How valid are these assumptions? Is the technology of testing sufficiently advanced to meet these demands? Glass's paper provides one answer in his indictment of the minimum competency movement.

Even those who do not share Glass's view recognize the problems that arise in trying a common set of skills that can be defined as "competence";

these problems exist at both the philosophic and practical levels. For example, historically there have been conflicting views of what constitutes the essential goals of education (Peters, 1978). Educating each individual to his/her fullest potential, for example, may be in direct conflict with educating individuals to meet a minimum standard. Educating to instill the love of learning may suggest different essential skills than educating to assume societal responsibilities. In a society where education is for the elite, one would expect the demands on education to be less diverse than in a democratic society where the number of people who are to benefit from education is far greater. This diversity suggests potential conflicts in goals.

Even if the potential value conflicts are resolved, and there is agreement that the minimum goal of schooling is to impart basic skills, there still exists the practical problem of defining the domain of basic skills. What is reading? Which skills in reading should be taught or mastered by students at each grade level? Traxter (1941) examined twenty-four reading tests and found that they conjointly measured forty-eight differently labeled skills. Until knowledge of skill hierarchies expands, we have little basis for choosing among skills or for making decisions about which are necessary and sufficient for "competent" reading performance.

The assumption that essential skills can be validly and reliably measured clearly presents another problem. As discussed in the previous section, the limits to the understanding of skill performance, and the paucity of accepted methodology for determining test quality render imperfect our measurement instruments, as well as the decisions based on these instruments.

Judgments of what constitutes a minimally acceptable standard of performance adds another layer of imperfection to the process. As Glass points out, it is not possible to define empirically minimum competence. Standard setting thus requires human judgment. While combining performance data with expert opinion is likely to produce sounder and more defensible standards (as Popham suggests), problems of error cannot be eliminated.

Nor can recent research on statistical methods for standard setting eliminate judgments. Here, the focus has been setting passing scores that minimize the probability of making a false positive and/or false negative decision (see, for example, Wilcox, 1977; Huynh, 1976.) Although each method requires the element of judgment at some stage of its execution, the resultant probabilities add another dimension that needs to be considered in standard setting. The question arises, what is an acceptable probability of misclassifying a competent student as incompetent, or vice versa?

Given that there are costs associated with each decision, it would be reasonable to study also the social, psychological, and economic costs associated with the probability of misclassification. For example, how much money is spent in providing remediation to one who has already mastered the skills tested? What is the psychological damage in wrongly retaining an individual? What is the cost to the society if individuals not having mastered the basic functional skills are passed through the educational system?

CONCLUSION

The issues raised in this book suggest some of the limits to current test use and imply that tests are being used to serve many functions which the technology cannot adequately support. For example, test results alone cannot answer evaluation or accountability questions, nor do they presently provide optimal information for instructional decision-making. Tests can provide but one source of information, and overreliance on this source is likely to yield faulty answers to critical questions. Test use in this context becomes misuse and abuse.

Baker poses the question, "Is something better than nothing?" She answers affirmatively, "*if* we can be fair." Fairness demands that testing be viewed from a perspective that recognizes present limitations and uses test results accordingly. Fairness would also seem to demand that teachers and students not be overburdened with tests that have limited value. Current tests do provide some gross level of useful information and therefore should not be abolished. However, rather than escalating the number of required tests, as seems to be the current trend, a wiser policy would be to devise testing programs that are more conservative of student time.

Certainly, testing has the potential to provide important information for decision-making. Future research, such as that outlined in this conference, will contribute to that potential. In the meantime, something may be better than nothing, but less is likely to be better than more.

REFERENCES

BAKER, E. L. (1973) "Beyond objectives: domain-referenced tests for evaluation and instructional improvement." Educational Technology.

Center for the Study of Evaluation (1979) "CSE Criterion-referenced test handbook." Los Angeles.

General Accounting Office (1976) "National assessment of educational progress: its results need to be made more useful." Washington, DC: Government Printing Office (HRD-76-113).

HOEPFNER, R. (1971) "Characteristics of standardized tests as evaluation instruments." Evaluation Comment 3.

HUYNH, H. (1976) "Statistical consideration of mastery scores." Psychometrika 41.

LINN, R. (1979) "Issues of reliability in measurement for competency-based programs," in M. Bunda and J. Sanders (eds.) Practices and Problems in Competency-Based Measurement. Washington, DC: National Council for Measurement in Education.

National Educational Association (n.d.) "Resolution of the National Representative Assembly of the NEA." Item 1972-28. Washington, DC.

PETERS, R. S. (1978) The Philosophy of Education. New York: Oxford Univ. Press.

POPHAM, W. J. and T. R. HUSEK (1969) "Implications of criterion-referenced measurement." Journal of Educational Measurement 6.

TYLER, R. (1977) "What's wrong with standardized testing?" Today's Education (March-April).

TRAXTER, A. E. (1971) The Nature and Use of Reading Tests. Chicago: Science Research Associates.

WHITE, R. and R. CLARK (1973) "A test of inclusion which allows for errors of measurement." Psychometrika 38.

WILCOX, R. (1977) "Estimating the likelihood of false-positive and false-negative decisions in mastering testing: an empirical Bayes approach." Journal of Educational Statistics 2.

18

ON TRADITIONAL TESTING

David Harman

The spread of mass education during the latter half of the nineteenth century and the first half of the twentieth has been accompanied by a growing use of testing and reliance upon it. Increasingly large student bodies, increasingly complex school systems, and increasing demands for more education have cohered to place an onus on school systems. Regulation of movement through the tiers of school systems, in an effort to preserve the notion of a meritocratically determined pyramid geared to the absorbent capacity of rapidly changing labor markets, has led to the creation of benchmarks and bottlenecks. In a purely anthropological sense, these way stations can be likened to rites of passage, a series of tests that determine both the direction and extent of subsequent movement of people.

"Processing" large numbers of students through the educational system, it has been contended, can best be achieved through standardization of achievement benchmarks and the establishment of measurement tools that assess attainments. Such benchmarks achieve two purposes: On the one hand, they establish standardized levels of educational development; and on the other hand, they provide a tool which permits comparisons among large groups of people. They indicate levels of desired proficiency, and then they indicate which people have attained those levels.

To be sure, testing is not a modern creation. Numerous types of tests have been used throughout time and across cultures. Just a few examples: the ancient Spartans tested the prowess of their youth in the martial arts; the rabbis of the ancient academies of Babylon assessed the intellectual abilities of their students; in many cultures, rites of initiation involved tests of various kinds; tests of knowledge and ability were frequently employed in apprenticeship situations; and, of course, tests have been a traditional tool of the schools. One might then ask, are contemporary "testologists" with their "art of testology" different from their forebearers in anything other than technique and sophistication? Is their function within the educational enterprise any different from that of testers of the past?

Unequivocally, the answer to both questions is yes. To a very real extent modern testing has become the fulcrum of educational policy development. An uneasy coalition of a concerned public and supposedly skilled and knowledgable policy-making groups derives its objectives, data, and feedback from the every-growing morass of standardized tests. A characteristic example: test results indicate that reading, writing, and arithmetic are "problem areas." Policy-makers take heed and establish a policy push toward the improvement of "basic skills" instruction in the schools. Test results continue to be disappointing. There arises a hue and cry over the lamentable lowering of standards. A concerned public applies greater pressure upon policy-makers, who respond by increasing expenditures on basic skills. The public, hungry for results, clamors for more tests; and policy-makers react by legislating "testable" levels of desired attainment. The buck, as President Truman was wont to say, must stop somewhere, and in university after university it has stopped. Regardless of test results it has been found necessary to establish various remedial courses in order to bring new students up to acceptable starting levels. But then, of course, even the results of remediation must be tested. Tests ultimately triumph.

There is also an historical argument that can be made to explain the differences in testing today. Roughly, until World War II, American higher education was characterized, it is contended, by socioeconomic class homogeneity and intellectual heterogeneity. Standardized testing has, in the decades since, changed the situation to one of intellectual homogeneity and socioeconomic heterogeneity. It is, however, difficult to believe that this change would not have occurred without tests, despite the social ferment of the past thirty years. The question remains: have standardized tests played a significant social role; will tests continued to be significant?

An examination of testing should be broadly based. One level of consideration is, or should be, purely educational. How important are tests in supporting the educational enterprise? Are they, as has been claimed, essential for dealing with the instructional needs of students? Such needs, presumably, are both diagnostic and instructional and, of course, raise questions as to the extent to which currently available tests perform in both these areas. In this regard one finds what is perhaps the most blatant inconsistency between accepted educational theory and an underlying basic characteristic of tests. At a time when individuation of instruction and pluralism of educational paths are becoming increasingly accepted educational practices, tests continue to set age- and grade-specific standards, essentially reinforcing the lockstep character of the enterprise. There is a fundamental conflict between these approaches which cannot be rectified through compromise.

Educational administrators and organizers, while employing the rhetoric of pluralism, nonetheless face issues of organizational import which they view as inconsistent with educational theory. Standardized benchmarks are convenient and allow for efficient administrative practice. Hence, the use of standardized tests is upheld and supported. In effect, one might argue that standardized tests serve an administrative, rather than an educational, function. If this is the case, there surely must be administrative means that could be devised and employed in their stead.

From a purely educational vantage point the advantages of standardized tests are less clear. Administered as they are, at grade- and age-specific intervals, they almost by definition cannot allow for differential development patterns. As diagnostic tools they are, at best, suspect. Research findings are available indicating that many observed differences fade away over time, rendering the diagnostic tools poor predictors of future performance and ability. A common citicism leveled at tests is that they test at a particular time and place, indicating—at most—abilities exhibited at that time, and neglecting, in the process, other factors.

On a philosophical level, standardization itself has been *decried.* The early lament of Walter Lippman in *The New Republic* when Binet tests were first introduced to the United States that standardization of any sort would be inimical to the American ethnic of individualism and pluralism, has been frequently echoed.

As instructional tools tests may be more harmful than helpful. They encourage the phenomenon of "cramming," raise anxiety levels unnecessarily, and may undo any systematic progress which instruction theoretically seeks to accomplish. In short, tests have been soundly attacked and are largely considered a nemesis by their detractors.

Their proponents argue that they serve to establish attainable basic standards and influence the entire curriculum accordingly. This pace-setting function, it is suggested, has had an impact on establishing basic standards for the school system. Moreover, it has been contended that tests have been effective in what might be labeled "gross diagnosis"; that is, they indicate major areas of concern and thus facilitate remediation.

It would seem, in light of the available evidence, that "pro" claims pale in comparison with "con" criticisms. Educational needs can best be served by a diversity of tests, probably derived from specific instructional contexts and differing accordingly. There are some ongoing developments in this direction, e.g., Project Torque, which point out various possibilities. Purists contend that testing is and should remain a classroom-specific process; that tests should be employed when teachers consider them relevant; and that they can serve as effective diagnostic and instructional tools. Other considerations aside, it would appear that standardized tests are used far too extensively and not always to the educational benefit of students.

One of the significant "other considerations" is social. Proponents of standardized tests maintain that they lead to meritocratically based rating rather than a more socioeconomically based standard. Tests allow people to be channeled through the system with achievement being the sole criterion. How true is this contention?

A major criticism of tests is that they are inherently culturally biased. They tend to reflect a white, middle-class culture, born out through norming procedures; and therefore, almost by definition, they discriminate against children from other sociocultural groups. The extent to which this is so belies the argument that they are an important tool in the quest for social egalitarianism. Current social mores, however, turn this into an academic question. Increasingly, it is becoming unthinkable to deny people admission to the various educational institutions on the basis of educational attainment alone. There now exists a clear social imperative to open institutional doors to students of diverse socioeconomic background, regardless of strict educational attainment. Where necessary, various remedial measures have been instituted, and now students are helped to achieve desired levels. Simultaneously, criteria for acceptance are being broadened, and the earlier emphasis on scholastic achievement is rapidly decreasing. Even if one assumes that tests played an important role in equalizing educational opportunity–a debatable point–one must concede that social events to a large extent are bypassing and outflanking tests.

Various educational factors have contributed to this situation, as has the rapidly changing demographic structure of the country. Alternative institutions, community colleges, "second" and "third chance" activities, all provide possibilities of maneuvering up the status ladder in ways formerly considered abnormative and unacceptable. The individual is presented with multiple paths up the ladder and need not fear termination as was once the case. At the same time, university enrollments are low and further decreasing as a result of diminishing size of age cohorts. Together these two factors have created a higher education crisis resulting in an active search for new roles. At least one of these is the acceptance of "nontraditional" students, to wit, those who in all likelihood would have been rejected or would never have reached application stages in the past. Dropout within the primary and secondary tiers has also diminished dramatically, in part due to new legislation mandating attendance and abolishing grade repetition.

Given these situations one might argue that tests and testing are anachronistic activities. Educationally, efforts might more profitably be directed at the improvement of instruction and curricula. Socially, the bottlenecks have been opened to such an extent that tests are no longer necessary gatekeepers. The gates have simply become so wide and multiple that the sacrosanctity of the "next tier" has been effectively breached.

What are the policy implications of this state of affairs or, in other words, what is the future of standardized achievement testing from a policy point of view? From a purely educational vantage point the value of standardized testing is highly questionable. It seems neither to help students directly nor to assist in providing corrective instruction. Indeed, it would appear that tests of this nature contribute to failure through early labeling and stratification.

Formal schooling has been subject in recent years to a variety of criticisms and demands. On the one hand, it has been contended that schools are failing in their primary mission of providing basic education–that they are graduating functional illiterates. On the other hand, many have argued that schools have ceased being relevant; that they are not providing their charges with the skills and knowledge necessary for proper functioning in today's complex world.

Torsten Husen, a distinguished Swedish educator, has analyzed both these criticisms and the actual situation in schools in industrialized societies in his recent book *The School in Question* (1979). Both criticisms, he posits, are justified; there is little question in his mind that major reforms are necessary. This conclusion was arrived at not only by Professor Husen, but also by a large group of educators on both sides of the Atlantic who participated in a series of workshops convened over a three-year period to discuss the future of schools and schooling in the West.

Standardized tests, as currently utilized, are an impediment to such reform. They impose upon schools both a structure and basic curriculum which permit only superficial reform. Such reform, however, is woefully inadequate. The surgery required is more radical. Changes may well be necessary in the structure of schooling as well as in core curricula. Notions of "plurality of excellence" (a term coined by Lord Bullock) must be translated from rhetoric into practice, most likely through multiple *tracks,* each with its own criteria for excellence. The lockstep nature of present school networks *will require modification* so that students might progress through the system in ways that suit their needs and characteristics. In theory, this is not a revolutionary notion. Twentieth-century educational thought has been replete with concepts of individuality and individualization of educational experience. To a very large degree, the rise of the "testing society" has mitigated against actualization of these theories.

In large part research into various developmental issues has provided support for the *lockstep.* Benjamin Bloom in his book *Stability and Change in Human Characteristics* (1964) summarized conclusively the findings of this research, indicating that there are terminal developmental phases. That is, if certain skills are not achieved by a certain age it is unlikely that corrective action will be effective. More recent investigation, however, has shown the fallacy in this conclusion. Characteristics do not necessarily become "fixed" at distinct stages but can be effectively influenced at other, later developmental phases (Brim and Kagan, 1980). Here, too, standardized tests could prove to be a barrier to change. Standardized and normed, as they are on age and grade basis, they do not permit for differential developmental paths; and they early on provide labels difficult to shake.

Educational policy must be allowed to develop unfettered by standardized tests. Tests in general need to revert to their more traditional function in education; that of tool rather than end. To do this requires that a hiatus or moratorium in their use be called; that over a period of several years both the nature of schooling and the nature of testing be reexamined so that each might be reformed without being unduly influenced by the other. The nature of reform necessary in schools is such that a relatively "clean slate" is a prerequisite. In turn, testing procedures have to be reassessed in light of the reforms attempted by the schools.

How realistic are these proposals? On the surface they might appear far-fetched. Too many constituencies and groups would have to agree to virtually cease activities. Educational institutions long accustomed to relying upon test results for admissions purposes would have to develop alternatives. An industry which relies on tests for profit would have to voluntarily forego regular income. However, without such a moratorium it is difficult to see how schools can effectively deal with the many questions and issues on their agenda and achieve the reforms they seek. The issues themselves are far from being clear-cut, and many incite controversy. Testing clearly has a constituency that would argue the case for the importance and continued use of tests. One could argue that it would be in their interest of this constitutency to instigate a reexamination of testing, particularly in view of current controversy on the subject.

Tests have become central issues in education. Much has been written about them, and they have been discussed repeatedly in numerous forums. Further improvement of test technology will not clear the air. Most educators find difficulty in understanding the intricacies of the technologies and cannot relate to them. Rather, they relate to the broader issues and their immediate policy connotations. These latter concerns are the problems that require urgent attention and should be uppermost on the agenda of the testing "community." There is a developing antitesting constituency, rapidly growing in fluence among the general public (see, for example, Houts, 1977). There is ample reason to accept the arguments being forwarded that tests as currently conceived and administered are anachronistic and serve as constraints to further educational reform. Those favoring the continued use of tests should heed these arguments and, rather than further polarize the issue, should seek to create partnerships among diverse constitutencies to assess the educational enterprise and jointly to seek ways to correct its course.

This review has not sought to comment on the papers collected in the present volume. Rather, it has attempted to place them in the wider context of the educational system which they purport to serve. Testing and the pursuit of excellence in the technology of testing are important aspects of the education system; they cannot, however, be separated from the larger context within which they are utilized. They must be aware of the pressures placed upon that system and the overall policy directions being considered. Ultimately, the education system is an integrated whole; and although its parts often appear to function without regard for each other, such separation is illusory.

Like other societal institutions, education cannot suffer stagnation. Its value to society is a function of the extent to which it can evolve and maintain its relevance. Evolution within education systems is complex and cumbersome, but systems nonetheless do change. Tests and testing must not stand as a barrier to such change. Those involved in the testing enterprise should seek to join in it and help provide directions to this change—a role that can only be performed by maintaining an open mind and fundamental malleability.

REFERENCES

BLOOM, B. (1964) Stability and Change in Human Characteristics. New York: John Wiley.

BRIM, Jr., O. and G. KAGEN, [eds.] (1980) Constancy and Change in Human Development. Cambridge, MA: Harvard Univ. Press.

HOUTS, P. L. [ed.] (1977) The Myth of Measurability. New York: Hart.

HUSEN, T. (1979) The School in Question. New York: Oxford Univ. Press.

ABOUT THE AUTHORS AND EDITORS

EVA L. BAKER, Director of the Center for the Study of Evaluation, is also Professor in the UCLA Graduate School of Education. She has written extensively on the topics of evaluation, testing, teacher education, and instructional research and development. Baker serves as editor for a number of journals and is an adviser to federal, state, and local educational agencies. She has held elective office in both the American Educational Research Association and the American Psychological Association.

PETER M. BENTLER is Professor of Psychology at the University of California, Los Angeles; Director of a National Institute on Drug Abuse research center on the psychosocial etiological bases of drugs and alcohol; and a Faculty Associate of the Center for the Study of Evaluation. He was a recipient of the Cattell Award for Distinguished Multivariate Research. His research interests include the development of psychometric and statistical models for multivariate analysis.

LEIGH BURSTEIN is Assistant Professor in the UCLA Graduate School of Education and Faculty Associate of the Center for the Study of Evaluation. He received his Ph.D. in educational measurement and statistics from Stanford University. He was Assistant Professor of Educational Psychology at the University of Wisconsin–Milwaukee before joining the UCLA faculty. Burstein served as Project Director of the Consortium on Aggregating Data in Educational Research. He currently directs CSE's project on analysis of multilevel data.

FRANK J. CAPELL, Senior Research Associate of the Center for the Study of Evaluation, is a doctoral student in the Department of Psychological Studies in Education at Stanford University. Prior to joining the Center staff in January 1978 he was a resident consultant at RAND Corporation for the Alum Rock Voucher Demonstration Project and worked with the ETS Head Start Longitudinal Study. He has worked on

CSE multilevel data analysis and the evaluations of the Community Services Administration's Basic Skills Learning Centers and California's School Improvement Program.

MICHELENE T. H. CHI is Research Associate at Learning Research and Development Center, University of Pittsburgh. She is currently investigating the cognitive processes underlying the induction of numerical relations. Her prior research centered mostly on the effect of capacity of memory development in young children. Dr. Chi received her Ph.D. in psychology from Carnegie-Mellon University in 1975. Her major interest lies in an information processing approach to cognitive development in the areas of individual differences, memory, and problem solving.

ROBERT E. FLODEN is Assistant Professor of Philosophy of Education and Statistics at Michigan State University and Senior Researcher at the Institute for Research on Teaching, where he coordinates the Intellectual Forum. His research is primarily in teacher education; he is currently studying the factors which influence teacher decisions about which content to present.

LAWRENCE T. FRASE is a member of the technical staff at Bell Laboratories. Prior to holding this position he was Head, Learning Division, Basic Skills Group, National Institute of Education. Frase has published extensively on learning and the instructional process, particularly prose learning; his current research is in computer applications relevant to test design. Frase, who received a Ph.D. from the University of Illinois, is a Fellow of the American Psychological Association and serves on the editorial board of several journals including the *Journal of Educational Psychology* and the *Educational Psychologist.*

DONALD J. FREEMAN is a Professor of Educational Psychology and Teacher Education at Michigan State University and Senior Researcher at the Institute for the Study of Teaching. His research interests include student teaching and other aspects of teacher education; he is currently studying the factors which influence teacher decisions about which content to present.

ROBERT GLASER is Professor of Psychology and Education at the University of Pittsburgh and Co-Director of the Learning Research and

Development Center. His special field of interest has been the psychology of instruction, and in this context he has carried out research in criterion-referenced testing, individual differences in learning, and systems for individualized instruction. His recent research interests are concerned with cognitive processes underlying aptitude and intelligence and the development of a theory of instruction. His achievements include the following: He was awarded a Guggenheim Fellowship to study abroad, was a Fellow at the Center for Advanced Study in the Behavioral Sciences, is a member of the National Academy of Education, and was awarded the 1976 AERA award for distinguished contributions to research in education.

GENE V GLASS is Professor of Education and Co-Director of the Laboratory of Educational Research at the University of Colorado. He was a CSE Visiting Scholar. In 1975 he was President of the American Educational Research Association and was co-winner of AERA's Palmer O. Johnson Award in 1969 and again in 1970; from 1968 to 1971 he edited the *Review of Educational Research.* Glass coauthored the textbook *Statistical Methods in Education and Psychology* and has authored some one hundred articles on statistical methods, evaluation methodology, law and social change, psychometrics, and psychotherapy.

DAVID HARMAN has been an Assistant Professor of Education at Harvard University and a tenured faculty member at Hebrew University of Jerusalem. Dr. Harman's interest transverses areas in social policy development, such as literacy, child and family policy, and health services delivery. As director of Research and Planning for the Joint Distribution Committee in Israel, he had the opportunity to supervise and assess the effects of interventions across the social and educational policy fields. Dr. Harman has served in numerous policy advisory capacities, including the National Academy of Sciences, the World Bank, UNICEF, and federal education agencies.

CHESTER W. HARRIS is Professor of Education at the University of California, Santa Barbara, and Faculty Associate, Center for the Study of Evaluation. Before joining the University of California, he was at the University of Wisconsin. Harris has published extensively and served as editor for several journals including *Psychometrika.* He is past president of AERA and holds fellowships in several other organizations. Harris, who received his Ph.D. in educational psychology from the University of

Chicago, has done some of the classic work in factor analysis. He is continuing research on measuring achievement and statistical techniques for characterizing achievement test items.

JOAN HERMAN is Assistant Director of the Center for the Study of Evaluation. She has been involved in evaluating large-scale school reform efforts funded by the State of California. Her areas of expertise include domain-referenced testing, formative evaluation, and training materials development. Herman received a B.A. in sociology from UC Berkeley and an M.A. and Ph.D. in learning and instruction from UCLA.

ROBERT L. LINN is a Professor at the University of Illinois, Champaign-Urbana holding joint appointments in educational psychology and psychology. He has been a Visiting Scholar at the Center for the Study of Evaluation and a Visiting Professor in the UCLA Graduate School of Education. He spent eight years at the Educational Testing Service where he was Director, Development Research Division. Linn served as editor of the *Journal of Educational Measurement* and associate editor, *Journal of Educational Statistics.*

JASON MILLMAN is Professor of Educational Research Methodology at Cornell University. He is past editor of the *Journal of Educational Measurement* and has held several offices in AERA. Millman is frequently called upon to assist federal, regional, state, and local educational agencies with testing and statistics. He is presently working on item generation schemes for criterion-referenced tests. Millman has been a Visiting Scholar at the Center for the Study of Evaluation and the Instructional Objectives Exchange.

W. JAMES POPHAM is a Professor in the UCLA Graduate School of Education and Director of the Instructional Objectives Exchange. He is former president of the American Educational Research Association and founding editor of the AERA journal, *Educational Evaluation and Policy Analysis.* He has authored many books and articles on the subject of testing and evaluation.

ANDREW C. PORTER is Professor of Education, Senior Researcher at the Institute for Research on Teaching, and Director of the School of Advanced Studies, College of Education, Michigan State University. He spent several years as a senior associate at the National Institute of Education, where he assisted in the formulation of the Center for the Study of Evaluation's planning.

EDYS S. QUELLMALZ, Senior Research Associate at the Center for the Study of Evaluation, received a Ph.D. in instructional research and development from UCLA. She was a member of the professional staff at Southwest Regional Laboratory for Educational Research and Development, responsible for development, revision, evaluation, and validation of educational programs. Quellmalz directed CSE workshop development and is conducting research on writing assessment.

WILLIAM H. SCHMIDT is Professor of Teacher Education and Statistics at Michigan State University and Senior Research Associate at the Institute for Research on Teaching. He is co-coordinator of a study on Time Allocation and Integration in Language Arts and is involved in the Content Determinants Project.

RICHARD E. SCHUTZ is Executive Director of SWRL Educational Research and Development. His professional background embraces research and development management, educational psychology, measurement and evaluation, and programmatic educational research and development. Dr. Schutz has served on several state and national advisory committees related to education and educational R&D. In addition, he has served as editor of the *Journal of Educational Measurement* and of the *Educational Researcher* and is editor of the *American Educational Research Journal.*

LEE S. SHULMAN is Director of the Institute for the Study of Teaching and Professor of Education at Michigan State University. He was recently named Fellow of the National Academy of Education and during the 1979-1980 academic year will be a fellow at the Institute for Advanced Studies in the Behavioral Sciences, Stanford University. Shulman is co-author of a recent book on clinical decision-making.

RAND R. WILCOX, Senior Research Associate at the Center for the Study of Evaluation, received a Ph.D. in educational psychology specializing in measurement and statistical methods at UC Santa Barbara. His numerous publications address various topics in achievement testing including indices of item stability and equivalence, models for stability and equivalence, partitioning populations, and other statistical techniques. He has referred papers for seven major journals and recently chaired a committee to review Baltimore's proficiency tests.

DAVID E. WILEY was recently appointed Dean of Education at Northwestern University. He was previously Co-Director, ML-Group for Policy Studies in Education, CEMREL, Inc., Chicago and was on the faculty of the University of Chicago. Dr. Wiley has been a visiting scholar or consultant to many national and international research organizations and serves on the National Advisory Board of the Center for the Study of Evaluation.

J. ARTHUR WOODWARD is Associate Professor, Psychology, at the University of California, Los Angeles. His research interests include psychometric theory, evaluation research, and the application of multivariate statistical models in the study of drug abuse. He was a recent recipient of the American Psychological Association Distinguished Scientific Contribution Award for an Early Career Contribution.

JENNIE YEH, Senior Research Associate at the Center for the Study of Evaluation, received a B.A. in education at National Chengchi University, an M.A. in counseling and guidance at the University of Northern Colorado, and an M.A. in statistics and measurement at UC Berkeley, and a Ph.D. in research methods and evaluation from UCLA. Before joining the CSE staff she was an evaluator for the Los Angeles Unified School District. Yeh has directed the statistical analysis for several large-scale evaluations and serves as statistical and research design consultant for other CSE projects.